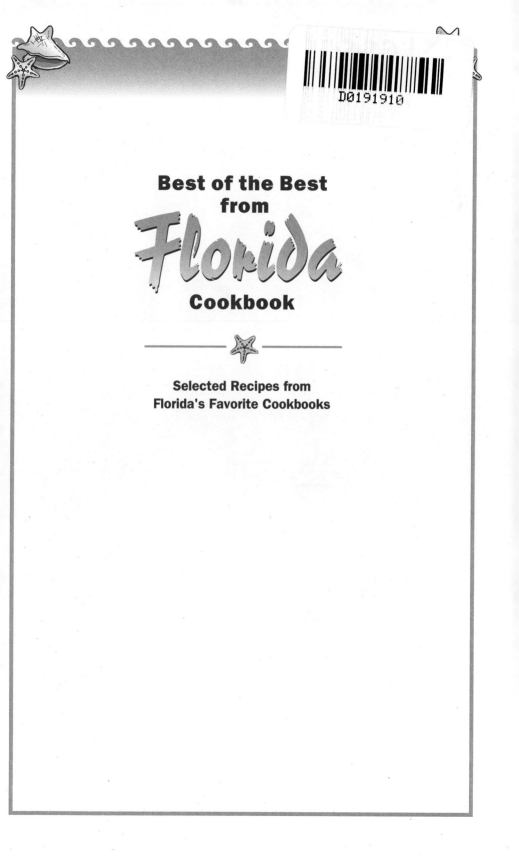

Best of the Best from
Florida
Cookbook

**Selected Recipes from
Florida's Favorite Cookbooks**

Flamingo Gardens, located in the Everglades, includes 60 acres of lush tropical vegetation showcasing rare, exotic, and native plants, along with sparkling waterfalls. It is a haven for flamingos and other wildlife.

Best of the Best
from
Florida
Cookbook

Selected Recipes from
Florida's Favorite Cookbooks

Edited by
GWEN McKEE
and
BARBARA MOSELEY

Illustrated by Tupper England

QUAIL RIDGE PRESS
Preserving America's Food Heritage

Library of Congress Cataloging-in-Publication Data

Best of the best from Florida cookbook : selected recipes from Florida's favorite cookbooks / edited by Gwen McKee and Barbara Moseley ; illustrated by Tupper England.
    p. cm.
    ISBN 1-893062-45-7
    1. Cookery, American 2. Cookery—Florida. I. Title: Florida cookbook II. McKee, Gwen. III. Moseley, Barbara.

TX715.B485615 2004
641.59759—dc21   2003064800

QUAIL RIDGE PRESS
P. O. Box 123 • Brandon, MS 39043 • 1-800-343-1583
email: info@quailridge.com • www.quailridge.com

Contents

PHOTO © LEN KAUFMAN / FLORIDA KEYS TDC

Kids enjoy building a sand castle on one of the many sand beaches found throughout Florida. The region's warm, clear waters enable families to enjoy beach activities any time of the year.

Preface

*F*lorida is the land of swaying palms and warm tropical breezes, of lapping ocean waves and bountiful orchards, of fun in the sun for every age. Just to think of Florida brings on a sunny smile. With no place more than a two-hour drive from the open sea, there are beaches everywhere, and boating, and fishing, and every imaginable water sport, and hunting, and ball fields, and golf courses, all with year-round seasons. Disney World and dozens of other theme parks host and delight people of all ages from every corner of the globe. Florida is not only the Sunshine State, it's considered the "fun-shine state" as well. And good food, naturally, goes along with good fun.

Naturally is a word that well describes Florida's abundance, because nature has truly blessed this beautiful state. The unique sandy soil and subtropical climate have proven to be ideal for growing citrus fruits like oranges, grapefruits, and tangerines, which alone account for one-third of the state's total agricultural yield. In addition, there are some 25 varieties of strawberries, melons, and winter vegetables that are produced in the rich mucklands of central Florida. And from the ocean flows a fantastic variety of seafood, from crab and shrimp, to oysters, to grouper, to swordfish. With such abundant resources, it is no surprise that creative Florida cooks have brought us such delicious recipes as Crab Island Bisque, Orange-Banana Yams, Mango Chicken . . . Yum!

The first edition of *Best of the Best from Florida* was published in 1986 and was the fourth volume in the BEST OF THE BEST STATE COOKBOOK SERIES, a series that now includes every state. With the passage of time came many new Florida cookbooks not included in the first edition, so many, in fact, we decided it was time to produce a completely new edition. Inside you'll find all new recipes, none of which were included in the original book—like Florida Pompano Baked in Sour Cream Sauce, White Chocolate Key Lime Cheesecake and Gator Gumbolaya. . . .

The 83 contributing cookbooks offer examples of some of the fine cuisine the state is noted for, including elegant, ethnic, and easy dishes. Cookbooks from groups, organizations, and individuals make up this outstanding collection. Admittedly, selecting recipes from all the fine cookbooks produced throughout the state was a real challenge. We have chosen exceptional recipes that we think you will want to make again and again. Cooks take pride in sharing their favorite recipes and we thank them for doing so. We have also included numerous tid-bits of information about the state scattered throughout the book, as well as photographs and illustrations that depict Florida.

As editors of this recipe collection, we thoroughly enjoyed working on *Best of the Best from Florida Cookbook* and getting to know the individuals and organizations behind the contributing cookbooks. Hearing their enthusiasm and pride in their cookbooks makes it all the more special for us to be able to showcase some of their signature recipes. We thank them for allowing us to share them, and invite you to review each of the contributing cookbooks in a catalog section that begins on page 255.

To everyone who worked so diligently on this cookbook, we offer our sincere gratitude. We appreciate the food editors, the bookstore and gift shop managers, and the many other individuals who helped us discover the state's most popular cookbooks. Thanks also to the tourism department and many chambers of commerce for providing historic and informative data. To our BEST OF THE BEST artist, Tupper England, we thank you for offering us a fun glimpse of the state through your illustrations. And to our assistant, Terresa Ray, whose diligence makes our work run smoothly, we give special thanks.

Welcome back to the sunny state of Florida.

Gwen McKee and Barbara Moseley

Contributing Cookbooks

An American Celebration
Bay Fêtes
The Best of Sophie Kay Cookbook
By Invitation Only
Calypso Café
Centennial Cookbook
Chilimania!
Christmas Memories
Citrus Lovers Cook Book
A Collection of Favorite Recipes
The Columbia Restaurant Spanish Cookbook
Cookin' in the Keys
Cookin' on Island Time
Cooking for Two, No Nonsense Cookbook
Cooking in Paradise
Cooking with Class
Cooking with People to People
Cooking with 257
Country Club Cooks
Crab Island Cookbook
The Cruising K.I.S.S. Cookbook II
Entirely Entertaining in the Bonnet House Style
The Essential Catfish Cookbook
Exotic Foods: A Kitchen & Garden Guide
Famous Florida Recipes
Favorite Florida Recipes
FCCD Cookbook
Feeding the Flock
Florida Cook Book
Florida Fixin's
Florida Seafood Cookery
Florida's Historic Restaurants and Their Recipes
4-U: 400 Recipes of 4 Ingredients
From Hook to Table
The Galley K.I.S.S. Cookbook
Garden of Eatin'
Gator Championship Recipes
Good Cooking
Gracious Gator Cooks
Great Recipes from Near and Afar
Gulf Coast Cooking
Heaven in a Pot

Contributing Cookbooks

Historic Spanish Point: Cooking Then and Now
Horse Tails
Intracoastal Waterway Restaurant Guide & Recipe Book
Kids at Work
Les Soups Fantastiques
Let's ACT Up in the Kitchen
Let's Talk Food from A to Z
The Life of the Party
Lighthouse Secrets
Made in the Shade
Marion Dragoons Chapter 2311 Cookbook
Mastering the Art of Florida Seafood
The Mongo Mango Cookbook
The Mostly Mullet Cookbook
Preserving Our Italian Heritage
Recipes and Remembrances
Recipes for Lori's Lighthouse
Recipes of Spruce Creek
Roberts Ranch Museum Cookbook
Sand in My Shoes
Savor the Moment
Simply Florida...Strawberries
Sing for Your Supper
A Slice of Paradise
Some Like it South!
Steinhatchee Village Seafood and Etc!
Strictly Scratch
The Sunshine State Cookbook
A Taste of Heaven
Tastes from Paradise
Tastes from Paradise: A Garden of Eating
Thymes Remembered
Treasured Recipes from Near and Far
Treasures
Treasures of the Tropics
Trinity Treats
Tropical Settings
Tropical Tastes and Tantalizing Tales
Under the Canopy
Village Royale: Our Favorite Recipes
The Woman's Exchange Classic Recipes

Beverages and Appetizers

Editor Barbara Moseley and family members enjoying their visit to historic Key West. This spot claims to be the southernmost point of the continental United States. A popular tourist destination for world travelers, a marker notes the distance as 90 miles to Cuba.

Cider Punch

3 cups apple juice
2½ cups unsweetened
   pineapple juice
2 cups cranberry juice

¼ cup brown sugar
2 cinnamon sticks
2 teaspoons whole cloves
2 teaspoons allspice

Mix juices and sugar, and pour into percolator coffeepot. Put spices in coffee basket. Perk and serve hot. Serves 6–8.

Christmas Memories

Bea's Best Punch

Everyone loves this punch.

3 (3-ounce) boxes raspberry
   Jell-O
13 cups water, divided
4 cups sugar
1 (16-ounce) bottle lemon
   concentrate

2 (46-ounce) cans pineapple
   juice
1 ounce almond extract
4 quarts ginger ale

Dissolve Jell-O in 4 cups boiling water. Add sugar, lemon concentrate, and all other ingredients except ginger ale. Seal in containers and freeze. Take out of freezer about 3 hours before serving. Add ginger ale just before serving.

Florida Fixin's

Hot Mulled Pineapple Juice

6 cups pineapple juice
2 cinnamon sticks
1 apple, cored and chunked
½ cup raisins

½ cup packed brown sugar
Grated rind of 1 orange
½ teaspoon whole cloves

Combine pineapple juice, cinnamon sticks, apple chunks, raisins, brown sugar, orange zest, and cloves in saucepan. Simmer 5 minutes. Remove and discard spices before serving. Serves 6.

Cooking with Class

Slushy Strawberry Daiquiris

7 (6-ounce) cans frozen lemonade	2½ (2-liter) bottles 7-Up
	½ gallon rum
6 (10-ounce) packages frozen strawberries	Fresh strawberries for garnish

Thaw and mix lemonade and berries. Add 7-Up and rum. Put in freezer for 3 days. Will be slushy. Scoop into pretty glasses and top each with a strawberry. Makes a 5-gallon bucket of daiquiris.

Country Club Cooks

Key Lime Daiquiri

Don't bother to buy daiquiri mix when you grow your own limes.

Juice of 2 limes	2 ounces white or dark rum
5–6 tablespoons sugar (use raw if you can find it)	Ice cubes
	Mint leaves for garnish

Put lime juice, sugar, and rum in blender. Use a blender that will crush ice; add ice cubes and more rum until mixture is of sherbet consistency. Spoon into chilled glasses and garnish with fresh mint.

Exotic Foods: A Kitchen & Garden Guide

Bourbon Slush

1 (12-ounce) can frozen lemonade concentrate	1 cup sugar, dissolved in tea
	1 cup bourbon
1 (6-ounce) can frozen orange juice concentrate	7 cups water
1 cup strong tea made with 4 tea bags	

Mix all ingredients together and place in container in freezer until slush forms. Can be served with ginger ale or alone.

Feeding the Flock

Mango Colada

A piña colada with mango. What could be more refreshing?

6 ounces coconut cream
6 ounces pineapple juice
4 ounces mango purée

4 ounces spiced white rum
8 ice cubes

Place all ingredients, except ice, in a blender and add ice cubes one at a time. Blend until smooth. Makes 4 servings.

The Mongo Mango Cookbook

Mango Smoothie

A great Florida refreshment.

Pulp of 2 mangoes
1 medium banana, peeled and
   sliced
1 scoop vanilla ice cream

2 tablespoons rum
2 tablespoons sugar
1 cup milk or orange juice

Place all ingredients in blender and blend until smooth. Pour over cracked ice in tall glasses.

Florida Cook Book

Mariposa

The name is Spanish for "butterfly." This frosty drink goes light on the tongue.

2 ounces white rum
1/2 very ripe banana
1/2 medium mango, cut into
   chunks
2 ounces coconut milk

1 teaspoon vanilla extract
2 tablespoons sugar (or equivalent
   amount of artificial sweetener)
1/2 pint vanilla ice cream
6 ounces milk

Place all ingredients in a blender and blend until smooth. Makes 2 servings.

The Mongo Mango Cookbook

Chicken Almond Spread

1 cup finely chopped, cooked
  chicken
½ cup finely minced celery
¼ cup finely chopped, blanched
  almonds

1 teaspoon lemon juice
Mayonnaise
Salt and pepper to taste
70 miniature toast cups

Combine chicken, celery, almonds, lemon juice, and enough mayonnaise to moisten. Stir until well combined. Season with salt and pepper to taste. Fill toast cups. Heat and serve warm or at room temperature.

Thymes Remembered

Garlic Feta Cheese Spread

1 clove of garlic, minced
¼ teaspoon salt
12 ounces cream cheese,
  chopped, softened
8 ounces feta cheese, crumbled

½ cup mayonnaise
¼ teaspoon crushed marjoram
¼ teaspoon crushed dill weed
¼ teaspoon crushed thyme
¼ teaspoon crushed basil

Mix garlic and salt in a bowl until of a pasty consistency. Process garlic mixture, cream cheese, feta cheese, mayonnaise, marjoram, dill weed, thyme, and basil in food processor until of the desired consistency. Spoon into crock.

Chill, covered, for 2 hours. Serve with assorted party crackers. May store in the refrigerator for up to one week. Makes 1½ cups.

Made in the Shade

Shrimp Log

1 (8-ounce) package cream
   cheese, softened
1 cup minced cooked shrimp
2 tablespoons chili sauce
2 tablespoons chopped stuffed
   olives

2 tablespoons chopped green
   onion
1 teaspoon lemon juice
Sliced stuffed olives

In bowl, stir cream cheese until smooth. Blend in cooked shrimp, chili sauce, chopped olives, onion, and lemon juice. Shape into a log, and garnish with sliced stuffed olives; chill thoroughly. To serve, spread on wheat crackers. Makes about 1½ cups.

Garden of Eatin'

Cheese-Olive Appetizers

These appetizers keep well in refrigerator for several weeks.

1 (9-ounce) bottle olives stuffed
   with pimento
2 tablespoons margarine, melted
½ cup all-purpose flour
Salt and pepper to taste

½ teaspoon mustard
3 tablespoons water
Few drops Tabasco
Few shakes paprika

Drain olives and set aside. Mix all other ingredients until mixture can be handled. Mixture may need a little more flour or water—up to 1 cup flour may be used. Use about 1 teaspoon of mixture to wrap around each olive. Roll in palm of hand. These should be frozen on a cookie sheet, then stored in freezer containers until ready to use. Bake on cookie sheet at 450° for 20 minutes. Serve hot.

Florida Fixin's

Deviled Pecan Ball

2 (8-ounce) packages cream
  cheese, softened
2 cups (8 ounces) shredded
  sharp Cheddar cheese
1 (2¼-ounce) can deviled ham
2 tablespoons chopped pimento
2 teaspoons Worcestershire
  sauce
2 teaspoons grated onion

1 teaspoon dried parsley flakes
1 teaspoon lemon juice
1 teaspoon dry mustard
¼ teaspoon salt
½ teaspoon seasoned salt
¾ teaspoon paprika
2–4 drops hot pepper sauce
2 cups chopped pecans

Combine first 3 ingredients, blending well. Stir in remaining ingredients except pecans. Chill 2 hours. Divide cheese mixture in half and shape into 2 balls; roll in pecans. Serve with crackers.

Sand in My Shoes

Bleu Cheese Ball

1 (8-ounce) package cream
  cheese, softened
1 (4-ounce) package bleu cheese,
  crumbled

1 (2-ounce) jar chopped black
  olives
1 teaspoon Worcestershire sauce
1 cup chopped pecans

Mix cream cheese, bleu cheese, olives, and Worcestershire sauce in a bowl. Shape into a ball and roll in pecans. Yields 20–30 servings.

Gator Championship Recipes

Gatorade was actually named for the University of Florida Gators (Gainesville) where the drink was first developed in order to help the football players combat dehydration.

Baked Crock of Artichoke, Brie and Lump Crab

1 leek, chopped
1 ounce minced garlic
1 Vidalia onion, diced
2 tablespoons olive oil
½ cup chopped spinach
½ cup chopped artichoke hearts
¼ cup Riesling wine
⅔ cup heavy cream
1 bunch mixed fresh tarragon,
   parsley, and dill, chopped

8 ounces Brie cheese, cut into
   cubes
1 pound fresh jumbo lump
   crabmeat
¼ cup Grey Poupon Dijon
   Mustard
2 tablespoons Tabasco sauce
Salt and pepper to taste

Preheat oven to 425°. Sauté leeks, garlic, and onion in oil in a large skillet until light brown. Add spinach and artichokes to skillet. Deglaze with wine and cook until spinach is soft. Add cream, tarragon, parsley, and dill. Bring to a slight simmer. Stir in cheese until blended. Remove from heat, and pour into a mixing bowl; cool.

In a separate bowl, combine crabmeat, mustard, and Tabasco sauce. Season with salt and pepper. Add to cheese mixture. Transfer mixture to a large casserole dish or individual ramekins. Bake 10 minutes or until slightly browned. Yields 6–8 servings.

Treasures of the Tropics

Hot Crab Dip in a Bread Basket

2 (8-ounce) packages cream
  cheese, softened
½ cup mayonnaise
¼ cup dry white wine
2 green onions, chopped
2 cloves garlic, minced

½ teaspoon Worcestershire sauce
1 pound crabmeat
¼ cup chopped pimento
1 (2-pound) round loaf bread
  (wheat or rye)

Mix and beat cream cheese until fluffy. Add mayonnaise, wine, green onions, garlic, and Worcestershire sauce. Mix until smooth. Stir in crabmeat and pimento. Scoop out center of bread to make basket. Place bread on baking sheet. Fill center with crab mixture. Bake at 350° for 45 minutes. Serve with crackers or fresh vegetables.

Crab Island Cookbook

Salmon Dip

This creamy salmon dip is ideal for entertaining. It can be prepared in advance and kept refrigerated until serving time.

1 (8-ounce) package cream
  cheese, softened
1 (16-ounce) can pink or red
  salmon, drained
¼ cup coarsely chopped onion
¼ cup coarsely chopped celery

1–2 tablespoons fresh lemon
  juice
2 tablespoons horseradish
½ teaspoon hickory smoked salt
Chopped fresh dill weed for garnish
Assorted crackers

Place all ingredients, except dill weed and crackers, in food processor or blender container. Blend until mixture is smooth and of spreading consistency. Chill before serving. Garnish top with fresh dill weed; serve with assorted crackers. Serves 8–10.

The Best of Sophie Kay Cookbook

Crab and Caper Dip

2 cups chopped onions
2 tablespoons margarine
2 cups mayonnaise
2 cups shredded Swiss cheese

1 (3½-ounce) jar capers, drained
1 (6-ounce) can fancy lump
  crabmeat
1 round loaf of bread

Preheat oven to 350°. Sauté onions in margarine until clear. Combine all ingredients, except bread, mixing well. Cut top off bread and hollow out (save soft bread to eat dip with). Put dip in hollowed loaf and put top back on bread. Wrap in foil and bake for one hour. Do not double or half recipe. Serves 16–20.

Gracious Gator Cooks

Shrimp Dip

2 (8-ounce) packages cream
  cheese, softened
½ pint Miracle Whip Salad
  Dressing
2 pounds cooked, chopped
  shrimp
1 clove garlic, minced
1 small onion, finely chopped
1 tablespoon vinegar

½ (8-ounce) bottle French salad
  dressing
6 drops Tabasco sauce
1 tablespoon horseradish
Juice of one lemon
1¼ teaspoons sugar
¼ teaspoon salt
¼ teaspoon pepper

Mix all ingredients well. Chill at least 4 hours, and serve with your favorite crackers.

Great Recipes from Near and Afar

Spicy Seafood Dip

This elegant hors d'oeuvre may be prepared a day in advance and baked just before serving.

1 large green bell pepper, chopped
1 tablespoon olive oil
1 pound small shrimp, shelled and deveined
2 tablespoons butter
2 (14-ounce) cans artichoke hearts, drained; chopped fine
2 cups mayonnaise
½ cup thinly sliced green onions
½ cup drained and chopped roasted red peppers

1 cup freshly grated Parmesan cheese
2 tablespoons fresh lemon juice
4 teaspoons Worcestershire sauce
3 pickled jalapeño peppers, seeded and minced
Dash of Tabasco
½ teaspoon salt or to taste
1 pound well-picked crabmeat
⅓ cup sliced almonds, lightly toasted
Pita Triangles

Preheat oven to 375°. In a heavy frying pan, cook green pepper in olive oil over moderate heat, stirring until peppers are soft; cool. Sauté shrimp in butter for 1½ minutes.

In a large bowl, mix bell peppers, artichokes, mayonnaise, green onions, roasted peppers, Parmesan cheese, lemon juice, Worcestershire, jalapeño peppers, Tabasco, and salt.

Gently stir in seafood and correct seasoning. Transfer to a large buttered baking dish and sprinkle with almonds. Bake at 375° for 25–30 minutes, or until top is golden and mixture is bubbly. Serve in a chafing dish with lightly buttered Pita Triangles. Serves 15.

PITA TRIANGLES:
8 large pita loaves
½ cup butter, melted
Salt

Freshly grated Parmesan cheese (optional)

Preheat oven to 375°. Cut each pita loaf into 8 wedges. Separate each wedge into 2 triangles. Place in a single layer close together on baking sheets, rough-side-up. Brush triangles lightly with butter and season with salt.

If preparing triangles to serve with salads or soups, sprinkle with Parmesan cheese before baking. Bake for 10–12 minutes, or until triangles are crisp and golden. Cool on cookie sheets. Makes 128 triangles.

Thymes Remembered

Blast-Off Black Bean Dip

4 slices bacon
1 medium onion, chopped
1 small red bell pepper, chopped
½ teaspoon cumin
½ teaspoon oregano
2 (15-ounce) cans black beans

1 teaspoon chopped seeded
  canned chipotle chiles
Salt and pepper to taste
½ cup sour cream
2 tablespoons chopped fresh
  cilantro

Fry bacon in a skillet until crisp. Drain, reserving 1 tablespoon bacon drippings. Sauté onion and bell pepper in reserved bacon drippings until onion is tender. Stir in cumin and oregano. Sauté for 1 minute. Stir in undrained beans and chipotle chiles.

Simmer over medium-low heat for 5 minutes or until slightly thickened, stirring occasionally. Process 1 cup bean mixture in a food processor until smooth. Return blended bean mixture to remaining bean mixture. Season with salt and pepper. Spoon bean dip into a serving bowl.

Chill, covered, for 2 hours. Stir half the bacon into the dip. Top with sour cream, and sprinkle with cilantro and remaining bacon. Serve cold or at room temperature with tortilla chips. Serves 10–12.

Note: Chipotle chiles canned in a spicy tomato sauce, sometimes called adobo, are available in Latin American markets, specialty food stores, and some large supermarkets.

By Invitation Only

Cape Canaveral is America's launch pad for space flights. The first U.S. satellite (1958), the first U.S. manned space flight (1961), and the first U.S. moon landing flight (1969), were all launched from Cape Canaveral. Space Shuttle *Columbia,* launched on April 12, 1981, was the first space shuttle launched at Cape Canaveral's Kennedy Space Center.

Chilled Shrimp Dip

1 (8-ounce) package cream
  cheese, softened
1 (10¾-ounce) can cream of
  mushroom soup
1 package unflavored gelatin,
  mixed with 3 tablespoons water
1 cup mayonnaise
1 cup diced celery

1 bunch green onions, green part
  only, chopped
1½–2 cups peeled and chopped
  shrimp
1 tablespoon lemon juice
⅜ teaspoon cayenne pepper, or to
  taste

Mix together cream cheese and soup. Add gelatin mixture. Add mayonnaise and all other ingredients. Spray mold with nonstick spray. Pour mixture into mold and chill for 24 hours.

Recipes for Lori's Lighthouse

Holiday Appetizer Pie

1 (8-ounce) package cream
  cheese, softened
½ cup sour cream
1 (2½-ounce) jar sliced dried
  beef (rinse and dry off)

2 tablespoons finely chopped
  green pepper
2 tablespoons finely chopped onion
½ cup coarsely chopped walnuts

Blend cream cheese and sour cream. Chop dried beef and stir into cream cheese/sour cream mixture. Add green pepper and onion. Mix well, and spoon into a 9-inch pie plate. Sprinkle walnuts over top. Bake for 15 minutes in a 350° oven. Cool, and serve with assorted crackers.

Under the Canopy

Sandpipers Onion Tart

SHELL:

1 cup flour
½ cup butter, melted

1 cup grated sharp Cheddar
  cheese

Preheat oven to 350°. Mix Shell ingredients to form a soft dough and press into pie plate or quiche pan.

FILLING:

3 large or 4 medium onions,
  chopped
¼ cup butter
¼ cup flour
1 cup milk

1 egg, beaten
¼ cup grated sharp Cheddar
  cheese
Dashes sea salt, pepper, and
  paprika

In a nonstick skillet, sauté onions in butter till translucent; sprinkle with flour to give a coated look. Add a little milk to the beaten egg, then the remaining milk to the onions. Slowly cook to make a white sauce; stir often.

Add egg and milk mixture to onions and cook for 1 minute on low heat. Add cheese, salt, and pepper, and mix well. Remove from heat and pour into prepared pie shell. Sprinkle with paprika, bake for 30 minutes. Serve warm. Serves 4–6.

Variation: Add a topping of ½ cup chopped broccoli or cauliflower florets just before baking.

The Cruising K.I.S.S. Cookbook II

The Best Mushroom Appetizer

These little black "bullets" are really the best—well worth the time.

4 pounds fresh mushrooms,
  cleaned
1 pound butter
1 quart Burgundy
1½ tablespoons Worcestershire
  sauce
1 teaspoon dill seed

1 teaspoon black pepper
1 teaspoon garlic powder
2 cups boiling water
4 beef bouillon cubes
4 chicken bouillon cubes
Salt to taste

Combine all ingredients in a large pot. Slowly bring to a boil and reduce heat to simmer. Cover pot and simmer 5–6 hours. Remove lid and simmer until liquid is reduced, another hour, barely covering the mushrooms. Salt to taste. Serve hot in chafing dish with little picks. Yields 1½ pints.

Historic Spanish Point: Cooking Then and Now

Shrimp and Corn Fritters

1 pound shrimp
1 cup corn
½ cup diced onion
½ cup diced red bell pepper
½ cup chopped scallion
½ cup chopped fresh cilantro
½ cup diced fresh jalapeño
  peppers

1½ cups buttermilk pancake mix
½ cup all-purpose flour
1 teaspoon salt
1 teaspoon black pepper
Juice of 1 lime
1 cup beer
Oil for frying

Cook shrimp. Chill, peel, and devein. Coarsely chop shrimp. Cook corn and drain. Combine shrimp, corn, and remaining ingredients, except oil. Refrigerate for at least 60 minutes. Using a small ice cream scoop or a soup spoon, drop batter into 350° oil. Fry 2–3 minutes or until golden brown. Place fritters on a paper towel to drain. Serve hot with cocktail or mustard sauce. Yields 6–10 servings.

Calypso Café

Shrimp, Scallop, and Mushroom Kabobs

My ever-imaginative friend from Sarasota describes this recipe as her latest attempt to solve the hors d'oeuvre dilemma.

2 quarts water
2 tablespoons prepared crab boil
2 pounds shrimp, shelled and deveined

2 pounds sea scallops
2 tablespoons butter
1 pound mushroom caps

Bring water to a boil; add crab boil, and simmer for about 20 minutes. Add shrimp and scallops and simmer about 2 minutes or until opaque. Drain and set aside.

Melt butter in a skillet and sauté mushroom caps until tender. Remove and combine with seafood in a shallow glass dish.

MARINADE:

2 tablespoons chopped capers
2 tablespoons chopped scallions
10 water-packed or freeze-dried green peppercorns

1 clove garlic, crushed
1 cup prepared Italian salad dressing
2 tablespoons lemon or lime juice

Mix capers, scallions, peppercorns, and garlic. Add salad dressing and juice and mix well. Pour over seafood. Refrigerate overnight.

Provide guests with a small plate, a cocktail fork, and a bamboo skewer for making their own kabobs.

Gulf Coast Cooking

Caribe Crab

1 pound cooked lump blue
  crabmeat
1 small onion, grated
2 tablespoons lime juice ($\frac{1}{2}$ lime)

$\frac{1}{4}$ teaspoon salt
$\frac{1}{8}$ teaspoon freshly ground black
  pepper

Carefully pick over the crabmeat to assure that all pieces of cartilage or shell has been removed. Add remaining ingredients and stir
lightly to mix. Divide between 2 bowls and serve. May be served
with crackers, if desired, but it's perfect just as it is. Serves 2.

Cookin' in the Keys

Crab Delights

1 package English muffins
1 (17-ounce) can crabmeat
1 stick margarine, softened
7 ounces grated sharp Cheddar
  cheese

2 tablespoons mayonnaise
1$\frac{1}{2}$ teaspoons salt
1 teaspoon garlic

Slice muffins in half and cut each half into fourths; place on cookie sheets. Mix remaining ingredients well. Spread on muffins and
freeze for 30 minutes. Broil until they puff up.

Favorite Florida Recipes

The sabal palm is the state tree. This palm is the most widely distributed in
the state, and grows in almost any soil.

Teriyaki Scallops

16 (30- to 40-count) sea scallops
8 bacon strips
6 tablespoons teriyaki sauce

2 tablespoons pineapple juice
Pinch of granulated garlic
Dash ground ginger

Wrap each scallop tightly with half a bacon strip, and secure with a toothpick. Place in a baking pan and pour mixture of teriyaki, pineapple juice, garlic, and ginger over scallops. Bake in 350° oven for 10–12 minutes until scallops are just done and bacon is medium. Arrange scallops on dishes and pour hot sauce over. Garnish dish with fresh fruit and tomato rose. Serves 2 as an appetizer.

Recipe from The Courtyard on Grove, Merritt Island
Intracoastal Waterway Restaurant Guide & Recipe Book

The Gibson Inn's Oysters Remick

⅓ cup mayonnaise
3 teaspoons chili sauce
1 level teaspoon horseradish

1 dozen Apalachicola oysters
2 slices Swiss cheese, grated

Combine mayonnaise, chili sauce, and horseradish; set aside. Place each opened and drained raw oyster on half of its shell, then place on a baking sheet. Top each equally with mayonnaise mixture and shredded cheese. Bake in a preheated 500° oven for 5 minutes, until cheese melts, or place oysters under the broiler for 2–3 minutes. Serves 2–4.

Florida's Historic Restaurants and Their Recipes

Oysters Rockefeller

20 oysters in shell
8 strips bacon
4½ tablespoons margarine, divided
4 tablespoons finely chopped celery
4 tablespoons finely chopped onion
2 tablespoons chopped parsley
5 ounces chopped frozen spinach, thawed and well drained
1 tablespoon anisette (optional)
2 tablespoons bread crumbs
Rock salt

Preheat oven to 450°. Shuck oysters. Leave oysters in deep half of shell. Fry bacon until slightly crisp; drain on paper towels. In 4 tablespoons margarine, sauté celery, onion, and parsley until slightly tender. Remove sautéed vegetables from stove. Add spinach and anisette.

Line baking trays with rock salt, ¼-inch deep. Place oysters in shells in rock salt and pack down. Sprinkle 1 teaspoon spinach mixture over each oyster. Sprinkle ½ teaspoon finely chopped bacon over each. Melt ½ tablespoon margarine and mix in bread crumbs. Sprinkle lightly on oysters. Bake for 10 minutes. Serve.

Note: Anisette is a clear, very sweet liqueur made with anise seeds and tasting of licorice.

Crab Island Cookbook

Tortilla Bits

1 (8-ounce) package cream
 cheese, softened
1 (8-ounce) carton sour cream
1 (4-ounce) can diced green
 chiles
1 small can or jar bacon bits,
 divided

1 (2-ounce) jar chopped pimentos,
 drained
4–5 green onion stalks,
 chopped
6–8 flour tortillas, or tomato basil
 tortillas
1 (16-ounce) jar picante sauce

Mix cream cheese, sour cream, green chiles, half the bacon bits, pimentos, and green onions; mix well. Spread some mixture on each tortilla. Roll each tortilla, and place seam-side-down in a large dish. Once all are rolled, cover tightly; chill 24 hours. Slice in 1-inch slices. Serve with picante sauce as a dip. Makes 36–40 individual servings.

Treasured Recipes from Near and Far

Sesame Chicken Fingers with Honey Dip

½ cup Hellmann's mayonnaise
1 teaspoon dry mustard
1 teaspoon chopped onion
¼ cup sesame seeds

½ cup fine dry bread crumbs
2 cups thinly sliced chicken
 breast

Mix mayonnaise, dry mustard, and onion together and set aside. Mix sesame seeds and bread crumbs together and set aside. Coat chicken first with mayonnaise mixture, then crumb mixture. Place on greased baking sheet and bake 12 minutes at 425°. Serve hot with Honey Dip.

HONEY DIP:
1 cup mayonnaise

2 tablespoons honey

Mix mayonnaise and honey.

Note: Use half the recipe if only a few people.

Cooking in Paradise

Sausage Blossoms

Won ton wrappers make this appetizer a snap to put together. The wrappers look like flower petals or blossoms, creating a pretty cup to hold the spicy sausage and cheese mixture.

2 pounds Italian sausage,
  casings removed
2 cups shredded Colby Jack
  cheese
2 cups salsa

1 (12-ounce) package won ton
  wrappers
Sour cream
Chopped green onions

Brown sausage in skillet, stirring until crumbly. Remove from heat and add Colby Jack cheese and salsa, stirring until cheese is melted. Press won ton wrappers into miniature muffin cups, leaving edges extending upward. Spoon a heaping tablespoon sausage mixture into each cup. Bake at 350° for 10 minutes or until won ton edges begin to brown. Remove to a serving platter and let stand for 5 minutes. Spoon a small amount of sour cream on top of each sausage blossom, and sprinkle with chopped green onions. Serve immediately. Yields 48 appetizers.

The Life of the Party

Spinach Balls

2 (10-ounce) packages frozen,
  chopped spinach
1½ cups herb stuffing mix
  (not cubes)

1 cup grated Parmesan cheese
3 eggs, beaten
¾ cup soft butter

Cook spinach; drain. Combine all ingredients. Roll in hands to bite-size balls (walnut). Put on cookie sheet and freeze. Take off sheet and store in container with wax paper between layers. Will keep a long time in freezer.

Before serving, bake (frozen) in 375° oven on foil-covered cookie sheet for about 10 minutes, or until lightly browned.

Sing for Your Supper

Spinach Phyllo

2 packages chopped spinach,
  cooked, drained
2 cups herb stuffing mix
1 onion, finely chopped
4 eggs, beaten
1¼ cups melted margarine,
  divided

½ cup grated Parmesan cheese
½ teaspoon garlic salt
¼ teaspoon pepper
1 package phyllo dough

Combine spinach, stuffing mix, onion, eggs, ¾ cup margarine, cheese, garlic salt, and pepper in a bowl and mix well. Chill for 30 minutes.

Work quickly with one sheet of phyllo dough at a time, keeping the remaining dough covered with wax paper topped by a damp towel. Cut each sheet into 2-inch-wide strips. Brush 3 strips of the dough with a small portion of the remaining ½ cup margarine; continue to keep the remaining dough covered.

Place one tablespoon of the spinach mixture on each strip. Fold over in triangle as you would a flag. Repeat the process with the remaining phyllo, margarine, and filling, keeping each triangle covered while you prepare the others. Place triangles in a nonstick baking pan. Bake at 350° for 10–15 minutes, or until golden brown. Yields 25–30 servings.

Gator Championship Recipes

DeFuniak Springs is home to Lake DeFuniak, one of the two naturally round lakes in the world (the other being located near Zurich, Switzerland). According to the *Atlas of Florida*, approximately 7,700 lakes (greater than 10 acres) cover the Florida landscape.

Guacamole

2 ripe avocados
Juice of 1 lime
½ teaspoon salt
½ teaspoon chili powder
2 teaspoons fresh onion juice

4 drops red hot sauce
½ (3-ounce) package cream
  cheese, softened
1 tablespoon minced pimiento
  (optional)

Peel avocados, remove pits, and mash with silver fork to prevent darkening. Add lime juice, then blend in seasonings and cream cheese. If pimiento is used, stir it in last. Use as a dip with potato chips or stuff tomatoes for salad. If guacamole must stand for some time, place in refrigerator with avocado pit placed in center and it will not darken.

Famous Florida Recipes

Sunchaser Salsa

1 (28-ounce) can whole tomatoes
1 large Spanish or Vidalia onion

4–10 jalapeño peppers
Salt to taste

Squish tomatoes with fingers; remove any remaining cores. Dice the onion fine; seed and dice jalapeño peppers. Mix all well. Serve with chips, Tostitos, or Doritos.

Variations: Add mashed, ripe avocado to make guacamole. Add sour cream or melted cheese for chile con queso. Add chopped fresh cilantro for flavor.

Cooking in Paradise

Hot Chili Salsa

2 cups diced ripe beefsteak
   tomatoes
⅓ cup finely chopped onion
¼ cup seeded, minced hot
   fresh chilies, or more to taste

Salt and pepper
2 tablespoons fresh lemon juice
¼ cup finely chopped fresh parsley
1–2 dashes Tabasco sauce
   (optional)

In a small mixing bowl, combine all ingredients at one time, and stir to mix together. Cover bowl, or place in a jar until ready to use. Makes approximately 3 cups.

Chilimania!

Seviche

This is a Latin American favorite—great as an appetizer, a first-course cocktail, or as a snack with cold beer. Is it raw fish? Not at all. Marinating in lime juice cooks it as thoroughly as any fire. Speaking of fire, the chile peppers and Tabasco sauce may be left out, if your prefer.

1 pound white-meat fish, cut in
   bite-size pieces
Salt
1 large onion, chopped or sliced
1 tomato, chopped fine (remove
   seeds)

1 small green pepper, chopped
   fine
2 chile peppers, chopped fine
Tabasco sauce, a few drops
4–6 limes or lemons

If you plan to serve as a snack or appetizer the same day, proceed as follows: put the fish in a crock or glass container. Salt liberally. Add the other ingredients; mix well, then add fresh-squeezed lime juice to cover. Marinate for a few hours until all pieces are white with no pinkish centers. As an appetizer, this serves 6–8. Serves fewer when offered as a snack with crackers and drinks.

   A slightly different approach is needed if you plan to make seviche and store it in the refrigerator for nibbling over the next few days. Do not include the chopped vegetables and other ingredients in the marinade, but simply marinate the salted fish in the lime or lemon juice until it turns white. Use a plastic or glass container with a lid. After marinating, drain the fish, add the chopped vegetables, mix and store.

From Hook to Table

Firecracker Chile Cheese Pie

Light up your taste buds with this festive appetizer.

1 cup crushed tortilla chips
3 tablespoons melted butter
16 ounces cream cheese, softened
2 eggs
1 (4-ounce) can chopped green chiles
2 fresh jalapeños, minced

4 ounces shredded Colby cheese
4 ounces shredded Monterey Jack cheese
¼ cup sour cream
Chopped green onions, chopped tomatoes, and sliced black olives for garnish

Mix crushed tortilla chips and melted butter in a bowl. Press over bottom of a 9-inch springform pan. Bake at 325° for 15 minutes.

Beat cream cheese and eggs in a mixing bowl. Mix in green chiles, jalapeños, Colby cheese, and Monterey Jack cheese. Pour over baked layer. Bake at 325° for exactly 30 minutes. Cool for 5 minutes.

Place on a serving plate. Loosen side of pan with a knife and remove. Spread sour cream over pie. Garnish with green onions, tomatoes, and olives. Serve with additional chips. Serves 8–10.

Savor the Moment

Southern Caviar

1 (10-ounce) can black-eyed
   peas, drained
2–4 small white onions, thinly
   sliced into rings
½ teaspoon Tabasco

½ teaspoon ground black pepper
⅓ (3-ounce) jar capers, drained
1 teaspoon minced garlic
⅓ (16-ounce) bottle Italian
   dressing

Mix all ingredients. Refrigerate at least 24 hours, stirring occasionally. Drain. Serve with salt-free crackers or pita chips. Yields 8–10 servings.

Historic Spanish Point: Cooking Then and Now

Bar Nuts

¼ pound each: peeled peanuts,
   cashews, brazil nuts, hazelnuts,
   walnuts, pecans, and whole
   unpeeled almonds or 1¼
   pounds unsalted assorted nuts
½ teaspoon cayenne

2 tablespoons coarsely chopped
   fresh rosemary
2 teaspoons dark brown sugar
2 teaspoons kosher salt
1 tablespoon butter, melted

Preheat oven to 350°. Toss nuts in a large bowl to combine and spread out on a cookie sheet. Toast in oven until they become light golden brown, about 10 minutes. In the large bowl, combine rosemary, cayenne, brown sugar, salt, and melted butter. Thoroughly toss warm toasted nuts with spiced butter and serve warm.

Horse Tails

Bread and Breakfast

John F. Kennedy Space Center was the departure site for the first human journey to the moon. It was also the starting point for hundreds of scientific, commercial, and applications spacecraft, and was the base for Space Shuttle launch and landing operations.

Bahamian Coconut Bread

Serve bread with honey, or use as a dessert by topping a slice with ice cream and amaretto.

3 cups unbleached flour
2 cups coarsely grated fresh
   coconut
1 cup sugar
1 tablespoon baking powder
1 teaspoon salt

1 teaspoon nutmeg
2 eggs
1 cup milk
2 tablespoons butter or margarine,
   melted, or oil
1 teaspoon vanilla

Combine flour and next 5 ingredients in a large bowl. In a separate bowl, beat together eggs and remaining 3 ingredients. Stir egg mixture into dry ingredients. Pour batter into a greased and floured 8-inch cast-iron skillet. Bake at 350° for 45–60 minutes or until a toothpick inserted in the center comes out clean. Cool in skillet. Yields 10–12 servings.

Calypso Café

Gruyère Cheese Bread

1 cup water
6 tablespoons butter
1 teaspoon salt
1/8 teaspoon pepper

1 cup flour
4 eggs
1 cup finely chopped Gruyère
   cheese, divided

Combine water, butter, salt, and pepper in a saucepan. Bring to a boil. Add the flour all at once. Cook, stirring constantly, until mixture forms a ball and leaves the side of the pan. Remove from heat. Beat in eggs one at a time. Set aside 2 tablespoons of the cheese. Stir remaining cheese into the dough. Arrange rounded tablespoonfuls of the dough in a circle on a greased baking sheet, leaving 2 1/2 inches in the center. Sprinkle reserved cheese over the top. Bake at 425° for 40–45 minutes or until puffed and golden brown. Yields 6–8 servings.

Entirely Entertaining in the Bonnet House Style

Lin's Tropical Banana Bread

1½ cups sugar
½ cup vegetable oil
¼ cup dark rum
2 ripe bananas, mashed
2 eggs
1 tablespoon milk
1 teaspoon vanilla extract
1¾ cups unbleached flour, sifted

2 tablespoons dry buttermilk blend
1 teaspoon baking soda
½ teaspoon salt
½ cup finely chopped walnuts
½ cup chopped pecans
¼ cup finely grated coconut
   (optional)
Rum Glaze

Combine sugar, oil, rum, bananas, eggs, milk, and vanilla in a mixer bowl. Beat until blended, scraping the bowl occasionally. Mix flour, buttermilk blend, baking soda, and salt in a bowl. Add to banana mixture, mixing just until moistened; do not overmix.

Spoon batter into a greased 5x9-inch loaf pan. Sprinkle walnuts, pecans, and coconut over top. Bake at 325° for 45 minutes or until edges pull from sides of pan. Remove bread from pan (pecans and coconut should be on top). Drizzle with warm Rum Glaze. Serve warm or chill for later use. Makes 1 loaf.

RUM GLAZE:
¼ cup sugar
2 tablespoons butter

2 tablespoons water
¼ cup dark rum

Combine sugar, butter, and water in a microwave-safe bowl. Microwave until boiling. Boil for 1–2 minutes. Stir in rum. May boil in a saucepan for 5 minutes.

Made in the Shade

Ybor City was once known as the Cigar Capital of the World with nearly 12,000 tabaqueros (cigar-makers) employed in 200 factories. Ybor City produced an estimated 700 million cigars a year at the industry's peak.

Mother's Yeast Rolls

½ cup sugar
2 teaspoons salt
6 tablespoons vegetable oil
1½ cups scalded milk
1 package yeast

½ cup lukewarm water
2 eggs, lightly beaten
6½ cups flour
Melted butter

Mix sugar, salt, and oil in a large bowl. Add milk. Set aside to cool to lukewarm. Dissolve yeast in lukewarm water. Add to the eggs in a bowl, and mix well. Add egg mixture to milk mixture. Add half the flour and beat until smooth. Work in the remaining flour. Place dough in a greased bowl. Chill, covered, overnight.

Roll out on a floured surface. Cut with a biscuit cutter. Spread with butter. Fold the rolls in half. Place in nonstick baking pans. Let rise for 3 hours. Bake at 425° for 8–10 minutes or until brown. Yields 36 servings.

Gator Championship Recipes

Jalapeño Corn Bread

1 cup yellow cornmeal
1 cup cream-style corn
1 cup sour cream
2 teaspoons baking powder
1 teaspoon salt
½ cup salad oil

2 eggs, slightly beaten
2 cups grated sharp Cheddar
 cheese
3 or 4 chopped jalapeño peppers
1 onion, diced

Combine ingredients and mix well. Bake in a greased, hot iron skillet or muffin pans at 350° for 1 hour for whole bread or 45 minutes for muffins. Serves 10–12.

Let's Talk Food from A to Z

Sour Cream Biscuits

A quick, rich biscuit that does not require butter when served.

1 cup margarine, melted　　　　**2 cups self-rising flour**
1 cup sour cream

Preheat oven to 400°. Combine melted margarine and sour cream.
Measure self-rising flour into a large bowl. Combine margarine and
sour cream with flour, stirring to mix thoroughly. Fill ungreased mini-
muffin pans with heaping tablespoons of batter. Bake 15 minutes.
Cool baked biscuits for 3 minutes before removing from pan.
Makes 30 mini-biscuits.

Thymes Remembered

Eva's Hush Puppies

2 cups self-rising meal　　　　**1 (16-ounce) can whole-kernel**
1 cup self-rising flour　　　　　　**yellow corn**
2 small onions, diced　　　　　　**1 tablespoon sugar**
1 small bell pepper, diced　　　**2½ tablespoons vegetable oil**
3 eggs

Mix meal, flour, onions, and bell pepper in a large mixing bowl, then
add corn, eggs, sugar, and oil. The batter should be fairly stiff, not
soupy like cornbread. Drop by tablespoonful into hot, deep oil. As
it cooks and browns on one side, it will flip over and brown on the
other side. Check with a fork on the first 2 or 3 to time the amount
of time needed for each batch.

Feeding the Flock

Zeppole

(Christmas Fried Dough)

1 package dry yeast	Oil for frying
Warm water, as needed	1 cup raisins
8 cups flour	1 cup pignoli nuts (pine nuts)
Salt and pepper to taste	2 ounces anchovy fillets (optional)

Soften yeast in 1 cup warm water. When yeast has dissolved and is foamy, add to flour, salt, and pepper. Add warm water to make a smooth elastic, almost runny dough. Work the dough through your fingers for about 5 minutes to blend all the flour. Set in a warm place to rise. When dough has doubled, work the dough down to rise a second time.

Heat oil; the oil is ready when a cube of bread pops to the surface and is lightly browned. Oil your fingers and sprinkle just a few raisins and pine nuts over the dough. Pull a piece of dough the size of a golf ball and lightly work in 3–4 raisins and nuts. Roll the dough around your fingers, shaping a ball. Drop gently into the hot oil and fry until golden brown. Continue to sprinkle just a few raisins and nuts over the dough as you fry each batch of zeppoles. May also add 2–3 pieces of anchovy fillets to raisins and nuts as you fry.

Preserving Our Italian Heritage

 Of the more than 17,000 golf courses in the United States, Florida boasts more than 1,250—more golf courses than any other state. Naples has the most per capita than anywhere else in the world with currently over 100 golf courses.

Piña Colada Muffins

1 (18¼-ounce) yellow or butter cake mix	1 cup coconut flakes
1 teaspoon coconut extract	½–1 cup chopped nuts
1 teaspoon rum extract	1 (8-ounce) can crushed pineapple, with juice

In a large mixing bowl, prepare cake mix following instructions on package. Add remaining ingredients and stir for one minute. Grease or add liners to a 12-cup muffin tin. Pour batter into eachh cup to ¾ full. Bake at 350° for 15–20 minutes or until golden brown. Makes 12 muffins.

Florida Cook Book

Sunshine Muffins

Laden with fruit and nuts, these muffins will bring a touch of tropical sunshine to any brunch or breakfast, and really don't need any additional spread.

½ cup milk	½ cup packed brown sugar
¼ cup vegetable oil	1 teaspoon cinnamon
2 eggs	½ cup shredded carrot
½ cup raisins	1 cup shredded apple
1½ cups rolled oats	1 (12-ounce) can crushed pineapple, drained
2 cups baking mix	
½ cup sugar	¼ cup chopped walnuts

Combine milk, oil, and eggs in a medium bowl, and beat lightly. Stir in raisins and oats. Let stand for several minutes. Add baking mix, sugar, brown sugar, cinnamon, carrot, apple, pineapple, and walnuts, and mix just until moistened. Spoon into greased muffin cups, filling ½ full. Bake at 400° for 20 minutes or until golden brown. Serves 12.

Tropical Settings

Cranberry Orange Scones

2 cups all-purpose flour
1 tablespoon baking powder
1/2 teaspoon baking soda
1/4 teaspoon salt
2 tablespoons sugar
1 tablespoon grated orange rind

1/2 cup butter, cut up
2/3 cup buttermilk
1 cup dried cranberries
1 tablespoon milk
1 tablespoon sugar

Combine first 6 ingredients. Cut in butter with a pastry blender until mixture is crumbly. Add buttermilk and dried cranberries, stirring until just moistened. Turn dough out onto a lightly floured surface; knead 5 or 6 times. Pat into an 8-inch circle. Cut into 8 wedges and place 1 inch apart on a lightly greased baking sheet. Brush with milk and 1 tablespoon sugar. Bake at 450° for 15 minutes or until scones are golden brown. Yields 8 servings.

Tastes from Paradise

Open-Face Cheese Buns

1 1/2 cups grated Cheddar cheese
1/2 cup mayonnaise
1 cup chopped or sliced ripe
   olives

1/2 teaspoon curry powder
1/2 cup chopped green onions
Hamburger buns

Mix together cheese, mayonnaise, olives, curry powder, and green onions. Spread on hamburger buns, open-faced. Bake at 450° or broil until bubbly.

Variations: Nice served with a tossed green salad or torn lettuce with chopped parsley, sliced green onion, and avocado, topped with Italian dressing.

Village Royale: Our Favorite Recipes

Strawberry Cream Cheese Coffeecake

2½ cups all-purpose flour
1 cup sugar, divided
¾ cup margarine
½ teaspoon baking powder
½ teaspoon baking soda
¼ teaspoon salt
¾ cup sour cream

2 eggs, divided
1 teaspoon almond extract
1 (8-ounce) package cream
    cheese, softened
½ cup strawberry preserves
½ cup sliced almonds, pecans or
    walnuts

Grease and flour bottom and sides of a 9- or 10-inch springform pan. In large bowl, combine flour and ¾ cup sugar. Using pastry blender, cut in margarine until it resembles coarse crumbs. Reserve 1 cup. To remaining crumb mixture, add baking powder, baking soda, salt, sour cream, 1 egg, and almond extract; blend well. Spread batter on bottom and 2 inches up sides of pan.

In a small bowl, combine cream cheese, remaining ¼ cup sugar, and 1 egg; blend well. Pour over batter in pan. Carefully spoon preserves evenly over cheese filling. In another small bowl, combine 1 cup reserved crumb mixture and nuts. Sprinkle over top. Bake until cream cheese filling is set and crust is deep golden brown. Cool 15–30 minutes, then refrigerate.

Note: You can use a 9x13-inch baking pan if you don't have a springform pan.

Christmas Memories

Florida Blueberry Streusel Coffee Cake

Florida's blueberries are the first to ripen in North America and are large and flavorfully sweet. Blueberries contain vitamins A and C, are a good source of fiber, iron, and potassium, and are high in antioxidants.

TOPPING:

½ cup packed brown sugar
3 tablespoons flour
2 teaspoons cinnamon
2 tablespoons butter, softened
¾ cup chopped walnuts

In a small bowl, combine all ingredients for Topping, except nuts, and stir until mixture resembles fine crumbs. Stir in the nuts, and set aside.

BATTER:

½ cup butter, softened
1 cup sugar
2 teaspoons grated lemon rind
3 eggs
2 cups flour
1 teaspoon baking powder
1 teaspoon baking soda
½ teaspoon salt
1 cup sour cream
2 cups blueberries

In a large mixing bowl, cream butter until fluffy; add sugar and grated lemon rind, and beat well. Add eggs, one at a time, beating well after each addition. In a bowl, combine dry ingredients. Add flour mixture to the creamed mixture alternately with sour cream, blending well after each addition. Spread batter into a greased 9x13-inch baking pan. Sprinkle blueberries and then topping over the batter. Bake at 350° for 30–35 minutes. Serve warm.

Florida Cook Book

Sour Cream Coffee Cake

2 cups all-purpose flour	2 eggs
1 teaspoon baking powder	1 teaspoon vanilla
1 teaspoon baking soda	1 cup sour cream
1/4 teaspoon salt	2 tablespoons cinnamon
1/2 cup margarine, softened	1/2 cup chopped nuts
1 1/2 cups sugar, divided	

Preheat oven to 350°. Mix together flour, baking powder, baking soda, and salt; set aside. In large bowl, cream together margarine and 1 cup sugar. Add eggs and vanilla; beat until light. Add dry ingredient mixture alternately with sour cream, mixing well after each addition. Set aside.

In small bowl, combine remaining 1/2 cup sugar, cinnamon, and chopped nuts. Pour half the batter into a well-greased 10-inch tube pan. Sprinkle half of the sugar mixture over batter. Add remaining batter, and top with remaining sugar mixture. Swirl with a knife. Bake 45–55 minutes.

Treasures

Chocolate Chip Coffee Cake

1 stick butter, softened	3/4 teaspoon baking soda
1 1/2 cups sugar, divided	1 teaspoon baking powder
2 eggs	1 teaspoon vanilla
1 cup sour cream	1/2 cup chocolate chips
2 cups flour	1/2 teaspoon cinnamon

Blend butter and 1 cup sugar well, then add eggs, sour cream, flour, soda, baking powder, and vanilla; blend again. In separate bowl mix chips, cinnamon, and remaining sugar. Grease tube pan and pour half of cake mixture in; sprinkle with half chips-sugar mixture. Pour remaining batter on top, then chips mixture again. Bake at 350° for 45–55 minutes. Test for doneness with toothpick.

The Galley K.I.S.S. Cookbook

Oatmeal Pancakes

2 eggs
1½ cups milk
1 cup uncooked quick rolled oats
¼ cup margarine or butter,
  melted

1 cup flour
1 tablespoon baking powder
1 teaspoon salt
2 tablespoons sugar

In large bowl, beat eggs. Stir in milk and oats. Let stand 5 minutes. Add margarine. Mix dry ingredients. Stir into oat mixture until just blended. Cook pancakes on a hot greased griddle until covered with bubbles. Turn and brown other side. A little bit of work, but delicious.

A Collection of Favorite Recipes

Grandma Benson's Swedish Toast

½ cup butter, softened
1 cup sugar
1 egg
½ teaspoon baking soda
2 cups flour
1½ teaspoons baking powder

½ teaspoon salt
½ cup sour milk
½ cup chopped almonds or
  pecans
Cinnamon sugar

Preheat oven to 350°. Cream butter and sugar. Add egg. Mix dry ingredients and add alternately with milk. Stir in nuts. Bake in a 9-inch-square pan 35 minutes or until center springs back. Cool slightly. Reduce oven heat to 250°. Slice into 1½-inch slices and then in half. Place on a cookie sheet; sprinkle with cinnamon sugar and dry in the oven about 10 minutes. Turn off oven and let toast remain 20 minutes longer. Broil lightly until just browned, if needed. Cool. Store airtight. Good for dunking in coffee or cocoa.

Strictly Scratch

Blintz Soufflé

12 small frozen blintzes, cut in
  half
1 pint sour cream
½ cup orange juice
½ cup sugar

2 teaspoons vanilla
½ teaspoon salt
6 eggs, beaten
1 stick margarine

Place blintzes in a 9x13-inch pan and cut in half. Blend together sour cream, orange juice, sugar, vanilla, salt, and beaten eggs. Pour mixture on top of blintzes. Cut up stick of margarine into slivers and place on top of mixture. Bake at 350° for 45 minutes. Serves 6.

Note: A blintz is an ultra-thin pancake. Delicious when topped with hot blueberries, cherries, or strawberries.

Cooking with Class

Brown Bears in an Apple Orchard

Cooking oil or butter
2–3 apples, sliced

1 package gingerbread mix

Line 8x8-inch baking pan with foil. Grease foil with oil or butter. Line bottom of pan with sliced apples. Mix gingerbread according to directions. Pour over fruit. Cover and bake at 350° for 25–30 minutes. Makes 8 servings.

Cooking with 257

Almost twice the size of Delaware, the Florida Everglades encompass some 4,000 square miles. Everglades National Park is the only subtropical preserve in North America. A swamp such as the Fakahatchee Strand in the Everglades functions in three major ways. First, its vegetation serves as a filter to clean the water as it makes its slow journey southward. Secondly, it is a major habitat for wildlife and plant life. Finally, it actually prevents flooding by slowing down the flow of water after heavy rains.

Christmas Morning Casserole

1 or 2 (8-ounce) packages
  crescent rolls
1 pound sausage
6 eggs
2 cups milk
Salt and pepper to taste
1 (24-ounce) package frozen hash
  brown potatoes
1 cup grated cheese

Spray a 9x13-inch baking pan, and place crescent rolls along the bottom. Brown and drain sausage. Beat eggs, milk, salt and pepper together. Layer sausage, egg mixture, potatoes, and top with cheese. Refrigerate overnight.

  Bake at 350° for 45 minutes. Serves 6.

Centennial Cookbook

Bacon-Cheese Brunch

1 pound bacon
1 (20-ounce) can apple slices,
  drained
2 tablespoons sugar
2 cups shredded Cheddar cheese
1½ cups Original Bisquick mix
1½ cups milk
4 eggs

Heat oven to 375°. Grease a 9x13-inch baking dish. Cut each bacon slice into fourths. Cook and stir over medium heat until crisp, then drain. Set bacon aside.

  Mix apples and sugar; spread in dish. Sprinkle with cheese and bacon. Beat remaining ingredients with hand beater until smooth. Pour over top. Bake, uncovered, until knife inserted in center comes out clean, 30–35 minutes. Cut in squares to serve. Serves 8–10.

Trinity Treats

Cheese-Whiz Grits

2 cups milk	1 stick butter or margarine
2 cups water	½ cup half-and-half
½ teaspoon salt	1 (5-ounce) container Cheese Whiz
1 cup quick cooking grits	Garlic powder to taste (optional)

Bring combined water and milk to a boil, and add salt and grits, stirring constantly with a wire whisk. Lower heat to medium-low and cover loosely. Watch mixture carefully as it thickens quickly. Stir occasionally with whisk to prevent lumps. Lower heat to low and continue cooking. When mixture is very thick, remove from heat, and stir in butter, half-and-half, Cheese Whiz, and garlic powder. Combine well and return to low heat (simmer), or place in preheated pan of water over low heat. Continue heating until piping hot. Careful not to scorch bottom. Serve with pat of butter or sprinkle with black pepper. Serves 10.

Cooking with Class

Grits Casserole

1 cup regular grits	4 eggs, beaten
3 cups boiling water	1 cup milk
½ teaspoon salt	¼ cup shredded Cheddar cheese
½ stick butter	

Pour grits into boiling water to which salt has been added. Mix well; cook until thickened. Add butter, beaten eggs, milk, and cheese. Mix well and place in a greased 2-quart casserole. Bake at 350° for 30 minutes. Yields 4–6 servings.

FCCD Cookbook

Green Chile Strata

6 (7½-inch) flour tortillas
4 (4-ounce) cans chopped green
  chiles, drained, divided
½ pound Canadian bacon or
  ham, cut into slivers, divided
4 cups grated Monterey Jack
  cheese, divided
5 eggs, beaten
2 cups milk
1 teaspoon salt

Generously grease a 9x13-inch baking pan. Cover bottom with tortillas. Sprinkle with half the chiles, half ham, half cheese; repeat layers and end with cheese. In medium bowl, combine eggs, milk, and salt. Pour over layered ingredients. Let stand in refrigerator ½ hour or overnight.

Bake at 350° for 45–60 minutes or until strata is slightly puffed and bubbly. Cool 5 minutes, then cut into squares.

Sing for Your Supper

Dianne's Best Frittata

4 medium unpeeled potatoes,
  thinly sliced
2 tablespoons butter
1 medium onion, chopped
Salt and pepper to taste
1 unpeeled zucchini, thinly sliced
6 eggs
2 tablespoons very hot water
2 ounces Monterey Jack cheese,
  shredded

Soak potatoes in cold water for 15 minutes, then dry. Heat butter in a 10-inch sauté pan with oven-proof handle. Add potatoes, onion, salt and pepper. Cover and simmer about 15 minutes, until potatoes are almost tender. Carefully turn the potatoes. Distribute zucchini slices over potatoes and re-cover the pan.

Meanwhile, beat eggs with a fork and add hot water, beating again. Pour into pan and tilt pan to distribute eggs evenly. Cover and cook over low heat about 10 minutes or until eggs are almost set. Top with cheese and place under the broiler on low until cheese melts and eggs are set. Cover, away from any heat, until ready to serve. Cut into wedges. Serves 6.

Strictly Scratch

Frittata Hot and Cold

1 tablespoon butter
1 tablespoon olive oil
1 medium green pepper, diced
1 large onion, diced
1 cup diced cooked ham or
  kielbasa sausage
7 large mushrooms, stems and
  caps, sliced

1 small zucchini, diced
6 large eggs
¼ cup freshly grated Parmesan
  cheese
½ cup Cheddar cheese
Salt and freshly ground pepper to
  taste

Melt butter in olive oil in a 12-inch skillet. Add all ingredients except eggs, cheeses, and seasonings. Sauté until vegetables are soft, but not browned. While vegetables and meat are sautéing, beat eggs until thick and foamy. Add cheeses and salt and pepper. Add to sautéed mixture. Let the egg mixture set up. Do not stir. When eggs are set and begin to bubble, place under broiler until top is browned. Serve immediately (hot). Serves 6.

To serve frittata cold: When the frittata is cooked as above, let it cool and place in refrigerator for at least 2–3 hours or overnight. The frittata will keep for 4–5 days in the refrigerator.

For each serving, toast half an English muffin and spread with 2 tablespoons Russian dressing. Place a 3-inch round of the frittata on each muffin. Add a large slice of ripe tomato and thin slices of ripe avocado, then cover with Russian dressing.

Let's Talk Food from A to Z

Strawberry Pineapple Jam

1 (10-ounce) package Birds Eye
   Quick Thaw Strawberries,
   thawed
1 (20-ounce) can crushed
   pineapple, drained

¼ cup water
3½ cups (1½ pounds) sugar
1 (1¾-ounce) box Sure-Jell Fruit
   Pectin
Paraffin

First, prepare the fruit. Thoroughly crush berries. Measure 1 cup strawberries and juice into a large saucepan; add pineapple and water.

Then make the jam. Measure sugar and set aside. Mix fruit pectin into fruit in saucepan. Place over high heat and stir until mixture comes to a hard boil. Immediately add all sugar and stir. Bring to a full, rolling boil and boil hard 1 minute, stirring constantly. Remove from heat, and skim off foam with a metal spoon. Then stir and skim for 5 minutes to cool slightly and prevent floating fruit. Ladle quickly into glasses. Cover at once with ⅛ inch hot paraffin. Makes about 5½ cups or 7 glasses.

Simply Florida...Strawberries

Soups, Chilies, and Stews

A diver greets a guest staying at the Jules' Undersea Lodge in Key Largo. The lodge is the first and only underwater hotel. Accomodating up to six people, the cottage-sized building has two bedrooms, a living room, showers, and a kitchen. The lodge actually began its existence as a research laboratory.

Cheeca Lodge's Jamaican Seafood Soup

SOUP BASE:

2 ounces apple-smoked bacon, chopped

⅓ cup diced yellow onion

½ cup diced celery

½ cup diced leek

2 tablespoons packed dark brown sugar

Pinch of cayenne pepper

1 ounce Jamaican jerk seasoning

2 cups fish broth

5 fresh plum tomatoes, diced

½ bunch fresh tarragon, chopped

Salt to taste

Croutons, sliced scallions, or yogurt for garnish

Cook bacon in a saucepan. Add onion, celery, and leek. Cook over low heat for 15 minutes or until vegetables are translucent. Add sugar and cook 3 minutes over low heat. Add cayenne pepper and jerk seasoning. Cook 1 minute. Stir in broth and tomatoes. Simmer 30 minutes. Add tarragon and salt.

SEAFOOD:

3 ounces shrimp, coarsely chopped

3 ounces snapper, dolphin, or grouper, coarsely chopped

3 ounces stone crabmeat, coarsely chopped

6 tablespoons butter

Cook shrimp, snapper, and crabmeat in butter over low heat until done. Place in soup bowls. Top with hot Soup Base. Garnish with croutons, sliced scallions, or yogurt. Yields 4 servings.

Calypso Café

Red Pepper Soup

Just a wonderful soup, and such a pretty color.

4 tablespoons olive oil
1 medium onion, chopped
5 red peppers, seeded and
  chopped
2 medium potatoes, diced

1 clove garlic, minced
5 cups chicken broth
1 cup evaporated milk
Chopped green onion and sour
  cream for garnish

Heat oil, then add onion, and cook until transparent. Add red peppers; cook until soft. Add potatoes, garlic, and chicken broth. Cook for 1 hour, then put in blender and mix; add milk. Serve with chopped onion and a dot of sour cream. Serves 8.

Les Soups Fantastiques

Taco Soup

2 whole chicken breasts
2 (14-ounce) cans chicken stock
1 (15-ounce) can whole peeled
  tomatoes, chopped
1 (15-ounce) can yellow hominy
1 (15-ounce) can creamed corn
2 (15-ounce) cans pinto beans
1 small onion, chopped
1 each: green, red, and yellow
  bell pepper, chopped

Taco seasoning to taste
1 teaspoon oregano to taste
1 medium onion, chopped, for
  garnish
1 large tomato, chopped, for
  garnish
½ pound Cheddar cheese,
  shredded, for garnish
Tortilla chips

In saucepan, cover chicken breasts with water and simmer until cooked through. Drain breasts and discard skin and bones. Using 2 forks, shred meat. In large stockpot, add shredded chicken, chicken stock, tomatoes, hominy, corn, beans, and onion. Simmer for 30 minutes.

Add peppers, taco seasoning, and oregano and cook 15 minutes. Serve in bowls and garnish with onion, tomato, and cheese. Serve with tortilla chips.

Cookin' on Island Time

Spanish Bean Soup
(Potaje de Garbanzos)

½ pound garbanzo beans, dried
(chickpeas)
1 tablespoon salt
2 quarts water
1 ham bone
1 beef bone
¼ pound salt pork, cut in thin
strips

1 onion, finely chopped
2 potatoes, peeled and cut in
quarters
½ teaspoon paprika
Pinch of saffron
1 chorizo (Spanish sausage),
sliced in thin rounds

Wash garbanzos. Soak overnight with 1 tablespoon salt in enough water to cover beans.

Drain salted water from beans. Place beans in 4-quart soup kettle; add 2 quarts of water and ham and beef bones. Cook for 45 minutes over low heat, skimming foam from top. Fry salt pork slowly in a skillet. Add chopped onion and sauté lightly. Add to beans along with potatoes, paprika, and saffron. Add salt to taste. When potatoes are tender, remove from heat and add chorizo. Serve hot in deep soup bowls. Serves 4.

The Columbia Restaurant Spanish Cookbook

Florida was owned by the British from 1763 to 1783. Spain gained control of Florida in 1783 as part of the Treaty of Paris which ended the American Revolution. Finally, Spain sold Florida to the United States in 1821 for $5 million.

Cabbage and Beef Soup

1 pound lean ground beef
½ teaspoon garlic salt
¼ teaspoon garlic powder
½ teaspoon pepper
2 celery ribs, chopped
1 (15- to 16-ounce) can kidney
  beans, undrained

½ medium head cabbage, chopped
1 (28-ounce) can tomatoes with
  liquid, chopped
1 tomato can water
4 beef bouillon cubes
Chopped fresh parsley

In a Dutch oven, brown beef; add all remaining ingredients, except parsley. Bring to a boil. Reduce heat and simmer, covered, for 1 hour. Garnish with parsley. Yields 3 quarts.

Treasured Recipes from Near and Far

White Chili Soup

On a diet? Try this!

1 medium onion, chopped
1 cup chopped green pepper
1 cup chopped red pepper
1 cup chopped celery
1 or 2 jalapeño peppers, chopped
3 medium cloves garlic, chopped
4 tablespoons olive oil
1 pound ground turkey meat,
  browned
2 tablespoons cumin powder

½ cup chopped fresh basil, or
  1 tablespoon dry basil
1 tablespoon thyme
2 tablespoons chopped parsley
3 cups cooked navy beans, or
  canned
1½ cups cooked barley
6 cups chicken broth
2 cups shredded Cheddar cheese
Chopped green onions for garnish

Cook the first 6 ingredients in olive oil until transparent. Add turkey and mix well. Add cumin, basil, thyme, and parsley. Mix again and add beans, barley, and chicken broth. Cook 15 minutes. Stir in cheese until thoroughly blended. Serve with chopped green onions. Serves 8.

Les Soups Fantastiques

Hearty Tortellini Soup

2 cloves garlic, crushed
1 tablespoon margarine
2 (14½-ounce) cans chicken broth
1 (8-ounce) package fresh or frozen cheese tortellini
1 (10-ounce) package frozen, chopped spinach, thawed
1 (16-ounce) can stewed tomatoes, undrained and coarsely chopped
Grated Parmesan cheese

In a large saucepan over medium heat, cook garlic in margarine for 2–3 minutes. Add broth and tortellini; heat to a boil. Reduce heat and simmer for 10 minutes. Add spinach and tomatoes; simmer 5 minutes more. Serve topped with cheese. Delicious. Serves 6.

Heaven in a Pot

Garlic Soup

This soup is so very healthy, it will do wonders for a cold or sore throat. Do not be afraid of the amount of garlic, as cooked garlic will lose some of its strength.

41 medium cloves garlic, peeled
1 cup chopped red pepper
1 cup chopped green pepper
1 cup chopped celery
1 medium onion, chopped
½ cup chopped fresh parsley
4 tablespoons olive oil
3 cups chopped or diced tomatoes, fresh or canned, with their juice
1 cup V-8 juice
6 cups chicken broth
1 cup white wine
½ cup sherry
½ cup raw rice or 1 cup cooked rice
1 tablespoon Italian seasoning
Black pepper to taste
Chopped green onions for garnish

Mix first 6 ingredients in a food processor. Cook processed ingredients in olive oil until very soft, mixing often. (If it sticks to the pot, add a little water and continue cooking very slowly.) Add all other ingredients and bring to a boil, stirring so the rice does not stick. Lower heat and cook for 1½ hours. Season with black pepper to taste. Serve with green onions for garnish. Serves 8.

Les Soups Fantastiques

Cream of Carrot Soup

We all know carrots are wonderful for the eyes.

1 onion, chopped
1 small green pepper, chopped
4 tablespoons olive oil
6 carrots, diced or sliced
2 medium potatoes, diced
2 cloves garlic, minced

6 fresh basil leaves
4 cups chicken broth
Salt and pepper to taste
1 cup evaporated milk
Basil leaf and Parmesan cheese for
   garnish

Cook onion and green pepper in oil until limp; add carrots, potatoes, garlic, and fresh basil. Stir in chicken broth, bring to a boil and simmer about 1 hour until carrots and potatoes are very tender. Salt and pepper to taste. Put in blender to blend; return to pot and add milk. Reheat to serve. Garnish with a leaf of fresh basil and grated Parmesan cheese. Serves 8.

Les Soups Fantastiques

Cheesy Broccoli Soup

½ cup margarine
1 medium onion, chopped
4 (15-ounce) cans chicken broth
2 broth cans water
1 (16-ounce) package frozen,
   chopped broccoli

1 pound Velveeta cheese, cubed
2 cups half-and-half
1 (8-ounce) package angel hair
   pasta
Garlic salt ot taste

Melt margarine in a large stockpot. Add onion; sauté until tender. Add chicken broth and water. Add broccoli. Combine cheese and half-and-half in a microwave-safe dish. Microwave on MEDIUM until cheese melts. Stir to blend well. Add cheese mixture and pasta to stockpot. Season with garlic salt. Cook over low heat until soup thickens (pasta will disintegrate). Yields 15–20 servings.

Gator Championship Recipes

Fresh Basil Soup

In Italy and Romania, basil is considered a love plant, so be romantic, try this soup with a loved one.

1 medium onion, chopped
4 tablespoons olive oil
2 medium potatoes, diced
2 bunches fresh basil, chopped

5 cups chicken broth
1 cup evaporated milk
2 tablespoons sour cream
Pepper to taste

Brown onion in olive oil until transparent; add potatoes, basil, and chicken broth, and slowly cook for 1 hour. Put in blender with milk and sour cream, then mix and serve with a leaf of fresh basil. Serves 8.

Les Soups Fantastiques

Chilled Strawberry Soup

2 oranges, peeled and thinly
    sliced
1 cinnamon stick
2 cups water
¼ cup sugar

2 cups sliced strawberries
Dash salt
1½ tablespoons cornstarch
1 tablespoon water

Simmer oranges and cinnamon stick in 2 cups water for 5 minutes. Remove cinnamon stick and set aside. Add sugar, strawberries, and dash of salt, and bring to a boil. Turn heat to low. Blend cornstarch and 1 tablespoon water, and stir into soup until clear. Chill with cinnamon stick.

Variation: May substitute peaches, apricots, cherries, or a combination of fruit.

Favorite Florida Recipes

Dr. John Gorrie of Apalachicola invented mechanical refrigeration in 1851.

Crab Island Bisque

1 pound Florida blue crabmeat
2 tablespoons finely chopped onion
2 tablespoons finely chopped celery
¼ cup margarine or butter, melted

3 tablespoons all-purpose flour
1 teaspoon salt
¼ teaspoon paprika
⅛ teaspoon white pepper
1 quart milk
¼ cup chopped parsley

Remove any remaining shell or cartilage from crabmeat. Cook onion and celery in margarine until tender, but not brown. Blend in flour and seasonings. Add milk gradually, stirring constantly; cook until thickened. Add crabmeat and heat. Just before serving, sprinkle with parsley. Yields 6 servings.

Crab Island Cookbook

Lobster Bisque

STOCK:
3 lobsters
Water
3 tablespoons ground cloves

3 tablespoons garlic powder
1 large sweet onion, peeled and chopped

Boil lobsters, reserving water. Remove lobster meat from shells and cut into bite-size pieces. Put all shells in leftover lobster water. Add cloves, garlic powder, and onion. Bring to a boil. Reduce heat, and simmer uncovered for about an hour and a half. Poke and stir occasionally to make sure all the good flavor gets into the stock.

BISQUE:
8 tablespoons butter
8 tablespoons flour

2 cups lobster stock
2 cups half-and-half (1 pint)

In a double boiler, melt butter. Add flour and stir until it is completely combined with butter. Add stock and half-and-half. Stir constantly until Bisque thickens. Do not stop stirring until it thickens. Add lobster pieces to Bisque and wait about 10 minutes for lobster meat to warm. Enjoy.

Favorite Florida Recipes

Bruce's Shrimp Bisque Thai Style

MARINADE:

2 pounds medium shrimp
⅓ cup fresh lime juice
1 tablespoon minced cilantro
1 tablespoon peeled fresh ginger
¼ teaspoon ground red pepper

1½ tablespoons grated lime rind
1½ tablespoons ground
  coriander
1½ teaspoons sugar
2 garlic cloves, crushed

Peel shrimp, reserving shells. Combine shrimp and remaining ingredients in large zip lock bag and refrigerate 30 minutes.

SHRIMP STOCK:

Shrimp shells
2 cups water mixed with
  ¼ cup dry white wine

1 tablespoon tomato paste

Prepare stock by combining shells, water, wine, and tomato paste in Dutch oven. Bring to a boil. Reduce heat; simmer until liquid is reduced to about 1 cup. Strain mixture over a bowl; discard solids and keep stock.

SOUP:

1 teaspoon olive oil
½ cup chopped onion
⅓ cup chopped celery
1 (14-ounce) can coconut milk
1 tablespoon tomato paste
¼ cup all-purpose flour

1 cup heavy cream
1 tablespoon lime rind
1 tablespoon minced fresh
  cilantro
½ teaspoon salt

Heat olive oil in Dutch oven over medium heat. Add onion and celery; sauté 8 minutes or until browned. Add Shrimp Stock, coconut milk, and tomato paste, scraping pan to loosen browned bits. Bring to a boil. Combine flour and cream in small bowl, stirring with a whisk. Add to pan; reduce heat and simmer until thick, about 5 minutes. Add shrimp and Marinade; cook for only 5 minutes. Stir in lime rind, cilantro, and salt. Makes 4–6 servings.

Recipes of Spruce Creek

Shrimp Gumbo

2 tablespoons flour
4 tablespoons oil, divided
2 pounds shrimp
2 onions, chopped
3 garlic cloves, minced
3 cups okra, sliced

1 can tomatoes, crushed
2 quarts water
1 bay leaf
4 hot peppers to taste
1 teaspoon salt

Brown flour and 2 tablespoons oil. Place cleaned shrimp in flour mixture. Cook until shrimp are pink. Set aside. Sauté chopped onion and garlic in remaining 2 tablespoons oil. Add okra, tomatoes, water, bay leaf, and peppers. Bring to a boil, then add flour and shrimp mixture. Simmer for 30 minutes, and salt to taste.

Cooking with People to People

Valencia Garden's Caldo Gallego

1 (1½-pound) ham hock
½ pound lean beef
½ pound salt pork
1 bunch turnip greens
Dash nutmeg
1 cup Great Northern white
    beans, soaked and drained

1 onion, chopped
1 green pepper, chopped
1 clove garlic, minced
3 tablespoons bacon grease
3 potatoes, peeled and cubed
2 chorizo sausages
Salt to taste

In a 4-quart pot, place ham hock, beef, and pork. Cover with water and bring to a boil. Skim several times. Cook over medium heat until tender, about one hour. Chop greens and add to meat. Add nutmeg and beans. Cook uncovered on low heat for 30 minutes. In a skillet, sauté onion, green pepper, and garlic in bacon grease. Add to soup. Add potatoes, chorizos, and salt. Cover and cook 45 minutes longer, until potatoes are done. Serves 6.

Florida's Historic Restaurants and Their Recipes

Western Hill Turkey Chili

1 teaspoon vegetable oil
1 onion, chopped
1 red bell pepper, finely chopped
1 green bell pepper, finely
  chopped
3 cloves garlic, minced
1½ pounds turkey breasts,
  coarsely ground
2 cups chicken broth
2 tablespoons chili powder
2 tablespoons ground cumin

2 tablespoons powdered cocoa
1–2 teaspoons cayenne pepper
¼ cup tarragon vinegar
¼ teaspoon salt
2 tablespoons strong brewed
  coffee
2 (14-ounce) cans plum tomatoes,
  crushed
2 tablespoons flour (optional)
2 cups cooked, black beans

Heat oil in a heavy skillet or Dutch oven. Sauté onion, bell peppers, and garlic until the onion is transparent, but not brown. Remove vegetables from cooking utensil, and set aside.

Cook turkey in remaining oil until it is grayish in color and not browned. Stir to break up turkey while cooking. Add vegetables to turkey and simmer, while adding chicken broth, after which the seasonings can be added. Add coffee and plum tomatoes. Bring kettle to a boil; reduce heat and simmer for 40–50 minutes. Stir in flour if chili mixture is too thin, or either a little water or tomato juice if it is necessary to thin the consistency. Add beans a few minutes before preparing to serve and heat them through.

Chilimania!

40 Minute Chili

2 tablespoons oil
1 onion, chopped
1 or 2 cloves garlic, minced
1 pound ground meat
2 (10¾-ounce) cans condensed
  tomato soup

2 (16-ounce) cans kidney beans
2 teaspoons chili powder
½ teaspoon salt
⅛–¼ teaspoon red pepper
  (optional)
Dash black pepper

In oil, sauté onion and garlic. Brown meat; stir in soup, beans, chili powder, salt, and peppers. Cover and simmer 30 minutes, stirring occasionally.

Chilimania!

Cold Weather Chili

1 (16-ounce) package dried pinto
  beans
2½ pounds lean ground beef
1 pound lean ground pork
3 medium green peppers,
  chopped
2 medium onions, chopped
2 cloves garlic, crushed
5 (16-ounce) cans whole
  tomatoes, undrained, cut up

1½ quarts water
4 tablespoons freshly chopped
  parsley
4 tablespoons chili powder
1½ teaspoons cumin seeds
1½ teaspoons salt
1 teaspoon freshly ground pepper
Dash or 2 hot sauce

Sort and wash pinto beans, placing them in a large Dutch oven. Add enough water so that beans are covered by about 2 inches of water. Let them soak overnight.

Next day, rinse beans, change the water, and bring to a boil. Reduce heat, cover, and let simmer until beans are tender, about 2 hours or so. Check for tenderness after 1 hour, and govern additional cooking time.

Sauté ground meats, green peppers, onions, and garlic in a skillet with a little oil, until meats are done and vegetables are tender. Stir with a wooden spoon to break and crumble meats as they cook. Drain excess fat from skillet, and mix in parsley and chili powder; simmer for 15 minutes.

Add meat mixture to Dutch oven, as well as all remaining ingredients. Bring to a boil; reduce heat to simmer, then cover, and cook for an additional hour, stirring occasionally. Uncover, and check for taste and desired consistency. If too thick, add a little water. If your chili is too thin, mix a little all-purpose flour with some water into a paste, and add to the chili, mixing thoroughly to blend. Leave pot uncovered, and cook over medium heat for an hour longer. Makes about a gallon of chili.

Chilimania!

Catfish Stew, Southern Style

2 slices bacon
1 large onion, chopped
1 large can tomatoes
2 large potatoes, diced
1 teaspoon salt
1 cup boiling water

2 tablespoons Worcestershire
  sauce
¼ cup ketchup
¼ teaspoon thyme
1¼ pounds skinned catfish
  fillets, cut into bite-size pieces

In Dutch oven or heavy saucepan, fry bacon; remove, then drain on paper and crumble back into pan with chopped onion. Brown onion lightly, then add water, tomatoes, and other ingredients except fish. Simmer for 30 minutes, covered. Add fish and simmer, uncovered, 15 more minutes. Serves 4.

From Hook to Table

Steel Pot Stew

1 pound ground beef
½ cup chopped onion
2 (16-ounce) cans kidney beans,
  rinsed and drained, divided
1 (14½-ounce) can beef broth
1 (16-ounce) can crushed
  tomatoes
4 cups chopped cabbage

3 potatoes, peeled, cut in bite-size
  pieces
½ teaspoon dried basil
½ teaspoon dried marjoram
½ teaspoon dried thyme
½ teaspoon salt
⅛ teaspoon pepper

In a Dutch oven or large stockpot, cook beef and onion until meat is browned and onion is tender; drain. In a small bowl, mash ¼ cup beans and ¼ cup beef broth. Add to pot remaining beans and broth, tomatoes, cabbage, potatoes, basil, marjoram, thyme, salt, and pepper. Cover and simmer for 30 minutes or until cabbage and potatoes are tender. Yields 6 servings.

Great Recipes from Near and Afar

Salads

Tucked at the edge of the Atlantic Ocean in Daytona Beach, the Daytona Beach Bandshell is one of the area's most recognizable landmarks. Constructed in 1936, the 48x114-foot bandshell is made of coquina rock.

Grilled Chicken Salad

2 boneless, skinless chicken
  breast halves
Garlic powder
Greek seasoning (optional)
Fat-free Italian dressing
4 cups torn salad greens

2 plum tomatoes, sliced
2 thin slices Bermuda onion
1/2 cup fat-free Cheddar or Feta
  cheese
Italian dressing or vinaigrette

Preheat grill. Pound chicken to 1/4-inch thickness with a mallet. Cut into 1-inch slices, but leave about 1/2 inch uncut at one end, so strips stay together. Sprinkle with garlic powder and Greek seasoning, if desired. Place on grill. Cook about 5 minutes on each side, until no longer pink. Baste both sides with fat-free dressing, and cook about 30 seconds on each side.

Meanwhile, divide and pile greens onto 2 plates. Spread one tomato over each pile, then separate onion slices into rings and add. Sprinkle cheese on top, and drizzle with vinaigrette to taste. Remove chicken from grill. Cut slices completely apart and lay on top of salad. Serve hot or cold. Makes 2 servings.

Cooking for Two, No Nonsense Cookbook

Mango Chicken

The hot mango chutney does not make this salad hot; it just gives it a spicy taste. This is a great salad. Can be served on a lettuce leaf, in a scooped-out tomato shell, or even on sandwich bread. Enjoy.

8 chicken breast halves
Water to cover
¾–1 cup sour cream
¾–1 cup mayonnaise
1 (9-ounce) jar hot mango
   chutney

½ teaspoon cumin
¾ teaspoon curry
1 cup finely sliced celery
½–1 cup golden raisins
   (optional)

Place chicken breasts in large pot and cover with water. Cook until chicken is very tender. Drain (freeze broth for later use), then cut chicken into small, bite-size pieces. Mix remaining ingredients and add to chicken. Stir until completely mixed. Place in refrigerator in covered container, and cool until about ½ hour before serving.

Christmas Memories

Crab-Potato Salad

4 cups cooked stone crabmeat,
   cartilage removed, lightly
   flaked with a fork
6 medium potatoes, boiled,
   chilled, peeled and cubed
4 eggs, hard-cooked, chilled,
   peeled and diced
½ medium green bell pepper,
   stem and seeds removed,
   finely diced

1 medium onion, finely diced
2 ribs celery, finely diced
2 cups mayonnaise
¼ cup sweet pickle relish
1 tablespoon salt
½ teaspoon freshly ground black
   pepper
Lettuce (optional)

Combine all ingredients except lettuce, and chill for several hours. Serve as is, or in crisp lettuce cups.

Variation: Substitute crawfish (Florida lobster), cut into bite-size pieces.

Cookin' in the Keys

Grilled Red Potato Salad

4 pounds new potatoes
½ cup olive oil, divided
Salt and freshly ground pepper
　to taste
12 ounces sliced smoked bacon
1 large red onion, thinly sliced
¼ cup plus 2 tablespoons white
　wine vinegar

1 tablespoon sugar
¼ cup coarsely chopped flat-leaf
　parsley
1 cup crumbled bleu cheese or
　feta cheese

Combine potatoes with enough water to cover in a saucepan. Bring to a boil. Boil until almost tender; drain. Cool slightly and cut potatoes into halves. Toss potatoes with ¼ cup olive oil in a bowl. Season with salt and pepper. Grill cut-side-down over hot coals for 3 minutes; turn. Grill for 2–3 minutes longer. Remove potatoes to a large bowl.

Heat a medium skillet on the stove top or grill until almost smoking. Add bacon. Cook until golden brown and crisp, turning occasionally. Remove bacon to a plate lined with paper towels to drain, reserving bacon drippings. Let bacon stand until cool and crumble.

Drain skillet, reserving 2 tablespoons of bacon drippings. Cook onion in reserved bacon drippings for 5–6 minutes or until tender. Stir in vinegar, remaining ¼ cup olive oil, and sugar. Cook until sugar dissolves, stirring frequently. Spoon onion mixture over potatoes. Add bacon and parsley and toss to mix. Season with salt and pepper. Spoon potato salad onto a large serving platter. Sprinkle with cheese. Serves 10–12.

Bay Fêtes

Built between 1845 and 1866, Fort Zachary Taylor in Key West was controlled by the Union during the Civil War. The fort was home base for a successful blockade of Confederate ships.

Pineapple Boat with Creamy Dill Shrimp Salad

A real tropical beauty. The pineapple boat is great stuffed with shrimp salad and garnished with fresh fruit. Magnificent!

CREAMY DILL SHRIMP SALAD:

10 ounces shrimp (medium or baby)
1/4 cup mayonnaise
3 tablespoons chopped celery
1 tablespoon chopped onion
1/4 lemon, squeezed for juice
1 tablespoon chopped dill
Salt and pepper to taste

Cook shrimp in a pot of boiling water. If using medium-size shrimp, it will take 1–2 minutes. When shrimp are done, remove from pot and cool with ice water. In mixing bowl, combine mayonnaise, celery, onion, lemon juice, and dill, and mix thoroughly. Next, add shrimp and toss gently together. Add salt and pepper to taste.

PRESENTATION:

1 medium pineapple
1/4 head leaf lettuce, washed
1/4 cantaloupe, peeled and diced
1/2 pint strawberries, washed
1/4 pint raspberries, washed
2 bunches red seedless grapes

Split pineapple in half lengthwise. If possible, also split the top in half. Cut out the inside of each pineapple half to form a boat. This is where you will place the Creamy Dill Shrimp Salad.

Now you will design the plate. First, cover plates with leaf lettuce, then set each half of pineapple on plates. The pineapple will be on one side of plate so fruit will sit in front. Fill each pineapple with shrimp salad. Clean and cut all fruit, and arrange neatly in front of pineapple boats. Serves 2.

Mastering the Art of Florida Seafood

Shrimp Macaroni Salad

¾ cup Miracle Whip
¼ cup ketchup
¼ head cabbage, shredded
1 cucumber, diced
4 stalks celery, cut fine

6–8 green onions, chopped
2 cups cooked, small shell
 macaroni
1 pound frozen cooked shrimp,
 thawed

Mix together Miracle Whip and ketchup, and combine with remaining ingredients in large bowl. Chill well. Serve with fresh fruit.

Sing for Your Supper

Shrimp Salad

3½ cups shrimp, cooked,
 peeled, deveined, and cut into
 bite-size pieces
1 cup chopped celery
⅓ cup finely chopped onion
1 cup chopped green pepper
2 hard-boiled eggs, chopped
¼ cup fresh lime juice
2 tablespoons catsup

2 teaspoons sugar
1½ teaspoons vinegar
1 teaspoon Worcestershire sauce
½ teaspoon salt
1 teaspoon Tabasco sauce or to
 taste
¾ cup real mayonnaise, not
 salad dressing

In a 2-quart mixing bowl, combine shrimp, celery, onion, green pepper, and eggs, and pour lime juice over all. In a small bowl, combine remaining ingredients, except mayonnaise. Pour over shrimp and stir. Add mayonnaise, and blend well. Chill; serve on lettuce.

Tropical Tastes and Tantalizing Tales

Holiday Pasta Salad

This looks like a lot of ingredients and a lot of trouble, but you can have the salad made in approximately 30 minutes. And besides, it is worth all the time and effort you put into it. Everyone loves this salad.

½ cup tarragon vinegar
1 (9-ounce) jar green olives,
   whole, drained and liquid
   reserved
¼ cup oil

1 clove garlic, minced
1 teaspoon oregano
3 (6-ounce) jars sliced mushrooms,
   drained

Mix vinegar, olive liquid, oil, garlic, and oregano; add mushrooms and olives. Marinate overnight, if possible.

2 cups Newman's Own Oil and
   Vinegar Salad Dressing

2 cups ranch dressing (regular, not
   light)

Mix well and reserve for salad. (If you should have any left over, the combination of these 2 dressings makes a great salad dressing.)

1 (8-ounce) package pasta (your
   choice, but colored, if possible)
1 medium red bell pepper, diced
1 medium green bell pepper,
   diced
1 medium sweet onion, thinly
   sliced (optional)

1 cup frozen small English peas,
   uncooked
1 (2-ounce) jar chopped pimento,
   drained
½ (12-ounce) jar mild banana
   pepper rings

Cook pasta according to directions on package, but do not over-cook. Drain and rinse. Add all remaining ingredients. Stir until completely mixed. Add marinade and salad dressing. This will keep in refrigerator for about 2 weeks, but it won't last that long if you have many pasta lovers.

Variation: Grilled chicken or baked ham can be added to your pasta salad to make it a meal.

Christmas Memories

Black Bean and Corn Salad

1 (16-ounce) can beans, rinsed and drained
1 (16-ounce) can garbanzo beans, drained
1 (8¾-ounce) can whole-kernel corn
12 ripe, stuffed green olives, thinly sliced
1 small onion, diced
2 tablespoons capers with juice, mashed
6 black olives, thinly sliced
½ cup finely chopped green bell pepper
1 large plum tomato, diced
2 tablespoons extra virgin olive oil

Place beans and corn in colander; rinse once, drain well. Place bean mixture into a large bowl; add remaining ingredients and toss lightly. Let sit for 5 minutes before serving, or chill until serving time. This salad stays fresh up to 3 days in the refrigerator. Serves 8.

The Cruising K.I.S.S. Cookbook II

Pesto Pasta Salad

PESTO:
6 ounces fresh basil, divided
2 cups olive oil, divided
3 large cloves garlic
2 cups grated Parmesan, divided
1½ teaspoons salt
½ teaspoon black pepper

Combine 3 ounces basil and 1 cup oil with garlic cloves in blender. Blend on high. Add 1 cup cheese; blend. Add remaining basil, oil, and Parmesan; blend. Add salt and pepper; blend.

PASTA SALAD (PER SERVING):
6 ounces tri-colored rotini
1 ounce Pesto
1 ounce sun-dried tomatoes
1 artichoke heart
Feta cheese
½ pita bread, torn

Combine rotini, pesto, and tomatoes in a bowl. Cut artichoke heart in half and place on either side of salad. Top salad with feta cheese. Add warmed pita bread.

Favorite Florida Recipes

Paella Salad

The flavors blend nicely when this salad is made 4–5 hours before serving. Try adding a few shakes of red pepper flakes for added zip. For a striking visual effect, alternate spinach leaves and quartered tomatoes in a circular pattern and mound salad in the center.

1 (10-ounce) package yellow rice
2 boneless chicken breasts, cooked, cut into 1-inch pieces
⅓ pound shrimp, cooked, peeled
½ red pepper, chopped
½ green pepper, chopped
3 scallions (including stems), chopped
2 medium tomatoes, seeded and chopped
⅓ cup olive oil
1 garlic clove, minced
2 tablespoons tarragon vinegar
⅛ teaspoon dry mustard

Cook yellow rice according to instructions on package. Add chicken, shrimp, peppers, scallions, and tomatoes; set aside.

In a jar, combine olive oil, garlic, tarragon vinegar, and dry mustard; shake until well mixed. Pour over rice mixture. Serve at room temperature or warm. Yields 5–6 servings.

A Slice of Paradise

Anything-Goes Marinated Salad

You can choose vegetables according to what's in season or to your own personal preference. It's important to blanche the broccoli and cauliflower before putting this recipe together. Note that this recipe requires 8–24 hours of marinating in the refrigerator, so make it about a day before you need it.

1 head broccoli
1 head cauliflower
1 bowl ice water
10–12 radishes
1–2 medium zucchini, sliced
1–2 medium yellow squash,
  sliced
1 large red, yellow, or Vidalia
  onion, chopped, or 5–7 green
  onions, sliced

8 ounces commercially prepared
  oil and vinegar (Greek or Italian
  salad dressing)
Salt and pepper to taste
1–2 ripe tomatoes, chopped
  (optional)
Fresh parsley or basil, chopped
  (optional)

Chop broccoli and cauliflower into bite-size pieces. Bring a large pot of water to a boil. Prepare a bowl of ice and water. Blanche broccoli and cauliflower in boiling water for 1–2 minutes. Put immediately into ice water. Drain well.

Mix all vegetables in a large bowl. Pour 6–8 ounces of prepared dressing over vegetables. Any oil-and-vinegar-based, non-creamy dressing will do.

Cover vegetables tightly and refrigerate for 8–24 hours. Invert container several times so all vegetables are covered by dressing. Taste before serving. Add salt and pepper to taste. Add ripe tomatoes and fresh parsley or basil as garnish, if desired. Serves 6–8.

The Essential Catfish Cookbook

 Serving only three days (January 3 through January 6, 1987), Wayne Mixson served the shortest term as Florida's governor. Mixson, who was previously lieutenant governor, was serving the remainder of the term of Bob Graham, who had resigned as governor to become a United States Senator.

Marinated Cold Broccoli

2 or 3 bunches broccoli
½–1 (16-ounce) carton sour
  cream
¼ cup vinegar
Garlic salt and fresh-ground
  pepper to taste

1 (15-ounce) can pitted, sliced,
  black olives
1 large red sweet pepper,
  chopped
1 medium red onion, sliced

Cook broccoli slightly until still a little crunchy. Leave flowers whole, and slice the stalks. Toss cooked broccoli with remaining ingredients. Chill at least 4 hours and serve cold as a vegetable or salad.

Cooking in Paradise

The O'Farrell's Salad

DRESSING:
¾ cup canola oil
⅓ cup apple cider vinegar
1 large clove garlic, minced

4–5 teaspoons sugar
½ teaspoon salt
Pepper to taste

Combine all ingredients and chill thoroughly.

SALAD:
1 large avocado, sliced
Lemon juice
1 head romaine lettuce, torn
1 head bibb lettuce, torn
1 large tomato, coarsely chopped

1 medium Vidalia or red onion,
  sliced
4 ounces bleu cheese, crumbled
8 ounces bacon, fried crisp and
  broken in ½-inch pieces

Sprinkle avocado with lemon juice to prevent browning. Combine lettuces, tomato, and onion in a large bowl. Add avocado and mix gently. Add bleu cheese, bacon, and Dressing 10 minutes before serving, tossing to mix. Serves 8.

Horse Tails

Green Bean Salad with Basil Vinaigrette

This easy, quick recipe can be prepared ahead, but do not mix in cheese until ready to serve.

2 pounds green beans, trimmed	**3 tablespoons olive or canola oil**
3 shallots, minced	**⅔ cup chopped fresh basil**
2 tablespoons balsamic or	**⅓ cup grated Romano cheese**
red wine vinegar	**Salt and pepper to taste**

Cook green beans in boiling, salted water to cover in a large Dutch oven just until crisp-tender. Drain, and rinse with cold water to stop cooking process. Arrange in a serving dish.

Combine shallots and vinegar in a bowl; gradually whisk in oil. Whisk in basil. Pour enough dressing over beans to coat; gently stir in cheese. Season with salt and pepper to taste. Yields 8 servings.

Lighthouse Secrets

Town and Country Salad

POPPY SEED DRESSING:

¼ onion, grated
½ cup sugar
½ cup salad oil, divided
⅓ cup apple cider vinegar,
  divided

1 teaspoon dry mustard
1½ teaspoons poppy seeds

Combine onion, sugar, half the oil, and a small amount of the vinegar in a bowl and mix well. Add remaining oil and vinegar gradually, mixing well. Stir in dry mustard and poppy seeds. Chill until serving time.

CARAMELIZED ALMONDS:

½ cup slivered almonds   ¼ cup sugar

Combine almonds with sugar in a skillet. Cook over medium heat until sugar melts and browns, stirring constantly. Spread on foil to cool.

SALAD:

Romaine, Bibb or red leaf
  lettuce, torn

Strawberries, sliced
Brie cheese, cubed

Combine lettuce, strawberries, and cheese in a serving bowl. Add dressing and toss to coat. Top with almonds. Serves 8.

Note: Do not use double-cream Brie for this recipe.

Variation: Add sliced, grilled chicken for a main course luncheon.

Savor the Moment

In 1903, President Theodore Roosevelt established Pelican Island National Wildlife Refuge in Indian River County, the United States' first and oldest national wildlife refuge.

Grand Avenue Mango Salad

Each summer, the Goombay Festival, a Bahamian arts, entertainment, and cultural extravaganza, is held along Grand Avenue in Miami's Coconut Grove. Traditional Bahamian foods are a big part of the fun. Along with chickpeas and rice and conch salad is this easy-to-make mango dish.

2 small to medium green mangoes, peeled and sliced	**Salt and pepper** **Apple cider vinegar**

Place mangoes in a flat-bottomed glass dish, such as a small casserole. Add salt and pepper to taste. Add enough vinegar to cover the slices and refrigerate for several hours before serving.

The Mongo Mango Cookbook

Warm Spinach-Orange Salad

½ (10-ounce) package fresh spinach, stemmed	**2 tablespoons cider vinegar**
1 orange, peeled and sectioned	**1½ tablespoons orange juice**
¼ cup sliced almonds	**1½ tablespoons olive oil**
	1½ tablespoons honey

Combine spinach, orange sections, and almonds in a large bowl. In a saucepan, bring vinegar, juice, oil, and honey to a boil over medium heat. Pour immediately over salad. Toss and serve.

Treasures of the Tropics

Tropical Carrot Salad

2 cups grated carrots
1 (11-ounce) can mandarin
 oranges, drained
1 (20-ounce) can pineapple
 chunks, drained
½ cup raisins

¼ cup coconut (optional)
1 (8-ounce) carton fat-free sour
 cream
2 tablespoons mayonnaise
½ cup chopped pecans or
 walnuts (optional)

Mix all ingredients and let chill a couple of hours. Serve as is, or on lettuce leaves. Makes about 6 servings.

Cooking for Two, No Nonsense Cookbook

Florida Sunshine Salad

1 (12-ounce) can apricot nectar
1 (3-ounce) package lemon
 gelatin
1 (6-ounce) can frozen orange
 juice, thawed

1 (3-ounce) package cream
 cheese, slightly softened
½ cup chopped pecans

Heat apricot nectar to boiling point. Dissolve lemon gelatin in this. Do not dilute. Add undiluted can of orange juice. Make small balls of the cream cheese to which pecans have been added, and place 3 small balls in each mold. Fill mold with juice mixture and refrigerate until jelled.

Cooking with People to People

Airman Benjamin Green, who was later to become a pharmacist in Miami Beach, invented the first suntan cream during World War II. This petroleum-based red-dye "goo" was used by soldiers for protection from the South Pacific sun. In 1944, on his wife's stove, Green concocted a more user-friendly mixture with cocoa butter and jasmine for his customers in Miami Beach, actually testing it on his own bald head. Green used his invention as the basis for Coppertone® Suntan Cream—the first consumer suncare product. The original bottle had an Indian with the slogan, "Don't Be a Paleface." In 1956, an illustrator of the Tally Embry Advertising Agency in Miami created the world-famous Little Miss Coppertone and dog icon.

Pear Salad with Arugula

1 head Boston lettuce
2 cups arugula, stems removed
⅓ cup walnuts, toasted
2 red pears with skin left on, cored and sliced thin (may substitute yellow or green)
1 small red onion, chopped
⅓ cup French Dressing
20 (¾- to 1-inch) cubes French bread
12 (¾-inch) cubes Fontina cheese

Preheat oven to broil. Tear and toss Boston lettuce and arugula. Add walnuts, sliced pears, and chopped onion. Toss with French Dressing to lightly coat salad greens.

On wooden skewers, alternate bread and cheese cubes, beginning and ending with bread. Place skewers under broiler to soften cheese and lightly toast bread. Remove skewers, and arrange bread and cheese cubes on individual plates mounded with salad. Serves 4.

FRENCH DRESSING:
½ cup olive oil
2 tablespoons red wine vinegar
2 tablespoons fresh lemon juice
1 teaspoon sugar
¼ teaspoon freshly ground pepper
½ garlic clove, crushed
¾ teaspoon dry mustard
½ teaspoon salt
⅛ teaspoon paprika
Dash cayenne pepper

Combine all ingredients in a jar. Cover and shake well. Refrigerate overnight to blend flavors. Makes ¾ cup.

Gracious Gator Cooks

Wilted Lettuce

1 pound leaf lettuce
2 cold boiled potatoes, diced
3 thick slices bacon
½ cup vinegar

Shred lettuce and mix lightly with diced potatoes. Fry bacon very crisp (reserve pan drippings), then crumble over lettuce. Mix vinegar with the bacon drippings and pour over salad.

4-U: 400 Recipes of 4 Ingredients

Almond Orange Garden Salad

Try this delicious dressing on all of your salad favorites.

SUNLIGHT SALAD DRESSING:

1 cup vegetable oil
¼ cup white wine vinegar
¼ cup sugar
1 teaspoon salt

1 teaspoon black pepper
3 teaspoons freshly chopped
  parsley, or 1 teaspoon dried
  parsley

Combine dressing ingredients in a jar, and shake until well mixed.

SALAD:

¼ cup sugar
1 cup sliced almonds
½ head iceberg lettuce
½ head romaine lettuce

6 green onions, chopped
1½ cups fresh oranges, peeled
  and sectioned, or 2 (10-ounce)
  cans Mandarin oranges, drained

Add sugar to frying pan with almonds, and cook over medium heat, stirring and watching closely. When almonds are browned, pour them onto foil and let cool. Tear clean lettuce into bite-size pieces and place in a salad bowl. Add onions and oranges. Pour Sunlight Salad Dressing over salad to taste, and toss lightly. Top with almonds and serve. Yields 8 servings.

A Slice of Paradise

Summer Fruit Salad

1 cantaloupe, peeled and cubed,
  or made into melon balls
1 (20-ounce) can pineapple
  chunks and juice
1 unpeeled apple, cubed
2 peaches, peeled and cut into
  wedges

2 cups watermelon balls
2 bananas, peeled and cut into
  ¼-inch slices
1 cup halved strawberries
1 (6-ounce) can frozen orange
  concentrate, thawed
Any other good fruits in season

Layer fruits in a large glass bowl in order given. Spoon orange juice concentrate on top. Cover and chill 6–8 hours or overnight. Yields 8–10 servings.

Some Like it South!

Blueberry Salad

2 (3½-ounce) packages grape
  or blueberry Jell-O
2 cups hot water
1 (20-ounce) can crushed
  pineapple

1 (20-ounce) can blueberry pie
  filling
1 cup chopped pecans

Dissolve Jell-O in hot water. Add other ingredients. Refrigerate until Jell-O is set.

TOPPING:

1 (8-ounce) package cream
  cheese, softened
½ pint sour cream

½ cup sugar
1 teaspoon vanilla
Chopped pecans

Mix cream cheese and sour cream. Add sugar and vanilla. Beat until it forms stiff peaks. Spread over Jell-O mixture. After it has set, sprinkle with pecans.

A Taste of Heaven

Orange Buttermilk Salad

1 (20-ounce) can crushed
  pineapple, undrained
1 (6-ounce) package
  orange-flavored gelatin

2 cups buttermilk
1 (8-ounce) carton frozen whipped
  topping

In a saucepan, bring pineapple to a boil. Remove from heat and add gelatin, stirring until dissolved. Add buttermilk, and mix well. Cool to room temperature. Fold in whipped topping. Pour into a 7x11x2-inch pan. Refrigerate several hours or overnight. Cut into squares.

Trinity Treats

Pineapple Cabbage Slaw

3½ cups shredded cabbage
2 cups shredded fresh pineapple

1 green pepper, chopped
½ cup salad dressing

Combine all and serve chilled.

Exotic Foods: A Kitchen & Garden Guide

Quick Coleslaw

Depending on your leanings toward mayonnaise or vinegar dressing, this easy recipe can be adjusted.

4 cups chopped or shredded
green cabbage
3 green onions, chopped
1 medium carrot, shredded or
grated
½ cup mayonnaise

2 tablespoons vinegar, cider or red
wine
1 teaspoon sugar
Salt and pepper to taste
1 teaspoon celery seed (optional)

Mix cabbage, onions, and carrot in a large bowl. Toss lightly. Combine mayonnaise, vinegar, and sugar. Taste and adjust seasonings. Add salt, pepper, and celery seed, if desired. Pour dressing over slaw, and toss lightly. Cover and refrigerate so the flavors blend. Serves 4–6.

The Essential Catfish Cookbook

Frozen Salad

1 pint sour cream (lite sour
   cream or yogurt is okay)
1/3 cup sugar
1 teaspoon lemon juice
1 cup pineapple tidbits, drained

1 or 2 bananas, sliced
1 (10-ounce) jar cherries,
   drained
1 cup seedless grapes, sliced into
   halves

Mix together sour cream, sugar, and lemon juice, then add remaining ingredients and mix well. Place muffin liners in muffin tins and fill with salad mixture. Place in freezer. When frozen, take from muffin tins (leave liners around salad) and place in a ziploc bag and return to freezer until 10 minutes before eating.

Note: It is pretty to serve them on a small lettuce leaf or other green.

Kids at Work

Watermelon Rind Pickles

The time and effort you put into making watermelon pickles is well worth it when the accolades are heaped on the cook. Wonderful with fried chicken or baked turkey, and you'll love them mixed into ham or chicken salad.

4 pounds watermelon rinds
2 quarts plus 1 pint water,
   divided
4 tablespoons coarse salt

2 quarts vinegar
4 1/2 pounds sugar
2 tablespoons whole cloves
10 (2-inch) cinnamon sticks

Use rind of a firm, not overripe, watermelon and, before weighing it, trim off outer green skin and pink flesh. Cut rind into 1-inch cubes, and soak 12 hours in 2 quarts of water mixed with salt. Drain, then cover with fresh water and cook for 10 minutes. Let stand overnight in cooking water. Drain.

   Combine vinegar, remaining 1 pint water, sugar, and spices tied loosely in cheesecloth. Add drained watermelon, and boil gently for 2 hours, or until syrup is fairly thick. Remove spice bag and pack rind into hot, sterilized jars; cover with spiced vinegar to within 1/4 inch of top. Seal immediately. Makes about 3 quarts.

Let's Talk Food from A to Z

Vegetables

PHOTO BY GWEN McKEE

The 50-foot-wide Tree of Life is the centerpiece of Disney's Animal Kingdom® Theme Park. This 14-story masterpiece with its tapestry of 325 animal carvings was sculpted by more than a dozen artisans. The Tree of Life is topped with more than 103,000 translucent, five-shades-of-green leaves that were individually placed and actually blow in the wind.

Asparagus Casserole

1 (16-ounce) can asparagus,
  drained
2 boiled eggs, sliced
1 (16-ounce) can English peas,
  drained
¼ cup grated cheese

1 (10¾-ounce) can cream of
  mushroom soup
½ cup milk
Bread crumbs
Butter

Spread asparagus in bottom of casserole dish. Top with sliced eggs. Top with English peas. Sprinkle cheese over top. Mix soup with milk, and pour over casserole. Top with bread crumbs and butter. Bake at 325° for 25 minutes.

Treasures

Squash Casserole

1 pound yellow squash, sliced
1 pound zucchini, sliced
1 (8-ounce) carton sour cream
2 carrots, grated
1 (10¾-ounce) can cream of
  chicken soup

½ cup grated Cheddar cheese
1 small onion, chopped
1 package Stove Top Cornbread
  Stuffing (reserve 1 cup)
1 stick margarine, melted

Cook squash in small amount of water until tender; drain. Combine other ingredients. Toss well, and top with reserved dressing mix.

This makes 2 casseroles, one of which can be frozen. Bake in greased casserole dish at 350° for 35 minutes.

Sing for Your Supper

Railroad and hotel magnate Henry Flagler brought tourism to Florida's east coast by purchasing and adding to existing railroad systems. He also connected Miami to Key West with his Overseas Railroad. Completed in 1912, the Overseas Railroad, later known as "Flagler's Folly," was a commercial failure, and in 1935, was partially destroyed by a hurricane. It did, however, lay the groundwork for the road bridges that exist today.

Corn Bread Casserole

2 large onions, chopped
6 tablespoons butter or
  margarine
2 eggs
2 tablespoons milk
2 (17-ounce) cans cream-style
  corn

1 (1-pound) package cornmeal
  muffin mix, or ½ pound corn
  meal muffin mix and ½ pound
  jalapeño cornmeal muffin mix
½ pint sour cream or yogurt
2 cups shredded sharp Cheddar
  cheese

Sauté onion in butter until golden brown. Set aside. In large bowl add eggs and milk; blend well. Next add corn and muffin mix; blend thoroughly. In a greased baking dish, spread layer of batter, then a layer of each of the following ingredients: onions, sour cream or yogurt, and grated cheese; continue layering and end with a layer of cheese. Bake at 350° for 35–40 minutes or until puffed and golden. Let stand 10 minutes before cutting. This can be served at room temperature as well.

The Galley K.I.S.S. Cookbook

Broccoli-Cauliflower Casserole

1 (16-ounce) package frozen
  broccoli cuts
1 (16-ounce) package frozen
  cauliflower flowerets
1 large onion, chopped
2 tablespoons margarine
2 tablespoons all-purpose flour
1 teaspoon salt
½ teaspoon garlic powder

½ teaspoon dried basil
¼ teaspoon pepper
1¼ cups milk
2 (3-ounce) cartons cream cheese
  with chives
¾ cup soft bread crumbs
3 tablespoons grated Parmesan
  cheese
2 tablespoons melted butter

Cook broccoli and cauliflower according to directions; drain, and set aside. Cook onion in butter until tender. Stir in flour, salt, garlic, basil, and pepper. Add milk; cook until thick and bubbly. Add cream cheese. Stir until cheese melts. Stir into vegetable mixture. Place mixture in 2-quart casserole dish. Toss together bread crumbs, Parmesan cheese, and melted butter. Sprinkle over vegetable mixture. Bake uncovered at 350° for 25–30 minutes.

Cooking with People to People

Shoe Peg Casserole

3 (11-ounce) cans shoe peg corn
2 (15-ounce) cans French-style
  green beans, chopped slightly
1 (10¾-ounce) can cream of
  celery soup
1 (10¾-ounce) can chicken soup
1 large onion, chopped and
  sautéed
1 large green pepper, chopped and
  sautéed
1 sleeve Ritz crackers
1 stick butter, melted

Combine corn, green beans, both soups, onion, and pepper. Pour into a greased 9x13-inch casserole dish. Crush crackers and crumble on top. Drizzle butter over crackers. Bake at 350° for 30 minutes.

Tastes from Paradise

Squash Bake

2 tablespoons chopped onion
2 tablespoons margarine
2½ cups cooked squash,
  mashed
½ cup half-and-half
½ cup crushed cracker crumbs
¾ cup grated sharp cheese
3 eggs, separated
Salt and pepper to taste
Buttered bread crumbs

Sauté onion in melted margarine until transparent; add to squash with half-and-half, cracker crumbs, cheese, and egg yolks, which have been slightly beaten. Season to taste with salt and pepper, then allow mixture to cool.

   Beat egg whites until stiff and fold into squash mixture carefully. Pour into greased, 2-quart casserole. Sprinkle with buttered bread crumbs, and bake in 350° oven for 20–30 minutes. Yields 6–8 servings.

Marion Dragoons Chapter 2311 Cookbook

Mushrooms Florentine

2 (10-ounce) packages chopped,
frozen spinach
½ teaspoon salt
¼ cup chopped onion
6 tablespoons butter or margarine,
melted and divided

1 cup grated white Cheddar
cheese, divided
1 pound mushrooms, sliced
¼ teaspoon garlic powder

Preheat oven to 350°. Cook spinach according to directions. Drain and squeeze dry. Spoon into shallow casserole. Sprinkle spinach with salt, onion, 2 tablespoons butter, and ½ cup grated cheese.

Sauté mushrooms in remaining 4 tablespoons of butter until tender. Spoon mushrooms over cheese layer. Sprinkle with garlic powder and top with remaining ½ cup cheese. Bake 20–25 minutes. Serves 6.

Gracious Gator Cooks

Vegetarian Moussaka

A new version of the popular Greek dish.

1 medium eggplant
1 teaspoon salt
1/2 cup vegetable oil, divided
1 pound zucchini, cut lengthwise
   into 1/8-inch slices
2 medium onions, sliced
1 (16-ounce) can whole tomatoes
1/8 teaspoon black pepper
Garlic salt to taste
10 cups water
2 teaspoons salt

1 tablespoon oil
4 cups (8 ounces) penne pasta,
   uncooked
1/4 cup milk
1 egg
1 tablespoon grated Parmesan
   cheese
2 tablespoons minced fresh
   parsley
1 cup (4 ounces) shredded
   mozzarella cheese

Oil a large baking sheet; set aside. Generously butter a 9x13-inch baking dish. Partially peel eggplant, leaving some lengthwise strips of peel. Slice crosswise 1/8-inch thick. Sprinkle with 1 teaspoon salt. Drain in a colander for 20 minutes. Rinse with cold water to remove salt. Lightly squeeze slices to remove excess water. Place on prepared baking sheet. Drizzle 1/4 cup oil over eggplant slices. Broil until golden brown, 10 minutes on each side. Remove eggplant slices.

Place lengthwise slices of zucchini on baking sheet. Drizzle with remaining 1/4 cup oil. Broil until golden brown, 10 minutes on each side. Remove zucchini. Pour excess oil into a small skillet. Add onions; sauté until golden. Set aside. Drain tomatoes, reserving juice. Slice tomatoes. Add pepper and garlic salt to reserved juice; set aside.

Bring water to a rapid boil in a heavy 5-quart pot or Dutch oven. Add salt and oil. Gradually add pasta, being sure water continues to boil. Cook pasta, uncovered, until tender but firm, stirring occasionally. Drain. Pour milk into a small bowl. Add egg, and beat with a fork or whisk until mixed well, but not frothy. Pour over cooked pasta. Mix well. Layer in the following order: pasta mixture, Parmesan cheese, broiled eggplant, sautéed onions, parsley, broiled zucchini, sliced tomatoes, tomato juice mixture, and mozzarella cheese. Place baking dish in cold oven. Set oven at 350°. Bake 30 minutes. Let stand 10 minutes before cutting. Makes 6 main-dish servings or 12 vegetable servings.

The Best of Sophie Kay Cookbook

Easy Italian Vegetables

1 small onion, sliced
2 medium zucchini, sliced
  lengthwise in 4 pieces
2 medium yellow squash, sliced
  lengthwise in 4 pieces

1 medium tomato, cut in
  into 8 wedges
½ cup Italian dressing

Preheat oven to 450°. Center onion on a sheet of heavy-duty aluminum foil. Layer zucchini, squash, and tomato over onion. Spoon salad dressing over vegetables. Bring up foil sides. Double-fold top and ends to form a packet, leaving room for heat circulation inside. Place on a cookie sheet and bake for 35–40 minutes.

A Collection of Favorite Recipes

Chinese Ginger Vegetables

1 tablespoon arrowroot
  (available at health food stores)
¼ cup water
12 whole button mushrooms
12 whole snow peas
1 stalk celery, sliced thin
1 green pepper, sliced
¼ cup sliced water chestnuts
1 cup chopped broccoli

2 stalks bok choy, sliced
1 carrot, thinly sliced
1 cup cauliflower, cut up
1 cup sliced zucchini squash
2 tablespoons peanut oil
¼ cup soy sauce
2 tablespoons white wine
1 teaspoon grated fresh ginger
1 clove garlic, crushed

Dissolve arrowroot in water and set aside. In skillet or wok, stir-fry mushrooms and vegetables in peanut oil until glossy. Combine soy sauce and wine, and dissolve spices in mixture. Add to vegetables and stir-fry about 10 seconds. Cover and steam about 1 minute. Remove lid; pull vegetables to one side, and add dissolved arrowroot to liquid in pan. Cook for another minute to thicken. Mix with vegetables. Serve with rice or cooked noodles.

Exotic Foods: A Kitchen & Garden Guide

Tomato Pie

12 slices bacon, cooked and
crumbled
4 large tomatoes, sliced and
laid on paper towels
8 scallions, sliced

1 cup shredded sharp Cheddar
cheese
1 cup real mayonnaise
4 garlic cloves, crushed
Pinch of basil

Mix all ingredients; pour into a 9-inch baked pie shell. Bake at 350°
for 35 minutes.

Garden of Eatin'

Thunder Pie

2 medium-large Vidalia onions,
thinly sliced
3 tablespoons butter
1 deep-dish pie crust, unbaked
3 eggs, beaten
1/2 cup half-and-half

1/2 cup sour cream
2 dashes Tabasco
1 cup shredded 4-cheese Mexican
blend
Salt and pepper to taste

Sauté onions in butter over medium heat until limp and transparent.
Place in pie crust that has been lightly greased to prevent soggi-
ness. Mix eggs, half-and-half, sour cream, Tabasco, cheese, salt
and pepper in a bowl, and pour over onions. Bake at 450° for 20
minutes, then turn oven to 300° and bake for an additional 20–25
minutes.

Cookin' on Island Time

Fresh Tomato Tart

1 (9-inch) pie pastry, unbaked	½ cup mayonnaise
3 large ripe tomatoes	½ cup freshly grated Parmesan
Seasoned salt	cheese
Freshly ground pepper	⅛ teaspoon garlic powder
1 tablespoon chopped fresh basil,	¼ cup cracker crumbs
or 1 teaspoon dried basil	

Line a 10-inch tart pan with pie pastry. Prick crust well, and bake according to package directions; cool.

Slice tomatoes, and place in layers in tart pan. Sprinkle with seasoned salt, pepper, and basil. In a small bowl, combine mayonnaise, Parmesan cheese, and garlic powder. Spread mixture over tomatoes. Mixture will not completely cover tomatoes. Sprinkle with cracker crumbs. Bake tart at 400° for 15 minutes. Makes 6 servings.

Thymes Remembered

Tomatoes Blue

6 (1-inch) slices large, ripe	2 ounces blue cheese
tomatoes	1 tablespoon Parmesan cheese
1 tablespoon butter or	1 tablespoon dried parsley
margarine	Dry bread crumbs

Place tomato slices on a baking sheet. In a small bowl, combine butter, blue cheese, Parmesan cheese, and parsley with a fork until well blended. Add enough crumbs to make a crumbly dough. Divide evenly among tomato slices and press to form a crust on each. Broil until topping is brown and bubbly and tomatoes are heated through. Serves 6.

Strictly Scratch

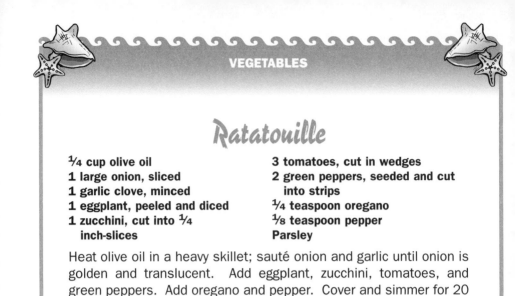

Ratatouille

¼ cup olive oil
1 large onion, sliced
1 garlic clove, minced
1 eggplant, peeled and diced
1 zucchini, cut into ¼
   inch-slices

3 tomatoes, cut in wedges
2 green peppers, seeded and cut
   into strips
¼ teaspoon oregano
⅛ teaspoon pepper
Parsley

Heat olive oil in a heavy skillet; sauté onion and garlic until onion is golden and translucent. Add eggplant, zucchini, tomatoes, and green peppers. Add oregano and pepper. Cover and simmer for 20 minutes, stirring occasionally. Sprinkle with parsley at serving time.

Tastes from Paradise: A Garden of Eating

Zucchini Fritters

2 cups grated zucchini
½ cup grated onion
2 eggs, beaten
½ cup grated Parmesan cheese

¼ teaspoon pepper
Chopped parsley
Flour
Oil

Combine ingredients, adding enough flour to hold shape when dropped by tablespoons into hot shallow oil. Brown on both sides; drain on paper towels. Serve immediately or reheat in oven.

Good Cooking

 More than 80 million visitors have explored the mysteries of the sea at SeaWorld® Orlando with up-close animal encounters with killer whales, dolphins, sea lions, stingrays and more.

Baked Spinach

1 (10-ounce) package chopped, frozen spinach, thawed
1 egg, beaten
1 cup grated sharp Cheddar cheese
½ (10¾-ounce) can cream of mushroom soup
½ cup finely chopped onion
½ cup mayonnaise (not diet)
Toasted, buttered bread crumbs

Mix all ingredients, except bread crumbs, well. Place in greased casserole dish and cover with toasted, buttered bread crumbs. Bake at 350° for 25–30 minutes. Serve hot.

Florida Fixin's

Vidalia Onion Tart

2 **pounds Vidalia onions**　　　1 **tablespoon flour**
1 **teaspoon salt**　　　　　　　3 **egg yolks, divided**
¼ **cup peanut oil**　　　　　　 6 **tablespoons heavy cream**
½ **cup water**　　　　　　　　 1 **crust pie pastry**
¼ **pound bacon, cut in strips**

Slice onions thinly and layer in large saucepan. Add salt to them and set aside to draw out the water for at least 30 minutes. Add oil and water. Steam onions until transparent and water is cooked out.

Meanwhile, place sliced bacon in a small amount of water in a shallow pan and blanch to remove excess fat. Bacon should be limp. Pour off liquid and coarsely chop bacon. When water is cooked out of onions, add flour and stir to dissolve. Remove from heat and add 2 egg yolks; cream with the onions. Stir constantly.

Roll pastry to about ½-inch thickness in a rectangular shape. Place pastry on an oiled baking sheet. Crimp edges of pastry. Beat remaining egg yolk with a pinch of salt and brush over entire pastry. (This is called "egg glazing" and helps the filling adhere to the pastry.) Pierce pastry with a fork in several places to prevent bubbles from forming while baking. Spread onion mixture over pastry and sprinkle the chopped bacon on top.

Bake at 300° for 10–15 minutes or until nicely browned. Cool slightly and cut into 1-inch squares. Serves 6.

Note: May be made a day ahead and reheated. Wait to cut until after heating, if made ahead. May be baked in individual tartlet pans or a pie plate.

Horse Tails

Creamy Potato Sticks

¼ cup all-purpose flour
½ teaspoon salt
1½ cups milk
1 (10¾-ounce) can condensed
  cream of celery soup, undiluted

½ pound American cheese,
  cubed
5–6 baking potatoes, peeled
1 cup chopped onion
Paprika

In a saucepan, combine flour and salt; gradually whisk in milk until smooth. Bring to a boil; cook and stir for 2 minutes. Remove from heat. Whisk in soup and cheese until smooth. Set aside. Cut potatoes into 4x½x½-inch sticks; place in a greased 9x13x2-inch baking dish. Sprinkle with onion. Top with cheese sauce. Bake uncovered at 350° for 55–60 minutes or until potatoes are tender. Sprinkle with paprika. Yield 6 servings.

Good Cooking

Potato Puffs

1½ cups mashed potatoes
1 egg, separated

¼ cup milk
3 tablespoons melted butter

Beat potatoes, egg yolk, milk, and butter until light. Fold in carefully stiffly beaten egg white. Drop by spoonfuls onto a greased baking sheet. Bake in 350° oven for 15 minutes or until golden brown.

4-U: 400 Recipes of 4 Ingredients

Fort Lauderdale is known as the "Venice of America" because of its 300 miles of navigable waterways. Islamorada is billed as the Sports Fishing Capital of the World. Key Largo is known as the Dive Capital of the World. Venice is known as the Shark Tooth Capital of the World. Titusville, known as Space City, USA, is located on the west shore of the Indian River directly across from the John F. Kennedy Space Center.

Garlic Gruyère Mashed Potatoes

6 medium potatoes, peeled and
  cut into 1-inch pieces
¾ cup milk, heated
½ cup sour cream
¼ cup (½ stick) butter or
  margarine, softened
½ teaspoon salt
⅛ teaspoon red pepper

1 garlic clove, minced
¼ cup shredded Gruyère
  cheese
2 green onions, thinly sliced
⅓ cup chopped baked ham
  (optional)
Sliced green onions (optional)

Combine the potatoes with enough water to cover in a saucepan. Bring to a boil. Boil for 15 minutes or until tender; drain. Mash potatoes in a bowl with a potato masher. Stir in the hot milk, sour cream, butter, salt, red pepper, and garlic.

Add the cheese, 2 thinly sliced green onions and ham to the potato mixture and mix well. Spoon into a serving bowl and sprinkle with sliced green onions, if desired. Serves 6–8.

Bay Fêtes

Sweet Potato Soufflé

This is a real winner.

3 cups sweet potatoes (yams),
  mashed
1 cup sugar
½ teaspoon salt (optional)
⅓ stick margarine, melted

½ cup milk
2 eggs, beaten
1 teaspoon butter flavoring
1 tablespoon orange juice

Mix all ingredients and pour into greased baking dish. Cover with Topping.

TOPPING:

1 cup brown sugar
⅓ cup flour

1 cup chopped pecans
⅓ stick margarine, softened

Mix thoroughly and sprinkle over soufflé. Bake at 350° for 35 minutes.

Florida Fixin's

Orange-Banana Yams

1 (23-ounce) can whole sweet
  potatoes in heavy syrup
1 tablespoon cornstarch
1/3 cup firmly packed light brown
  sugar

1 cup orange juice
1 tablespoon butter
1 tablespoon grated orange rind
3 medium bananas

Drain sweet potatoes and save syrup for other use. Slice potatoes in half, lengthwise. Place in a single layer in an oblong, 1½-quart glass baking dish.

Stir together cornstarch and brown sugar in small saucepan. Gradually stir in orange juice, keeping smooth. Stir constantly over moderate heat until clear and thickened. Remove from heat. Stir in butter and orange rind.

Peel bananas. Score by drawing a fork lengthwise down sides. Slice crosswise about ¼-inch thick. Arrange bananas over sweet potatoes. Spoon orange sauce evenly over top so yams, and especially bananas, are covered with it.

Bake in preheated 400° oven until bubbling hot, 15–20 minutes. Serve at once. Serves 6.

Citrus Lovers Cook Book

Sweet Potato Pudding

1 egg, beaten
½–¾ cup whole milk
1 cup grated raw sweet potato

Scant ½ cup sugar
2 tablespoons butter, melted
Pinch of salt

Combine all ingredients in casserole dish. Place casserole in larger pan of water and bake at 350° for 1½ hours. Remove from pan of water and continue baking on oven rack another 30 minutes.

The Woman's Exchange Classic Recipes

Black Beans and Rice

1 pound dried black beans,
  washed and drained
6 cups water
½ cup olive oil
1 large onion, coarsely chopped
1 green bell pepper, stem and
  seeds removed, coarsely
  chopped
1 clove garlic, minced
2 bay leaves

2 teaspoons salt
¼ teaspoon black pepper, freshly
  ground
1 smoked ham bone (optional)
1 slice bacon, minced
¼ cup wine vinegar
Cooked yellow rice
Raw rings of onion or scallions,
  cut into ¼-inch rounds

Cover beans with water. Bring to a boil and boil for 2 minutes. Remove from heat; cover pan and let stand for 1 hour.

Heat olive oil in skillet. Add onion, pepper, and garlic. Sauté for about 5 minutes. Add to beans. Add bay leaves, salt, pepper, ham bone, and bacon. Bring to a boil and simmer, covered, for 2 hours or until tender, adding more water if necessary. Remove bay leaves and add wine vinegar. Serve with yellow rice, and garnish with onion rings. Serves 6–8.

Variation: This dish can be improved through the use of any flavorful stock (chicken, ham, vegetable, dry white wine, etc.), rather than water. Also for added flavor: as dish simmers, consider adding ½ cup sliced, pimiento-stuffed olives, 1 teaspoon ground oregano, and/or ¼ teaspoon ground cumin.

Note: To cook yellow rice, just cook rice as you normally do, but add a drop or 2 of yellow food color. In Key West, most cooks use an inexpensive condiment called BIJOL, which gives rice a rich yellow color.

Cookin' in the Keys

Meats

A registered National Historic Landmark, the Hemingway Home and Museum offers guided tours of Ernest Hemingway's home, writing studio and Key West's first swimming pool. Of the 60 cats that roam the grounds, over half are polydactyl, which means they have extra toes. All are descendants of Hemingway's pets.

Tea Marinated Florida Beef Roast

1 (3- to 5-pound) Florida chuck or shoulder-cut beef roast
2–3 tablespoons fat

Pitcher of strong tea
Sauce

Brown roast well in Dutch oven on top of stove in fat. Make enough very strong tea to cover roast ¾ way. Simmer 3–5 hours, until meat is fork tender. Drain off tea and place meat in baking dish. Pour half of Sauce over meat and baste several times during baking.

SAUCE:

1 cup chili sauce
3 tablespoons brown sugar
Juice of 2 lemons
1 tablespoon Worcestershire sauce
¼ teaspoon celery salt

⅓ cup grated onion
2 tablespoons bacon fat
1 cup water
1 teaspoon paprika
3 tablespoons vinegar
1 teaspoon salt

Combine all ingredients, and stir to blend. Pour half over meat; save half. Bake uncovered at 325° for 45 minutes. Serve hot Sauce with meat.

Famous Florida Recipes

Marinated Roast Beef

This makes a wonderful buffet item.

1 (5- to 6-pound) chuck roast
1 bottle Wishbone Italian Dressing
3 cups sliced onions
Bay leaves
2 cups vegetable oil

1 cup white vinegar
4 tablespoons capers with juice
3 teaspoons celery seed
2 teaspoons salt
2–3 drops Tabasco sauce
2 ounces pimento

Pierce meat all over, and cover with Italian dressing. Cook in Dutch oven, covered, at 350° for 3 hours. Let cool. Slice paper thin (butcher can do it best) and layer with onion slices and bay leaves (about 8 bay leaves per layer) in large glass bowl. Mix remaining ingredients, and pour over layers. Marinate 1 hour at room temperature and at least 24 hours in refrigerator before serving. Serve cold. Yields 20–30 servings.

Some Like it South!

Medallions of Beef au Vin

2 (8-ounce) beef tenderloin filets
1 teaspoon oregano
Salt and pepper

2 tablespoons olive oil
1/3 cup Burgundy wine
1/3 cup brown sauce

Cut each filet into 3 or 4 medallions. Sprinkle both sides with oregano, salt and pepper. Heat oil; brown medallions on both sides over medium-high heat about 5–6 minutes. Remove medallions and keep warm. Add wine to pan and deglaze. Add brown sauce and heat through. Pour over prepared medallions and serve. Serves 2.

The Best of Sophie Kay Cookbook

Pan-Seared Filet Mignon Medallions

4 (4-ounce) tenderloin filets
Salt and pepper to taste
2 ounces olive oil
2 tablespoons chopped scallions
2 teaspoons prepared mustard
1/2 teaspoon tarragon

1/2 cup dry white wine
1 cup brown sauce
1/2 cup heavy cream
4 artichoke hearts
2 tablespoons butter

Season filets with salt and pepper, and sauté in hot olive oil until desired doneness. Remove and set aside. Add scallions, mustard, tarragon, and white wine to pan and reduce slightly. Add brown sauce and cream, and simmer one minute.

Quarter artichokes, add to sauce, and simmer 2 minutes. Check seasoning; return filets to warm and stir in butter. Arrange filets on plates and spoon sauce over. Serve with hot vegetable medley. Serves 2.

Intracoastal Waterway Restaurant Guide & Recipe Book

Sirloin with Grilled Shrimp and Brie

2 (12-ounce) New York strip
  steaks
Olive oil
Salt and pepper to taste
2 long thin slices Brie cheese,
  room temperature

4 slices avocado
4 large shrimp, butterflied,
  seasoned, grilled
Classic Madeira Sauce

Brush both sides of the steaks with olive oil and sprinkle with salt and pepper. Grill steaks over hot coals to desired degree of doneness. Remove steaks from grill and arrange on 2 serving plates. Top each steak immediately with 1 slice of Brie, 2 slices of avocado, and 2 shrimp. Drizzle Classic Madeira Sauce over and around steaks. Serve immediately. Serves 2.

CLASSIC MADEIRA SAUCE:

¼ cup chopped carrots
¼ cup chopped celery
¼ cup chopped shallots
½ teaspoon chopped fresh
  thyme

2 tablespoons olive oil
½ cup Madeira
1 (10-ounce) can beef
  consommé
1 consommé can water

Sauté carrots, celery, shallots, and thyme in olive oil in a skillet for 3–5 minutes or until vegetables are tender. Stir in the wine. Cook for 2 minutes or until liquid is reduced by one half. Process the wine mixture in a food processor or blender until puréed. Return the purée to the skillet.

Add consommé and water to the purée and mix well. Cook over medium heat for 12–14 minutes or until the mixture is reduced and thickened, stirring frequently. Remove from heat. Cover to keep warm. You may prepare in advance and store, covered, in the refrigerator or freezer. Reheat before serving. Serves 2.

Bay Fêtes

Beef Parmesan

1½ pounds good round steak
½ cup grated Parmesan cheese
½ cup bread crumbs
2 eggs, beaten
⅓ cup vegetable oil
1 medium-size onion, chopped
1 teaspoon salt
¼ teaspoon black pepper

1 teaspoon sugar
½ teaspoon marjoram
Garlic to taste (about 3 cloves)
1 (6-ounce) can tomato paste
1 cup hot water
1 (8-ounce) package mozzarella
  cheese slices
Buttered noodles

Place meat between 2 pieces of wax paper; lay on cutting board and pound thin. Cut into thin, small, bite-size pieces. Mix Parmesan cheese and bread crumbs. Dip meat in beaten eggs, then roll in bread crumbs. Heat oil and brown steak. Place in baking dish. In same skillet, cook onion until soft. Stir in seasonings and tomato paste. Add hot water and stir. Pour part of sauce over meat; top with cheese slices and add remaining sauce. Bake at 350° for 1 hour. Serve over buttered noodles. Serves 4–6.

Note: Great to prepare in advance and freeze. If you plan to freeze it, cook for 45 minutes instead of 1 hour. When ready to serve, thaw and cook about 30 minutes.

Sand in My Shoes

Cabbage and Beef Casserole

2 pounds lean ground beef
1 large onion, chopped
2 tablespoons brown sugar
Salt and pepper to taste

2 (14-ounce) cans tomatoes,
  cut up
1 medium cabbage, chopped
Parmesan cheese

In a large skillet, brown ground beef with onion, brown sugar, and salt and pepper to taste. Add tomatoes. Add chopped cabbage. Bring to a boil, and simmer for 30 minutes. Sprinkle with Parmesan cheese. Serves 6–8.

Cooking with 257

Braciole

1 pound top round steak
4–6 mozzarella slices
4–6 teaspoons butter
$\frac{1}{3}$ cup Parmesan cheese
2 garlic cloves, chopped or garlic
  powder

$\frac{1}{4}$ cup raisins
Salt and pepper
Olive oil
Tomato sauce

Cut steak into 4–6 pieces, and pound each piece to flatten very thin. Place mozzarella and butter on each piece, then sprinkle with Parmesan, garlic, raisins, salt and pepper. Roll each piece, and tie securely with string.

    Sauté in olive oil with salt and pepper until steak rolls are browned on all sides. Drop into your favorite tomato sauce and simmer $1\frac{1}{2}$ hours or until fork tender. Remove from sauce, let cool slightly, then carefully remove string and serve with your favorite pasta.

Preserving Our Italian Heritage

La Gaceta is the only tri-lingual (English, Spanish, and Italian) newspaper in the country and has served the Tampa area for more than 80 years.

Cajun Meat Loaf

2 tablespoons margarine
¼ cup diced onion
¼ cup chopped celery
¼ cup diced green pepper
1 teaspoon minced garlic
1 bay leaf
½ teaspoon black pepper
½ teaspoon cayenne pepper
¼ teaspoon cumin

¼ teaspoon ground nutmeg
½ tablespoon Worcestershire sauce
1 teaspoon hot pepper sauce
¼ cup ketchup
¼ cup evaporated milk
1 pound ground beef
1 egg
½ cup dry bread crumbs

In frying pan, melt margarine and sauté onion, celery, green pepper, and garlic. Add bay leaf, black pepper, cayenne pepper, cumin, and nutmeg; stir to blend. Mix in Worcestershire, pepper sauce, ketchup, and milk. When mixture begins to simmer, turn off, remove from heat, and allow to cool. In a large bowl, mix together the ground beef, egg, and bread crumbs; add cooled vegetable mixture. Combine all ingredients and form into loaf. Bake in loaf pan at 350° for one hour.

Great Recipes from Near and Afar

Mexican Goulash

2 pounds lean ground beef
1 medium onion, finely chopped
1 (15-ounce) can cut green beans, drained
1 (15-ounce) can whole-kernel corn, drained

1 (8-ounce) can tomato sauce with bits
Fritos, crushed

Brown ground beef and onion together. Drain off any grease. Add beans, corn, and tomato sauce with bits. Place in baking dish. Bake in a 300° oven for 30–45 minutes. Serve with Fritos or other corn chips to cover top of casserole.

Kids at Work

Cuban Beef Hash
(Picadillo)

4 tablespoons vegetable oil
1 cup finely chopped onions
2 large green peppers, finely chopped
6 medium-size firm ripe tomatoes, peeled, seeded, and finely chopped, or 2 cups canned whole tomatoes, drained and chopped
2 teaspoons minced garlic
2 pounds lean boneless beef (preferably chuck), trimmed of excess fat and ground

1 teaspoon oregano
4 bay leaves
½ teaspoon ground cumin
2 teaspoons salt
Freshly ground pepper to taste
1 tablespoon white vinegar
¼ cup seedless raisins
½ cup small pimento-stuffed green olives
¼ cup burgundy

In a 10- to 12-inch skillet, heat oil over medium heat until a light haze forms above it. Sauté onions and peppers, stirring frequently, for about 5 minutes, or until vegetables are soft, but not brown. Add tomatoes and garlic. Still stirring, cook briskly until most of the liquid in the pan has evaporated. Add ground beef, oregano, bay leaves, and cumin. Stir until meat is no longer red. Add salt, pepper, vinegar, raisins, olives, and wine. Cook at low temperature for approximately 15 minutes. Picadillo is traditionally served with fluffy white rice and, when available, fried ripe plantains. Serves 4–6.

The Columbia Restaurant Spanish Cookbook

With over 2.5 million Floridians born outside the United States, Florida has one of the most culturally diverse populations in the U.S. Florida also has the third-highest immigrant population in the United States behind New York and California.

Oven BBQ Beef Brisket

3 tablespoons liquid smoke
1 (3- to 4-pound) boned beef
   brisket
Celery salt
Onion salt

Garlic salt
Salt and pepper
3 tablespoons Worcestershire
   sauce
1 (6-ounce) bottle BBQ sauce

Pour liquid smoke over meat. Generously sprinkle both sides of brisket with celery, onion, and garlic salts. Cover and refrigerate overnight.

Do not drain meat. Sprinkle with salt, pepper, and Worcestershire sauce. Cover and bake at 250° for 5 hours. Pour BBQ sauce over meat and bake uncovered 1 more hour with temperature raised to 350°.

Cooking with 257

Spiced Brisket a la Toby

1 (4-pound) brisket of beef
2 tablespoons oil
2 onions, sliced
1/3 cup chili sauce

1/2 cup A-1 sauce
Dash Worcestershire sauce
1/2 cup water
Salt, pepper, and garlic to taste

In Dutch oven, place meat on top of oil and cook on high for about 3–4 minutes. Turn heat down, add onions and remaining ingredients, and simmer for 1 1/2 hours. Remove meat, slice thin, and return to pot and cook an additional 30 minutes.

If you have a pressure cooker, cook meat on high heat for 3–4 minutes. Add remaining ingredients; cover and cook under pressure for 20 minutes. Shut off and let pressure drop of own accord. Remove meat, slice thin, then return to cooker and simmer, uncovered, for 15 minutes.

The Galley K.I.S.S. Cookbook

Barbecue Beef

1 (6- to 8-pound) top round roast
2 large Bermuda onions, sliced
   thin
2 cups ketchup
½ cup Worcestershire sauce

½ cup wine vinegar
1 cup beef consommé
2 tablespoons brown sugar
Salt, pepper, and garlic powder to
   taste

Place meat in deep baking pan. Add onions, ketchup, Worcestershire, vinegar, consommé, brown sugar, and seasonings to taste. Cover with heavy-duty foil. Bake at 300° for about 8 hours. Shred meat with a fork and serve on rolls.

Heaven in a Pot

Tangy Honey Sauce for Meat and Chicken

½ teaspoon ground nutmeg
1 tablespoon prepared mustard

¼ cup honey
1 cup ketchup

Mix all ingredients well. To serve, spread on meat loaf, pork loin, ribs or chicken pieces during last 15 minutes of baking, or serve as dipping sauce.

FCCD Cookbook

Easy Ribs

2 tablespoons cooking oil
1¾ pounds lean spareribs, cut in
   half lengthwise
Pinch of salt

2 tablespoons brown sugar
¼ cup soy sauce or
   Worcestershire sauce

Heat oil in frying pan. Fry ribs until meat color has just changed from pink to gray. Add salt, sugar, and sauce; mix well. Pour enough water over ribs to barely cover. Keep uncovered and bring to a boil, stirring occasionally. When liquid thickens, stir constantly (approximately ½ hour) until ribs are well glazed and almost no liquid is left. Makes 4 servings.

Under the Canopy

Citrus Spareribs

4–5 pounds spareribs, cut in
   serving pieces
1 (6-ounce) can frozen orange
   concentrate, thawed, undiluted
¾ cup ketchup

2 tablespoons molasses
1 teaspoon Worcestershire sauce
½ teaspoon Tabasco sauce
2 teaspoons salt
4 teaspoons grated onion

Place spareribs in large pot. Cover with water and bring to a boil. Reduce heat and simmer, covered, for 30 minutes. Drain and refrigerate until ready to grill.

   Mix orange concentrate with remaining ingredients. Place spareribs on grill set about 8 inches from heat. Cook 15 minutes. Turn and brush with orange sauce. Cook 15–30 minutes longer, turning and brushing frequently with sauce. Serves 4–6.

Citrus Lovers Cook Book

Pacific Pork Kabobs

3 tablespoons lime juice	1 envelope onion soup mix
¼ cup water	1 pound boneless lean pork loin
1 teaspoon ground ginger	

In a medium bowl, combine lime juice, water, ginger, and soup mix. Cut pork into 1-inch squares and add to marinade. Add a little more water to cover, if necessary. Cover bowl and refrigerate overnight.

Thread pork on kabobs and grill until done, about 20 minutes, brushing once or twice with marinade. If desired, thread a chunk of your favorite vegetable between each pork cube. Could make 4 servings, but this flavorful, tender dish may only serve 2, as it will go fast.

Cooking for Two, No Nonsense Cookbook

Citrus Pork Chops

6 pork chops (½–¾ inch thick)	2 tablespoons honey
2 tablespoons shortening	¼ teaspoon cinnamon
1 teaspoon salt	¼ teaspoon ginger
⅛ teaspoon pepper	1 teaspoon sugar
½ cup orange juice	2 oranges, sectioned
1 teaspoon lemon juice	Flour for thickening

Brown chops in shortening. Pour off drippings. Season chops with salt and pepper. Combine juices, honey, spices, and sugar. Pour over chops. Cover tightly, and cook slowly 45 minutes, or till done. Add orange sections and cook just until heated through. Remove chops. Thicken pan liquid with flour for gravy, and spoon over hot chops.

Citrus Lovers Cook Book

Roast Pork with Gingered Fruit Sauce

GINGERED FRUIT SAUCE:

1 cup orange marmalade
2 tablespoons orange juice
2 tablespoons lemon juice
1½ teaspoons prepared
  horseradish

1 small piece fresh gingerroot,
  peeled, crushed
1 teaspoon dry mustard

Process marmalade, orange juice, and lemon juice in a blender or food processor until combined. Spoon into a bowl. Add horseradish, gingerroot, and dry mustard and mix well. May be stored in the refrigerator for several weeks.

1 (3-pound) boneless pork loin
1 large onion, chopped
2 garlic cloves, crushed
2 tablespoons vegetable oil
½ cup soy sauce

1 tablespoon brown sugar
1 teaspoon curry powder
1 teaspoon pepper
1 teaspoon oregano (optional)
Gingered Fruit Sauce

Place pork in a large bowl. Combine onion, garlic, oil, soy sauce, brown sugar, curry powder, pepper, and oregano in a small bowl and mix well. Pour over pork. Marinate, covered, in refrigerator for 4 hours, turning occasionally. Drain and place in a shallow roasting pan. Roast at 375° for 1½ hours or to 145° on a meat thermometer. Serve with Gingered Fruit Sauce. Yields 10–12 servings.

Entirely Entertaining in the Bonnet House Style

Pork Chop Casserole

6 pork chops
½ cup flour
Salt
Pepper
4 sweet potatoes, peeled, sliced, divided

½ cup brown sugar
1½ cups sliced apples, divided
Sugar
½ cup apple juice

Coat chops with flour, salt, and pepper. Brown in heavy skillet. Arrange in greased 2-quart casserole. Arrange ½ of sweet potato slices over top. Sprinkle with brown sugar. Top with ½ the sliced apples. Sprinkle with sugar. Top with remaining potatoes and apples, and pour juice over all. Cover. Bake at 350° for 1½ hours. Remove cover for last 15 minutes.

Cooking with 257

Applesauce-Stuffed Tenderloin

1 (1-pound) pork tenderloin
2 tablespoons dry vermouth
   or apple juice
2 tablespoons finely chopped dry
   roasted peanuts

⅓ cup chunky applesauce
⅛ teaspoon finely crushed fennel
   seed
Salt and pepper

Using a sharp knife, form a pocket in tenderloin by cutting a lengthwise slit down center almost to, but not through, bottom of tenderloin. Place in a glass baking dish. Pour vermouth in pocket and over tenderloin. Cover dish and marinate about 1 hour.

Preheat oven to 375°. Spray a 10x15-inch jellyroll pan or shallow baking pan with nonstick cooking spray. Combine remaining ingredients and salt and pepper to taste in a bowl and blend well. Spoon mixture into pocket in tenderloin. Secure stuffed pocket with toothpicks. Place stuffed tenderloin in prepared pan. Roast about 30 minutes. Let stand 5–10 minutes before slicing.

Horse Tails

Pork Chops Pizzaiola

6 (¾-inch-thick) loin or shoulder
  pork chops, trimmed
2 tablespoons olive oil
1½ cups marinara sauce
½ teaspoon dried rosemary
½ cup sliced black olives
Salt and pepper to taste
½ cup fresh grated
  Parmigiano-Reggiano cheese

Brown chops in hot oil in a skillet over medium heat; drain. Stir in marinara sauce and next 3 ingredients. Cover, reduce heat, and simmer 30 minutes. Uncover and simmer 15 minutes or until meat is tender. Sprinkle with cheese. Yields 6 servings.

Lighthouse Secrets

Feta-Pesto Stuffed Pork Chops

PORK CHOPS:

3 tablespoons crumbled feta
  cheese
4–5 tablespoons purchased
  pesto, divided
1 tablespoon pine nuts, toasted
4 (1¼-inch-thick) pork chops
1 tablespoon balsamic vinegar
2 tablespoons jalapeño jelly

Preheat grill. Make a stuffing by combining feta, 2 tablespoons pesto and pine nuts in a small bowl. Trim fat from pork chops. Cut a horizontal slit in each chop, starting at edge and going to bone. Spoon stuffing into pockets, and secure each with a toothpick, if necessary. Combine vinegar, remaining 2–3 tablespoons pesto, and jelly in a small saucepan. Heat over low heat until jelly melts.

RUB:

1 teaspoon minced garlic
1 teaspoon black pepper
½ teaspoon crushed fennel
  seeds
¼ teaspoon ground cumin
½ teaspoon cayenne pepper
½ teaspoon celery seed
¼ teaspoon dried thyme

Mix all Rub ingredients. Rub seasoning mix over both sides of chops. Grill chops over medium heat for 35–40 minutes or until juices run clear. Brush with jalapeño glaze during last 10 minutes, turning once during that time to glaze other side. Yields 4 servings.

Treasures of the Tropics

Pork Roast with Cranberry-Pecan Butter Sauce

1 (3½-pound) boneless pork
  loin roast
1 (16-ounce) can whole cranberry
  sauce, divided
¼ cup apricot preserves
¼ cup butter, divided
½ cup green onions

1 bay leaf
¼ cup port wine or orange juice
½ cup chicken broth
1 tablespoon balsamic vinegar
½ cup pecans
Salt and pepper

Heat oven to 350°. Place tied roast in shallow roasting pan. Roast for 1 hour. In cup, combine ¼ cup cranberry sauce and apricot preserves. Spoon glaze over roast. Return to oven, and continue roasting 30–45 minutes longer or until meat thermometer registers 155° or 160°. Remove from oven and let stand 10 minutes before slicing.

In medium skillet, melt 1 tablespoon butter. Add chopped green onions and bay leaf. Cook 1 minute. Stir in wine or orange juice. Cook over medium heat until mixture has reduced to thick glaze, about 4 minutes. Stir in remaining cranberry sauce, broth, vinegar, and chopped pecans. Cook over medium heat until sauce thickens slightly, about 5 minutes. Reduce heat and stir in remaining butter until combined. Season to taste. Yields 6–8 servings of pork roast and about 2½ cups sauce.

Recipes of Spruce Creek

Cranberry Orange Lamb Chops

4 lamb loin chops, cut 1½
   inches thick
⅛ cup browning sauce
½ cup chopped onion
1 cup orange juice
1 cup fresh or frozen cranberries

½ cup sugar
1 tablespoon flour
1 tablespoon Dijon mustard
1 teaspoon grated orange peel
½ teaspoon allspice

Place lamb in a shallow, 9-inch-round dish; brush with browning sauce (like Kitchen Bouquet) and top with onions. Cook in microwave oven on MEDIUM-HIGH (70% power) 12 minutes, turning once. Drain. May freeze at this time.

Place remaining ingredients in large glass measuring cup. Cook on HIGH 6 minutes or until it comes to a boil, stirring twice. Pour sauce over lamb. Cook on MEDIUM-HIGH 5 minutes.

From frozen, cook on DEFROST 10 minutes. Then cook on MEDIUM-HIGH for 15 minutes. Stir once, halfway through cooking time. Let stand, covered, 5 minutes. Yields 4 servings.

A Slice of Paradise

Gator Piquante

1½ pounds farm-raised alligator
¼ cup chopped celery
½ cup chopped green onions
½ cup chopped bell pepper

1 (16-ounce) can diced tomatoes
¼ teaspoon salt
⅛ teaspoon white pepper
⅛ teaspoon red pepper

Cut gator into 1-inch cubes. Cook meat in nonstick skillet over medium heat until all natural juices have evaporated. Add chopped vegetables; sauté until tender. Add tomatoes, salt, white pepper, and red pepper. Simmer until meat is tender.

Roberts Ranch Museum Cookbook

Blackened Alligator Steaks

1 teaspoon salt
1 tablespoon paprika
1 teaspoon ground cayenne
pepper
½ teaspoon freshly ground
black pepper
½ teaspoon freshly ground
white pepper

½ teaspoon dried thyme
½ teaspoon dried oregano
½ teaspoon dried chives
1 teaspoon garlic powder
4 (6-ounce) alligator steaks, from
the tail
3 tablespoons butter, melted

Mix seasonings in a bowl. Pour onto a plate. Brush steaks with 2 tablespoons melted butter. Dip both sides of each steak into seasoning mix. Place a dry, heavy cast-iron skillet over high heat for 5–7 minutes. Place steaks in pan and sear for 2 minutes; turn, brush with remaining butter, and cook for 1–2 minutes. With thicker steaks, it may be necessary to finish in a 350° oven for 4–5 minutes. Serves 4.

Horse Tails

Editor's Extra: This sizzles and smokes, so be sure to turn on your vent.

Long an unofficial symbol of Florida, the American alligator (*Alligator mississippiensis*) was designated the official state reptile in 1987.

Gator Gumbolaya

Gators love to travel to away games, and one of their favorite places is Baton Rouge for a Florida/LSU match-up. Tiger fans are great cooks and love to share their Cajun food with everyone (including us Gators).

1 pound bacon
5 pounds boneless, skinless
   chicken fillets
1 cup flour
1¼ cups vegetable oil
4 green bell peppers, chopped
5 pounds onions, chopped
2 bunches shallots, chopped
1 stalk celery, chopped
3 cans mushroom steak sauce
2 (12-ounce) cans tomatoes with
   green chiles
1 (10-ounce) bottle
   Worcestershire sauce

1 (3-ounce) jar garlic powder, or to
   taste
1 (3-ounce) jar Italian seasoning,
   or to taste
6 (15-ounce) cans chicken broth
4 (15-ounce) cans beef broth
Salt and pepper to taste
MSG to taste (optional)
6 pounds lean pork cubes or
   chopped ham
6 pounds smoked sausage, cut
   into halves lengthwise, sliced

Fry bacon in a large skillet until crisp. Crumble bacon and set aside. Brown chicken in the bacon drippings in the skillet. Add enough water to cover chicken. Simmer until cooked through. Remove chicken and let cool. Cut chicken into bite-size pieces and set aside.

Cook a mixture of flour and oil in a large heavy skillet over medium heat until rich brown, stirring constantly; watch carefully to avoid burning. Add green peppers, onions, shallots, and celery. Cook until vegetables are tender.

Pour vegetable mixture into a large stockpot. Add mushroom steak sauce, tomatoes, Worcestershire sauce, garlic powder, Italian seasoning, chicken broth, beef broth, salt, pepper, and MSG, and mix well. Simmer for 10 minutes. Add chicken, pork cubes, bacon, and sausage. Simmer for 2 hours.

Serve over rice. Recipe may be cut in half. May be prepared ahead and frozen. Yields 6 gallons.

Gator Championship Recipes

Sausage-Stuffed Rigatoni

SAUSAGE STUFFING:

1 pound hot bulk pork sausage
³/₄ cup dry Italian bread crumbs
  with Romano cheese

¹/₃ cup milk
1 egg, lightly beaten

Brown sausage in a skillet, stirring until crumbly; do not drain. Stir in bread crumbs, milk, and egg. Spoon sausage mixture into a bowl. Chill, covered, in refrigerator.

ITALIAN TOMATO SAUCE:

1 large onion, chopped
3 tablespoons olive oil
4 cups water
1 (28-ounce) can crushed Italian
  tomatoes
1 (14-ounce) can diced tomatoes

2 (6-ounce) cans tomato paste
1 tablespoon sugar
1 tablespoon salt
¹/₂ teaspoon pepper
¹/₂ teaspoon oregano
¹/₂ teaspoon basil

Sauté onion in olive oil in a Dutch oven until tender. Stir in water, undrained tomatoes, tomato paste, sugar, salt, pepper, oregano, and basil. Simmer, covered, for 1 hour, stirring occasionally.

RIGATONI:

16 ounces rigatoni
Olive oil
Italian Tomato Sauce

1 (6-ounce) package shredded
  Parmesan cheese

Cook pasta using package directions until al dente; drain and rinse. Toss pasta with just enough olive oil to coat in a bowl. Spray a 9x13-inch baking dish with nonstick cooking spray. Ladle just enough of the Italian Tomato Sauce over bottom of prepared dish to form a thin layer.

Shape Stuffing into several small logs to make it process easier. Stuff enough pasta shells with Stuffing for 2 complete layers, serving leftover pasta with your favorite sauce. Arrange stuffed pasta in rows in a single layer in prepared baking dish. Ladle ¹/₂ remaining Italian Tomato Sauce over pasta and sprinkle with ¹/₂ cheese. Layer with another row of stuffed rigatoni. Top with remaining Italian Tomato Sauce and sprinkle with remaining cheese. Bake at 350° for 1 hour. Let stand for 10–15 minutes before serving. You may prepare in advance and freeze, covered, for future use. Adjust baking times as needed. Serves 8–10.

Bay Fêtes

Poultry

PHOTO BY BARBARA MOSELEY

Extending across the southern tip of the Florida peninsula and most of Florida Bay, Everglades National Park is the only subtropical preserve in North America and the only place in the world where alligators and crocodiles exist side by side.

Chicken Asparagus with Tarragon

Tarragon and balsamic vinegar add a special touch.

2 large whole chicken breasts,
  deboned, skinned, split in half
  lengthwise
1½ teaspoons salt, divided
¾ teaspoon black pepper,
  divided
¼ cup all-purpose flour
2 tablespoons olive oil
2 tablespoons butter
1 cup chopped onion
2 cloves garlic, pressed
1 pound asparagus, trimmed, cut
  diagonally
½ pound mushrooms, sliced
2 cups chopped fresh tomatoes
½ cup chicken broth
2 tablespoons chopped fresh
  tarragon, or 1½ teaspoons
  dried tarragon
1 tablespoon balsamic vinegar
1 teaspoon sugar
1 cup freshly grated Parmesan
  cheese, divided
1 pound fettuccini or linguine,
  cooked

Flatten chicken by pounding lightly between 2 pieces of wax paper. Sprinkle with ½ teaspoon salt and ¼ teaspoon pepper. Coat lightly in flour; set aside.

Heat olive oil and butter in large skillet over medium heat. Sauté onion and garlic until onion is golden. Add chicken; cook on both sides until golden. Remove chicken; set aside. Add asparagus to drippings. Sauté 3 minutes. Add mushrooms, and sauté 2 more minutes. Add tomatoes, chicken broth, tarragon, vinegar, sugar, remaining 1 teaspoon salt and remaining ½ teaspoon pepper. Cook and stir about 8 minutes over low heat. Stir ¾ cup Parmesan cheese into asparagus mixture. Cook and stir until thickened. Add cooked chicken. Heat through. Toss cooked fettuccini or linguine lightly with remaining ¼ cup Parmesan cheese. Arrange chicken over pasta, and pour sauce over fettuccini or linguine. Makes 4 servings.

The Best of Sophie Kay Cookbook

Chicken Saltenbuca

½ pound spinach, cleaned and stemmed
4 large chicken breasts, skinned and boned
1 pound ham, sliced
½ pound provolone cheese, sliced
¾ pound prosciutto, sliced thin
3 bunches basil, chopped fine
3 cups heavy cream
Salt and pepper to taste

Sauté spinach in a small amount of oil; set aside. Pound chicken breasts flat. Divide ham evenly over breasts. Add layers of provolone cheese and spinach. Roll chicken and wrap with prosciutto. Bake at 400° for 15 minutes or until done. Turn rolls frequently while baking.

While chicken bakes, prepare a sauce by combining basil and cream in a saucepan. Cook and reduce sauce until thick and creamy. Season with salt and pepper. To serve, slice chicken rolls and top with sauce. Yields 4 servings.

Calypso Café

Bacon-Wrapped Chicken

6 boneless, skinless chicken breast halves
1 (8-ounce) carton whipped cream cheese with onions and chives
1 teaspoon butter or margarine, chilled
Salt to taste
6 bacon strips

Flatten chicken to ½-inch thickness. Spread 3 tablespoons cream cheese over each. Dot with butter and sprinkle with salt. Roll up. Wrap each with a strip of bacon. Place seam-side-down in a greased 9x13x2-inch baking pan. Bake, uncovered, at 400° for 35–40 minutes or until juices run clear. Broil 6 inches from the heat for 5 minutes or until bacon is crisp. Serves 6.

Centennial Cookbook

Apricot Salsa Chicken

½ cup flour
¼ teaspoon pepper
1 teaspoon salt
¼ teaspoon paprika
6 boneless, skinless chicken
  breasts (about 1½ pounds)

3 tablespoons vegetable oil
1 (16-ounce) jar salsa
1 (12-ounce) jar apricot preserves
½ cup apricot nectar (can use
  juice from canned apricots)

In a shallow bowl, combine flour and seasonings. Add chicken; turn to coat. Brown chicken in hot oil; drain. Stir in salsa, preserves, and nectar; bring to a boil. Reduce heat; simmer, uncovered, for 15 minutes or until sauce thickens and meat juices run clear. Or you may bake in oven for 30 minutes at 350°. Serve over hot, cooked rice. Serves 4–6.

Recipes of Spruce Creek

Florida Orange Chicken

1½ cups uncooked long-grain
  rice
4 boneless, skinless chicken
  breasts
½ cup sliced fresh mushrooms

2 cups orange juice
1 cup fat-free chicken broth
½ teaspoon salt and pepper
2 oranges, sectioned, membrane
  removed

Spread rice in greased, shallow 3-quart baking dish. Top with chicken and mushrooms. Pour orange juice and broth over all. Sprinkle with salt and pepper. Cover with foil and bake at 350° for 50 minutes or until rice is tender. Makes 4 servings.

Country Club Cooks

Orange juice became Florida's official state beverage in 1967.

Cranberry Chicken

4 whole chicken breasts, boned, skinned and split	1 (8-ounce) bottle Catalina dressing
Salt and pepper to taste	1 (16-ounce) can whole cranberry sauce
Garlic powder (optional)	
1 jar mushrooms	1 package Lipton Onion Soup Mix

Season chicken with salt, pepper, and garlic powder, if desired. Place chicken in large greased casserole; add mushrooms. Combine dressing, cranberry sauce, and soup mix. Pour over chicken. Bake for 1 hour, uncovered, at 350°. Serve over rice. Serves 8.

Tastes from Paradise

Firehouse Four's Key Lime Chicken

3 cloves garlic	1 cup oil
2 jalapeño peppers	10 skinless chicken breasts
¼ cup Key lime juice	

Chop garlic and peppers and mix with lime juice and oil. Marinate chicken breasts in this mixture for several hours or overnight.

Grill chicken over charcoal or on stove until done.

KEY LIME SAUCE:

1 pound unsalted butter	1 cup white wine
1 shallot	⅓ cup Key lime juice
3 jalapeño peppers	½ cup heavy cream

Soften butter to room temperature. Chop shallot and peppers. Put in saucepan with wine and lime juice and simmer. Add butter and boil 5–7 minutes to reduce, stirring continuously and being careful not to scorch. Add heavy cream slowly over low heat, being careful not to add too much at one time. Stir to make creamy and smooth. Pour over chicken breasts and serve. Serves 10.

Recipe from Firehouse Four, Miami
Florida's Historic Restaurants and Their Recipes

Chicken Kelley

3 chicken breasts, skinned,
  boned, cut into bite-size pieces
2 eggs, beaten
1 cup Italian bread crumbs
Oil

1 tablespoon margarine
¾ pound fresh mushrooms, sliced
Shredded mozzarella cheese
2 cubes chicken bouillon
1 cup hot water

Coat chicken pieces with eggs. Put bread crumbs into a sealable plastic bag and add chicken. Shake until coated. Brown chicken in oil and drain on paper towels. Melt margarine in 9x13-inch pan. Put chicken in bottom of pan, then mushrooms; cover with cheese. Dissolve bouillon cubes in water and pour over casserole. Cover and bake in 350° oven for 45 minutes.

Treasured Recipes from Near and Far

Islander Chicken

1 bottle Chablis wine
3 boneless, skinless chicken
  breasts, quartered
4 ounces butter
4 large garlic cloves, crushed

1 cup orange juice
2 tablespoons soy sauce
¼ teaspoon cinnamon
2 medium mangoes, peeled and
  sliced lengthwise into spears

Pour Chablis into a large skillet. On high heat, poach chicken breasts in wine for about 7 minutes. Reserve 1 cup of liquid and pour off and save remainder. Add butter and garlic to pan and slowly pan-fry chicken until brown and completely cooked. Return reserved liquid to pan and add orange juice, soy sauce, cinnamon, and mangoes. Cover and simmer for 10 minutes. Makes 4 servings.

The Mongo Mango Cookbook

 There are 882 islands or "keys" in the Florida Keys which are large enough to be shown in hydrographic maps. Florida is home to an additional 4,510 islands 10 acres or larger, second only to Alaska's total island acreage. The Florida reef tract, extending 200 miles from Key Biscayne to the Dry Tortugas, contains approximately 6,000 coral reefs.

Pecan-Crusted Chicken with Banana Salsa

A favorite entrée at the world-famous Boca Raton Resort & Club, this recipe is a wonderful marriage of bananas and chicken.

BANANA SALSA:

3 cups (1/8-inch) banana slices
1/3 cup chopped red bell pepper
1/3 cup chopped yellow bell pepper
1 1/2 jalapeño chiles, seeded, chopped, or to taste
3 tablespoons chopped cilantro
Juice of 1 1/2 limes
1 1/2 tablespoons brown sugar
Salt and pepper to taste

Combine bananas, bell peppers, jalapeño chiles, cilantro, lime juice, brown sugar, salt and pepper in a bowl and mix well. Let stand for one hour or longer.

CHICKEN:

1 egg
1/2 cup milk
1 1/2 cups bread crumbs
1 1/2 cups chopped, toasted pecans
6 (6-ounce) boneless, skinless chicken breasts
Salt and pepper to taste
3 tablespoons Dijon mustard
1/2 cup flour
3 tablespoons vegetable oil

In a medium bowl, beat egg with milk.

In a separate medium bowl, mix bread crumbs and pecans. Season chicken with salt and pepper. Spread with Dijon mustard, and coat lightly with flour. Dip into egg mixture, then pecan mixture, pressing to coat well.

Heat oil in a nonstick sauté pan and add chicken. Sauté until golden brown on both sides, turning once. Remove to a baking dish. Bake at 350° for 15–20 minutes or until cooked through. Serve with Banana Salsa, smashed potatoes and fresh green beans. Serves 6.

Savor the Moment

Blue Bayou Chicken Breasts

6 boneless chicken breasts with skin attached
6 tablespoons butter, divided
5 scallions or green onions, chopped
2 cloves garlic, minced
12 ounces fresh mushrooms, chopped
6 ounces bleu cheese, crumbled
1 cup fresh bread crumbs
1 pound linguine, freshly cooked
1 (10-ounce) package frozen chopped spinach, defrosted and squeezed dry
2 tablespoons minced parsley
Parsley sprigs for garnish
Sliced tomatoes or tomato roses for garnish

Preheat oven to 350°. Rinse and pat dry chicken breasts. Separate skin from flesh of breast, leaving one side attached; set aside. Melt 2 tablespoons butter in a large skillet, and sauté onions until transparent. Add scallions and garlic, and continue to sauté until onions are lightly browned. Using a slotted spoon, transfer onion mixture to a large bowl.

Add mushrooms to drippings in skillet. Sauté, stirring often until most of the liquid evaporates. Add mushrooms to onion mixture. Stir in bleu cheese and bread crumbs, mixing well. Spoon cheese mixture between skin and flesh of each chicken breast. Tuck skin edges under breast; secure with wooden picks, if necessary. Place breasts skin-side-up in a shallow baking dish.

Melt remaining 4 tablespoons butter and brush on each breast. Bake uncovered at 350° for 40–50 minutes, basting occasionally with pan juices. Remove chicken breasts from baking pan; set aside to keep warm. Add freshly cooked linguine to drippings in baking dish, and toss along with chopped spinach. Spread linguine on a serving platter and arrange chicken breasts on top. Sprinkle chicken with minced parsley and garnish with parsley sprigs and tomatoes. Makes 6 servings.

Note: Boneless thighs with skin can be substituted for the breasts.

Recipes and Remembrances

Spinach-Stuffed Chicken in Apricot Sauce

1 (10-ounce) package frozen, chopped spinach, thawed
½ cup 1% fat cottage cheese
⅓ cup bread crumbs
1 tablespoon minced shallot
1 egg white
⅛ teaspoon garlic powder
⅛ teaspoon nutmeg
Salt to taste

6 (4-ounce) boneless, skinless chicken breast halves
1 tablespoon vegetable oil
1 cup apricot nectar
3 tablespoons Dijon mustard
1 tablespoon tarragon vinegar
2 teaspoons brown sugar
6 (2-ounce) unpeeled fresh apricots, cut into wedges

Press spinach between paper towels to remove excess moisture. Combine with cottage cheese, bread crumbs, shallot, egg white, garlic powder, nutmeg, and salt in a bowl and mix well. Rinse chicken and pat dry. Spoon spinach mixture onto chicken and roll to enclose filling; secure with wooden picks. Chill in refrigerator for 1 hour.

Brown chicken rolls in heated oil in a large skillet for 7 minutes on each side. Remove chicken to a warm platter. Add apricot nectar, mustard, vinegar, and brown sugar and mix well. Bring to a boil and reduce heat. Simmer for 7 minutes. Add apricots. Simmer until sauce thickens to desired consistency. Serve over chicken. Serves 6.

Tropical Settings

Chicken Breasts Stuffed with Feta and Dried Tomatoes

½ cup finely chopped red onion
2 tablespoons olive oil, divided
1½ teaspoons minced garlic
¼ cup pine nuts, lightly toasted
½ cup oil-packed, sun-dried
  tomatoes, drained, rinsed,
  dried and cut into thin strips
¼ pound feta cheese crumbled
  (approximately 1 cup)
2 tablespoons Parmesan cheese
1 tablespoon fresh marjoram or 1
  teaspoon dried marjoram
2 whole boneless chicken
  breasts, halved

Sauté onion in 1 tablespoon oil in a medium saucepan over moderate heat, stirring until softened. Add garlic and cook for 1 minute. Transfer to a bowl and let cool. Stir pine nuts, tomatoes, cheeses, and marjoram into onion mixture; season with salt and pepper.

Preheat oven to 350°. Insert knife into thicker end of chicken breast and cut a lengthwise pocket, making it as wide as possible. Fill each breast with ¼ cup filling. Secure opening with toothpicks, if necessary. Heat remaining 1 tablespoon oil in large skillet until hot; brown chicken for 5 minutes. Place in shallow baking dish and bake for 20 minutes or until just cooked through. Use any extra filling for garnish on the plate. Yields 4 servings.

A Slice of Paradise

Walnut Chicken

5 tablespoons oil, divided
5 teaspoons soy sauce, divided
3 teaspoons cornstarch, divided
2 whole boneless chicken
  breasts, skinned and cut
  in 1-inch pieces
½ cup chicken broth
½ teaspoon ginger
½ teaspoon dried red pepper
1 medium onion, cut into 1-inch
  pieces
1 clove garlic, minced
½ pound fresh broccoli, cut into
  1-inch pieces
½ cup chopped walnuts
1 (10-ounce) can mandarin
  oranges (optional)

Mix 1 tablespoon oil, 2 teaspoons soy sauce, and 1 teaspoon corn-starch in small bowl. Stir in chicken to coat. Cover and refrigerate 30 minutes. Meanwhile, mix chicken broth, ginger, and remaining 3 teaspoons soy sauce and 2 teaspoons cornstarch; set aside. Heat remaining oil in large skillet. Stir-fry refrigerated chicken mix-ture and dried pepper over medium heat until chicken is no longer pink. Remove chicken from skillet. Stir-fry onion and garlic until onion is tender. Add broccoli; stir-fry until tender. Add chicken and broth. Cook, stirring constantly, until thickened. Stir in walnuts and oranges. Serve with rice.

Recipes of Spruce Creek

The Navy's famous Blue Angels flying squadron is based in Pensacola and was established in 1946 to enhance recruiting. Their first air show was held at Craig Field in Jacksonville on June 15, 1946. The fastest speed flown during an air show is about 700 mph (just under Mach 1) and the slowest speed is about 120 mph.

Chicken Normandy

2 apples, peeled and sliced	4 tablespoons honey
1 chicken, cut up in small pieces	5 tablespoons cider or wine
4 tablespoons raisins	Dash each: salt and pepper

Place apples in a pie dish. Place chicken on top followed by remaining ingredients. Cover and cook in hot (400°) oven for 45 minutes, basting from time to time. Eat and enjoy.

The Galley K.I.S.S. Cookbook

Chicken and Mango

Cooked in a pressure cooker.

1 ripe medium to large mango, peeled and cubed	3 tablespoons dried herb seasoning
1⁄3 cup soy sauce	1⁄2 cup water
1 large sweet onion, thinly sliced	1⁄4 teaspoon sea salt
1 large green pepper, cut into strips	1⁄8 teaspoon ground black pepper
1 (3- to 3½-pound) chicken, quartered	1⁄8 teaspoon red pepper flakes

Combine mango, soy sauce, onion, and bell pepper in bowl; set aside.

Rinse chicken, and pat dry with paper towel. Place chicken and remaining ingredients into pressure cooker. Secure cover, then bring up to pressure and cook for 12 minutes. Remove from heat; allow pressure to drop of its own accord.

Place cooked chicken on platter; add mango mixture to hot chicken juices. Stir, then simmer uncovered for 2 minutes or until peppers are fork-tender. Pour mixture on top of chicken. Serve with cooked rice. Serves 4.

Note: May substitute 1 small can of Mandarin orange slices for fresh mangoes; drain slightly.

The Cruising K.I.S.S. Cookbook II

Chicken and Yellow Rice Valenciana

An Ybor City specialty.

1 (2½-pound) frying chicken,
  quartered
½ cup fresh olive oil
2 onions, chopped
1 green pepper, chopped
1 clove garlic, chopped fine
2 tablespoons salt
1 bay leaf
1 (14½-ounce) can tomatoes,
  drained

¼ teaspoon pepper
2½ cups rice
5 cups water plus 2 chicken
  bouillon cubes
½ cup sherry wine (optional)
⅛ teaspoon saffron
1 cup green peas
1 dozen green olives
1 (2-ounce) jar pimientos

Brown chicken in olive oil over medium heat. Add onions, green pepper, and garlic. Continue cooking until slightly brown, about 5 minutes. Return chicken to pot and stir in salt, bay leaf, tomatoes, and pepper. Add rice, water (in which 2 chicken bouillon cubes have been dissolved), and wine. Dissolve saffron in small amount of water and add to pot (or use a few drops of yellow food coloring mixed with water). Bring to a boil. Bake in preheated oven at 350° for 20 minutes. Garnish with green peas, olives, and pimientos. Makes 4 servings.

Famous Florida Recipes

In April of 1513, explorer Juan Ponce de León landed on the northeast coast of Florida near present-day St. Augustine. He called the area La Florida, in honor of Pascua Florida ("Feast of the Flowers"), Spain's Easter-time celebration.

Chicken Fiesta

Chicken Fiesta is a spectacular party dish. It travels well and makes excellent picnic fare when served at room temperature. When prepared with small drumsticks, it makes a delicious hors d'oeuvre.

2 chickens, cut up
1 small head garlic, minced
2 tablespoons fresh oregano
1 teaspoon salt
½ teaspoon freshly ground
  pepper
¼ cup red wine vinegar
¼ cup olive oil
¼ cup pitted, green Spanish
  olives

1 cup sliced fresh mushrooms
¼ cup capers with 1 tablespoon
  juice
2–3 bay leaves
½ cup light brown sugar
½ cup dry vermouth or white
  wine
2 tablespoons minced fresh
  parsley

In a large bowl, combine chicken pieces, garlic, oregano, salt, pepper, wine vinegar, olive oil, olives, mushrooms, capers, juice, and bay leaves. Cover and let marinate in refrigerator overnight.

Preheat oven to 350°. Arrange chicken in a single layer in a large, shallow baking pan, and spoon marinade over it evenly. Sprinkle chicken pieces with brown sugar, and pour vermouth around them. Bake at 350° for 50 minutes, basting frequently with pan juices.

With slotted spoon, transfer chicken, olives, mushrooms, and capers to a serving dish. Spoon pan juices over chicken and sprinkle with parsley. Serve remaining pan juices in a sauceboat. Yields 6 servings.

Some Like it South!

Florida is the number one destination state for overseas visitors. New York is second and California, third.

Chicken Potacchio

(Chicken with Red Wine Vinegar, Marchigana Style)

6–8 tablespoons olive oil
1 frying chicken, cut into as many small pieces as possible
Salt and pepper to taste

20 garlic cloves, peeled to the last thin skin
2 tablespoons rosemary leaves
½ cup red wine vinegar

In a heavy cast aluminum frying pan with a tight cover, heat olive oil. Add chicken, salt and pepper. Cook chicken quickly to a nice golden brown, stirring often. Add garlic, rosemary, and vinegar. Lower heat; cover and let cook gently for 15–20 minutes. When chicken is fork-tender, remove cover, then turn up heat to reduce liquid in pan. Stir chicken pieces until well coated in pan juices. Serve with crescia (flat bread) and sautéed escarole.

Preserving Our Italian Heritage

Eggplant and Chicken in a Skillet

1 (2- to 3-pound) frying chicken,
  cut into serving portions
Paprika
2 teaspoons salt, divided
¼ teaspoon pepper
2 tablespoons butter or
  margarine
½ cup chicken broth

1 clove garlic, crushed
1 medium-size eggplant, peeled
  and diced
1 onion, chopped
2 tomatoes, peeled and diced
¼ teaspoon thyme
1 tablespoon chopped parsley

Sprinkle chicken with paprika, 1 teaspoon salt and ¼ teaspoon pepper. Melt butter or margarine in large skillet. Add chicken and brown lightly. Remove from skillet. Add broth, scraping the brown particles from bottom of skillet into the broth. Add garlic, eggplant, onion, and tomatoes. Sprinkle with remaining salt and thyme and parsley. Arrange pieces of chicken on top of this mixture in the skillet. Cover and simmer for 30 minutes. Serves 4–6.

The Sunshine State Cookbook

Chicken with Marinated Artichoke Hearts

2 (2½- to 3-pound) chickens
2 medium onions, sliced thin
1 pound mushrooms, sliced
1 stick butter
3 (14-ounce) jars marinated
  artichoke hearts, drained
  (reserve oil from 1½ jars)

½–1 cup dry sherry
½ cup flour
1 (10¾-ounce) can cream of
  chicken or mushroom soup

Skin and cut up chicken. Sauté onions and mushrooms in butter. Stir in artichoke hearts. Place chicken pieces in greased casserole and cover with onion mixture. Mix together artichoke oil, sherry, flour, and soup, and pour over top. Bake at 350° for 45–60 minutes. Serves 6–8. May be prepared the night before.

The Woman's Exchange Classic Recipes

Editor's Extra: To avoid lumps when mixing flour with liquid, use a whisk, or shake in a jar.

Pollo Milanese

The secret to this crispy chicken cutlet dish is to make the chicken slices as thin as possible. If necessary, ask the butcher to cut them. Also invest in a chunk of imported Parmigiano-Reggiano cheese; the flavor is incredible! It is the finest brand of Parmigiano cheese in the world, and once you try it, you will never go back to canned American Parmesan cheese.

1½ cups plain or Italian bread
  crumbs
½ cup freshly grated
  Parmigiano-Reggiano cheese
1 teaspoon salt

16 (¼-inch) chicken breast
  cutlets
2 large eggs, beaten
½ cup extra-virgin olive oil
2 tablespoons butter

Mix bread crumbs, cheese, and salt in a shallow dish. Dip chicken cutlets into beaten eggs in a separate dish, allowing excess to drain back into dish; coat with bread crumb mixture. Heat olive oil and butter until foamy in a skillet over medium heat. Add chicken and cook until golden brown on both sides. Remove to serving platter and garnish with lemon wedges. Yields 8 servings.

An American Celebration

Beer Can Chicken

1 medium-size chicken	Poultry seasoning
Salt and pepper	¾ can lite beer

Preheat oven to 250°. Clean chicken. Sprinkle chicken inside and out with salt, pepper, and poultry seasoning. Cut off top of the can and put can (¾ full) in roaster pan; position chicken to sit on top of beer can (with beer in the can). Chicken will sit up in upright position. Cook 2 hours or until golden brown.

Good Cooking

Hot Chicken Salad Sandwich

2 cups finely diced, cooked chicken	12 slices extra thin sandwich bread, divided
2 hard-boiled eggs, chopped	1 (10¾-ounce) can cream of chicken soup
½ cup sliced mushrooms	
½ cup sliced stuffed olives	1 cup sour cream
½ cup mayonnaise	Cheddar cheese, grated

Combine the first 5 ingredients to make chicken salad. Remove crust from bread. Lay 6 slices in bottom of oiled 9x13-inch baking dish. Add chicken salad, then top with remaining 6 slices of bread. Combine soup and sour cream, and spread on top of sandwiches. Cover and let sit overnight in refrigerator.

Bake at 325° for 25–30 minutes. Add grated cheese at last few minutes, and continue to cook until cheese melts.

Note: Chicken can be cooked in crockpot ahead of time.

Trinity Treats

One-Dish Chicken Shortcake

4 tablespoons margarine
1 cup chopped onion
2 cups coarsely chopped, cooked
  chicken
1 cup sour cream
1/2 teaspoon thyme
1/4 teaspoon sage
1/4 teaspoon salt
1 (4-ounce) can mushroom
  pieces, drained

1 cup grated Cheddar cheese,
  divided
1 cup yellow cornmeal
1 1/2 teaspoons baking powder
1 teaspoon salt
1/2 cup flour
1/3 cup milk
1 egg, lightly beaten
1 (17-ounce) can cream-style corn
Dash of cayenne pepper

Preheat oven to 425°. Melt margarine in a 10-inch sauté pan; add onion and sauté until soft. Remove from heat and add chicken, sour cream, thyme, sage, salt, mushrooms, and 1/2 of the grated cheese. Set aside.

In a medium bowl, combine cornmeal, baking powder, salt, flour, milk, egg, corn, and cayenne. Stir until just mixed. Pour cornmeal batter into a greased 9x9x3 1/2-inch pan. Top with chicken mixture. Bake 15 minutes. Remove from oven and top with remaining cheese. Continue baking 25–30 minutes longer or until lightly browned and bubbly. Allow to stand 10 minutes before cutting into squares. Serves 4–6.

Strictly Scratch

Thirty-six percent of all U.S. hurricanes hit Florida. Hurricane Andrew, which hit Florida in 1992, was the third fiercest hurricane ever recorded on mainland America. Gusts reached 145 miles an hour and the cost of the damage was estimated at about $25 billion, making Andrew the most expensive natural disaster in U.S. history. The most fierce hurricane was an unnamed storm that hit the Florida Keys in 1935, and the second fiercest was Hurricane Camille which hit Mississippi in 1969.

Chicken Enchiladas

1 medium-sized onion, finely
  chopped
¼ pound sliced fresh mushrooms
1 tablespoon margarine
3 cups finely chopped, cooked
  chicken breast
1 (10-ounce) can cream of
  mushroom soup, undiluted
1 (8-ounce) carton sour cream
1 (4-ounce) can chopped green
  chiles, drained

½ cup sliced almonds
½ teaspoon dried whole oregano
¼ teaspoon salt
¼ teaspoon pepper
10 (7- to 8-inch) flour tortillas
1 (10-ounce) can cream of chicken
  soup, undiluted
1 (12-ounce) jar medium picante
  salsa
2 cups (8 ounces) shredded sharp
  Cheddar cheese

Sauté onion and mushrooms in margarine until tender. Combine chicken breast, cream of mushroom soup, sour cream, chiles, almonds, oregano, salt and pepper; mix well. Spoon about ½ cup mixture in center of each tortilla; roll up and place seam-side-down in a lightly oiled 9x13x2-inch baking dish.

Combine cream of chicken soup, picante salsa, and grated cheese; spoon over tortillas. Bake uncovered at 350° for 30–35 minutes. Serve while hot.

Sand in My Shoes

Chicken Pot Pie

3 chicken breasts
2 cups sliced carrots
2 cups diced potatoes
2 cups diced onions
1 (8-ounce) can Le Sueur peas,
  drained
1 (10¾-ounce) can cream of
  chicken soup
1 (10¾-ounce) can cream of
  celery soup
½ cup chicken broth
1 stick margarine, melted
1 cup self-rising flour
1 cup milk

Cook chicken breasts, carrots, potatoes, and onions in water to cover. Cut chicken into bite-size pieces. Line the bottom of a 9x13-inch dish with chicken. Layer vegetables plus can of peas over chicken. Pour mixture of soups and broth over chicken layers. Mix margarine, flour, and milk. Pour over mixture. Bake at 350° for 30 minutes; increase temperature to 375° and bake for 15 minutes.

Centennial Cookbook

E-Z Chicken Pot Pie

2 ready-made pie crusts
1 (14-ounce) can mixed
  vegetables, drained
1 (10¾-ounce) can cream of
  mushroom soup
1 (10¾-ounce) can cream of
  potato soup
½ cup milk
1½ cups cubed, cooked chicken

Put one crust into bottom of 1-quart casserole dish, bringing crust up sides. Mix remaining ingredients, except remaining crust, thoroughly. Place in casserole dish on top of crust and top with other crust; seal the 2 crusts by pinching them together. Bake at 350° for 45 minutes.

Kids at Work

Chicken and Dumplings

4 boneless, skinless chicken
  breasts
6 cups water
1 (10¾-ounce) can cream of
  chicken soup

1 (12-ounce) package frozen
  dumplings
Salt and pepper to taste

Boil chicken breasts in salted water. Turn to low heat and cook for 1 hour. Remove chicken. Add soup to chicken broth, then add frozen dumplings. You can break each strip into 4 pieces, if desired. Bring to a boil, then cook, covered, for 45 minutes on low heat. Chop chicken breasts, and add to dumplings at end of cooking time; cook on low heat for 15 minutes. Season to taste.

Treasures

Egg Foo Yong

1 cup diced, cooked chicken or
  turkey
½ cup chopped onion
1 (16-ounce) can bean sprouts,
  drained
1 tablespoon soy sauce
¼ teaspoon salt
3 eggs

Oil for deep frying
1½ cups prepared chicken
  bouillon
1 teaspoon molasses
1 dash soy sauce
1 teaspoon cornstarch, mixed with
  2 tablespoons water
3 tablespoons chopped scallions

Place meat, veggies, 1 tablespoon soy sauce, and salt in bowl; mix well. Break eggs and stir lightly into mixture. Using soup ladle, scoop out some of the mixture and fry in hot oil. Fry until they rise up, then turn and fry second side.

In separate small saucepan, heat bouillon, molasses, dash of soy sauce, and cornstarch mixed with water until thickened. Serve on top of foo yong; sprinkle with scallions.

The Galley K.I.S.S. Cookbook

Seafood

PHOTO © STEPHEN FRINK / FLORIDA KEYS TDC

The 327-foot former Coast Guard cutter Duane *was intentionally sunk in 120 feet of water off Key Largo in 1987 to create an "artificial reef." Artificial reefs are an important part of the marine environment in the Keys, providing essential habitats for marine life, as well as recreational opportunities for divers and fishermen.*

Shrimp St. George Sauté

Good and easy!

1 pound medium shrimp, peeled and deveined	½ teaspoon salt
	½ teaspoon white pepper
1 teaspoon paprika	3 tablespoons butter

Thaw shrimp, if frozen. Pat shrimp dry with paper towels. Combine shrimp, paprika, salt, and pepper; mix well and set aside. Melt butter in frying pan until hot, but not smoking. Add shrimp and cook on medium heat for 30 seconds. Stir shrimp and cook for 45 seconds longer, stirring constantly. Remove from heat; serve immediately. Serves 6.

The Woman's Exchange Classic Recipes

Shrimp Delight

1½ pounds medium raw shrimp	2 tablespoons parsley flakes
4 tablespoons butter	¼ teaspoon salt
1 teaspoon Worcestershire sauce	⅛ teaspoon freshly ground black pepper
1 clove garlic, minced	¼ cup grated Parmesan cheese
2 tablespoons chopped chives	¼ cup dry bread crumbs

Shell and devein shrimp. Pat dry with paper towels. Melt butter in a medium skillet. Add shrimp, Worcestershire sauce, garlic, chives, parsley flakes, salt, and pepper. Sauté for about 5 minutes, stirring constantly, until shrimp just turn pink.

With a slotted spoon, transfer shrimp to a casserole dish. Sprinkle with cheese and bread crumbs. Pour butter in which shrimp were cooked over all. Bake in a preheated 400° oven for 8–10 minutes, until golden brown. Serve with drawn butter, garnished with a sprig of parsley and a lemon wedge. Serves 4.

Cookin' in the Keys

Grilled Marinated Shrimp

Simple, devine and always a hit. For a different presentation that is also aromatic, thread the shrimp on the woody end of rosemary branches, leaving some of the leaves on the end.

½ cup vegetable or canola oil
¼ cup soy sauce
¼ cup lemon juice
2 tablespoons chopped fresh
  gingerroot

2 garlic cloves, minced
2 pounds fresh jumbo shrimp,
  peeled, deveined

Combine oil, soy sauce, lemon juice, gingerroot, and garlic in a bowl and mix well. Add shrimp to the mixture, tossing to mix well. Chill, covered, for 2–3 hours. Thread shrimp onto skewers. Grill over hot coals for 3–4 minutes on each side or until shrimp turn pink. If using wooden skewers, soak in water for 15 minutes before threading. Yields 8–10 servings.

The Life of the Party

Shrimp Sanibel

4–5 large shrimp per person
1 cup olive oil
4 cloves garlic, peeled and
  pressed

½ cup white wine
Juice of 2 lemons
Chopped parsley to taste

Peel and devein shrimp, and place in a large bowl. Add remaining ingredients and marinate at least 2 hours. Thread shrimp on skewers and grill over hot coals, 3 minutes per side. Serve.

Let's ACT Up in the Kitchen

Florida's Sanibel and Captiva islands are home to hundreds of species of seashells. Sanibel is one of the unique barrier islands of the world, having an east-west orientation when most islands are north-south. Therefore the beaches act as a net, catching an abundance of shells.

Soppin' Shrimp

¼ pound butter
⅔ cup lemon or lime juice
2½ teaspoons black pepper

1 teaspoon grated lemon rind
1½ cups Italian dressing
2 pounds raw shrimp, with shells

In medium saucepan, melt butter. Add juice, pepper, rind, and dressing, and bring to a boil. Add shrimp and simmer 6 minutes. Divide shrimp and sauce among 6 bowls. Serve with hot, crusty bread for soppin'. Yields 6 servings.

Historic Spanish Point: Cooking Then and Now

Feta Shrimp

2 large onions, thinly sliced
⅓ cup olive oil
4 large tomatoes, peeled and
   coarsely chopped
3 tablespoons finely chopped
   parsley
½ teaspoon dried dill weed
¼–½ teaspoon freshly ground
   black pepper

¼ teaspoon sugar
1 clove garlic, minced or mashed
2 pounds large raw shrimp, peeled
   and deveined
¾ pound Greek feta cheese
1 large whole tomato, peeled
   (optional)
Parsley or dill

In an oven-proof skillet or Dutch oven, sauté onions in oil until tender. Add chopped tomatoes, chopped parsley, dill, pepper, sugar, and garlic. Cover and simmer 30 minutes, stirring occasionally. Add shrimp, dipping them down into the sauce and arranging in a circle. Crumble feta cheese over shrimp. Place whole tomato in center, if desired. Bake, uncovered, in 450° oven for 10–15 minutes or until shrimp are done and cheese is melted. Garnish with parsley or fresh dill sprigs.

Recipes and Remembrances

Shrimp in Tomato and Feta Cheese Sauce à la Grecque

This recipe originated in the Tarpon Springs area, where a small but colorful Greek community carries on the sponge-fishing industry started in the early years of this century. Flavorful Greek ingredients are combined with tomatoes, shrimp, and feta cheese to make a dish that is good for serving a crowd because it is easily multiplied. Chunks of fish can be substituted for the shrimp or mixed with the shrimp for variety.

½ cup olive oil
2 cloves garlic, crushed
1 large onion, sliced thin
⅔ cup dry white wine
4 large tomatoes, peeled and
  chopped
¼ cup chopped Italian (flat-leaf)
  parsley

1 teaspoon chopped fresh oregano,
  or ½ teaspoon dried
1 teaspoon salt
½ teaspoon ground pepper
2 pounds shrimp, shelled,
  deveined, and halved lengthwise
½ pound feta cheese
Sprigs of parsley

In a shallow oven-proof casserole, heat oil and sauté garlic and onion until transparent. Add wine, tomatoes, herbs, and seasonings; simmer about 30 minutes or until mixture has thickened. Add shrimp and stir to coat thoroughly.

Crumble feta cheese over top of casserole. Preheat oven to 450° and bake for about 15 minutes or until shrimp is cooked and cheese has melted. Garnish with parsley sprigs and serve over rice or with crusty bread. Serves 6.

Gulf Coast Cooking

Coconut Fried Shrimp with Mango Sauce

MANGO SAUCE:

2 cups cider vinegar
1 cup firmly packed light brown
   sugar
2 mangoes, peeled, seeded, and
   chopped
4 shallots, thinly sliced
4 cloves garlic, thinly sliced
½ ounce fresh gingerroot

1 ounce tamarind paste
2 inches sliced lemon peel
2 inches sliced orange peel
1 teaspoon cayenne pepper
⅓ teaspoon cinnamon
⅓ teaspoon ground cardamom
1 tablespoon kosher salt
8 bananas, peeled

In heavy, stainless steel saucepan (not aluminum), place vinegar and sugar; bring to a boil. Reduce heat and simmer until thick syrup forms and thickens (238° on candy thermometer). Add all other ingredients except bananas; simmer 45 minutes, stirring frequently. Remove from heat and chill. In blender or food processor, purée mango mixture and bananas until smooth and well blended. Store, covered, in a glass container in refrigerator until needed. Serve cold with hot, freshly cooked coconut shrimp. Dip and enjoy.

2 pounds raw shrimp
1 cup all-purpose flour
½ teaspoon sugar
½ teaspoon salt

1 egg, slightly beaten
2 tablespoons vegetable oil
⅔ cup grated coconut

Thaw shrimp, if they are frozen; shell and devein, leaving tails intact. Blot shrimp dry with paper towels. In large bowl, combine flour, sugar, salt, egg, and oil. Dip shrimp into batter, then into coconut. Fry in deep fat fryer at 375° until golden brown. Serve with Mango Sauce. Serves 4–6.

Florida Seafood Cookery

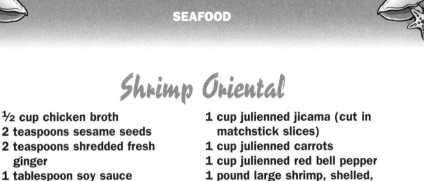

Shrimp Oriental

½ cup chicken broth
2 teaspoons sesame seeds
2 teaspoons shredded fresh
  ginger
1 tablespoon soy sauce
¼ teaspoon red hot pepper
  sauce
1 teaspoon cornstarch
2 tablespoons oil

1 cup julienned jicama (cut in
  matchstick slices)
1 cup julienned carrots
1 cup julienned red bell pepper
1 pound large shrimp, shelled,
  deveined
2 cloves garlic, minced
3 cups cooked rice

Blend together in a large bowl the broth, sesame seeds, ginger, soy sauce, hot pepper sauce, and cornstarch. Set aside.

In a large nonstick skillet or wok, heat oil. Stir-fry jicama and carrots for 3 minutes; remove from pan and set aside. Add more oil, if needed, and stir-fry pepper, shrimp, and garlic for 3 minutes or until shrimp turns pink and opaque.

Stir sauce again; pour into center of work or skillet and cook until mixture bubbles. Return jicama and carrots to the pan; cover and cook for 2 minutes or until heated through. Serve over hot cooked rice. Serves 4.

The Cruising K.I.S.S. Cookbook II

Grits a Ya Ya

(Shrimp and Grits)

CHEESE GRITS:

2 cups chicken stock
1 quart heavy cream
8 ounces grits

½ stick butter
½ pound smoked Gouda cheese, diced

Bring stock and cream to boil. Add grits and cook on high heat for 5 minutes, stirring rapidly. Add butter and cook on low heat for 10 minutes. Add smoked Gouda cheese. Stir to incorporate to smooth consistency.

SAUCE:

8 strips bacon
1 tablespoon minced garlic
1 tablespoon minced shallots
3 tablespoons butter
White wine
1 pound peeled and deveined jumbo shrimp

1 portabello mushroom cap, sliced
¼ cup diced scallions
2 cups chopped fresh spinach
2 cups heavy cream
Salt, pepper, and hot sauce to taste

Heat a large saucepan over medium heat. Add bacon and cook for about 3 minutes, then add garlic and shallots. Sauté, then add butter and a splash of white wine. When butter is half melted, add shrimp. When the down sides of shrimp become white, flip them and add mushroom slices, scallions, and spinach. Sauté for 2 minutes. Remove shrimp. Pour in heavy cream and let simmer while stirring. When reduced by ⅓, add salt, pepper, and hot sauce to taste. Return shrimp to sauce and combine. Spoon sauce and shrimp onto heaping mounds of Cheese Grits.

Recipes and Remembrances

The St. Johns River is one of the few rivers that flows north instead of south.

Yummy Shrimp Casserole

1 (16-ounce) package medium
  egg noodles
2 (10¾-ounce) cans cream of
  mushroom soup
1 cup sour cream

⅓ cup sliced green onions
½ teaspoon dill weed
1 pound shrimp, cooked, peeled,
  deveined, and cut
1 cup shredded Cheddar cheese

Cook noodles as directed on package, and drain well. Combine and mix soup, sour cream, onions, and dill weed. Stir in noodles. Fold cut shrimp and cheese into noodle mixture. Spoon into 2-quart baking dish. Bake 30–35 minutes at 350°. Casserole may be made a day ahead; increase baking time by 10–15 minutes.

Centennial Cookbook

Shrimp Florentine

¼ cup finely chopped onion
¼ cup butter
¼ cup flour
1 teaspoon salt
½ teaspoon dry mustard
2 cups milk
½ cup grated Swiss cheese
1 cup grated Parmesan cheese,
  divided

2 (10-ounce) packages frozen
  chopped spinach, cooked and
  drained
1 (8-ounce) can water chestnuts,
  drained and sliced
1 tablespoon lemon juice
1½ pounds shrimp, boiled and
  peeled
Paprika

Preheat oven to 400°. Cook onion in butter until tender. Stir in flour, salt, and dry mustard. Add milk. Cook, stirring constantly, until thickened. Remove from heat. Add Swiss cheese and stir until melted. Fold in half the Parmesan cheese.

Combine spinach and water chestnuts and spread in a shallow, greased 1½- to 2-quart baking dish. Drizzle lemon juice over spinach. Add shrimp, then sauce; top with remaining Parmesan cheese. Garnish with paprika. Bake for 15–20 minutes or until hot. Yields 6 servings.

Some Like it South!

Shrimp Marinara and Spaghetti

1 cup chopped onion	1 teaspoon sugar
1 clove garlic	1 cup white wine
¼ cup olive oil	1 pound raw shrimp, shelled and
6 tomatoes, peeled, quartered	cleaned
Salt and pepper to taste	1 pound spaghetti, cooked

Cook onion and garlic in oil until golden. Add tomatoes and cook slowly for 30 minutes. Season to taste with salt, pepper, and sugar. Add wine and shrimp. Bring to a boil and cook about 8 minutes. Serve over cooked spaghetti.

FCCD Cookbook

Shrimp or Lobster and Angel Hair Pasta

1 (8-ounce) package angel hair	1 tablespoon white wine
pasta	Salt and cracked pepper to taste
4 large shallots	1 pound shrimp, boiled and peeled,
½ cup plus 2 tablespoons	or 1 lobster, boiled and cleaned
butter, divided	

Cook angel hair pasta according to package directions. Drain and set aside. Thinly slice shallots. Melt ½ cup butter in large saucepan. Add shallots and cook slowly until soft. Add wine, salt and pepper. Cook gently for 5 minutes. Add shrimp or lobster to shallots, and cook until heated. Add remaining 2 tablespoons butter and heat until just melted. Pour over drained cooked pasta. Mix.

Steinhatchee Village Seafood and Etc!

Pasta Sauce—Florida Style

2 garlic cloves, minced
1 onion, chopped
3 stalks celery, chopped
2 tablespoons olive oil
1/4 teaspoon thyme
1/4 teaspoon basil
1/2 teaspoon oregano
2 (14 1/2-ounce) cans diced
   tomatoes

2 (6-ounce) cans tomato paste
1/2 teaspoon salt
1/2 cup dry white wine
2 (8-ounce) bottles clam juice
4 (4.5-ounce) cans minced clams,
   drained
1 pound boiled shrimp, shelled
1/2 cup parsley, chopped

Sauté garlic, onion, and celery in oil. Add thyme, basil, oregano, tomatoes, tomato paste, salt, and wine. Simmer, uncovered for one hour. Add clam juice and continue to simmer 30 minutes. Add clams and shrimp and simmer an additional 10 minutes. Garnish with parsley. Serve over favorite pasta. Makes 6 servings.

Gracious Gator Cooks

Fast Eddie's All-Purpose Linguini Sauce

3 tablespoons olive oil
1 large garlic clove, minced
3 (4 1/2-ounce) cans clams,
   minced, drained, and juice
   retained
1 tablespoon cornstarch
1/4 cup lemon juice
1/2 cup finely chopped fresh
   parsley

3 tablespoons finely chopped fresh
   basil, or 1 teaspoon dried basil
1/2 teaspoon dried thyme
1 (8-ounce) package linguini,
   cooked and drained
1 cup freshly grated Parmesan
   cheese
Salt and pepper to taste

In a large skillet, add olive oil and sauté garlic briefly to release flavor. Add clams and cornstarch; heat just to boiling, stirring frequently. Lower heat; stir in clam juice, lemon juice, parsley, basil, and thyme. Remove from heat and add linguini. Toss mixture lightly. Add Parmesan cheese, salt and pepper to taste, and toss again. Serve hot.

Great Recipes from Near and Afar

Shrimp Creole

½ cup chopped onion
2 tablespoons butter
2 tablespoons flour
1 bay leaf
1 tablespoon minced parsley
½ cup minced green pepper
½ teaspoon salt

¾ can Ro-Tel tomatoes
1 (8-ounce) can tomato sauce
1 cup water
1 onion, thinly sliced
2 cups cooked and cleaned
   shrimp

Sauté onion in butter. Blend in flour, making a roux. Cook until blended well, but not dark. Add remaining ingredients, except shrimp, and simmer until sauce thickens. Add shrimp. Simmer until shrimp are hot. Serve on rice.

Village Royale: Our Favorite Recipes

Greek Shrimp and Scallops

½ pound pasta
1½ tablespoons minced garlic
⅓ cup olive oil, divided
1¼ cups chopped fresh
   tomatoes
½ cup dry white wine
Salt and pepper to taste

1 tablespoon basil
½ teaspoon oregano (fresh,
   if desired)
1 pound peeled and deveined
   shrimp or Steinhatchee scallops
½ teaspoon red pepper flakes
Feta cheese

Cook pasta of choice according to package directions. Briefly sauté garlic in half the olive oil, then add tomatoes and cook briefly. Add wine, salt, pepper, basil, and oregano, and simmer on low about 10 minutes. Sauté seafood in remaining olive oil. Add all together with spices and tomato mixture. Put feta cheese on top and bake about 20 minutes in 350° oven. Serve over pasta with salad and bread of choice.

Steinhatchee Village Seafood and Etc!

Grilled Marinated Grouper

⅓ cup lemon juice
1 teaspoon lemon rind
2 teaspoons prepared
  horseradish
½ garlic clove
½ teaspoon oregano
½ teaspoon basil

½ teaspoon salt
¼ teaspoon pepper
⅓ cup olive oil
8 (4-ounce) grouper fillets or other
  white fish
Vegetable cooking spray

In electric blender or food processor, combine lemon juice, lemon rind, horseradish, garlic, oregano, basil, salt and pepper. Turn blender or processor on low, and gradually add olive oil in a slow, steady stream. Set aside.

Arrange fish in a 9x13x2-inch baking dish. Pour marinade over fish, turning to coat both sides. Cover and refrigerate 8 hours or overnight.

Arrange fish in a fish grill basket coated with cooking spray. Grill, covered, over medium hot coals 7–8 minutes on each side, or until fish flakes easily when tested with a fork, basting frequently with marinade. Yields 8 servings.

Cookin' on Island Time

Grouper à la Rusa

(Cherna à la Rusa)

2 (6-ounce) grouper or snapper
   fillets
Garlic powder, salt, and pepper
   to taste
1 cup flour
2 eggs, beaten lightly

1 cup bread crumbs
1 stick butter, divided
1 lemon, thinly sliced
1 hard-boiled egg, chopped
⅓ cup chopped parsley

Season fish fillets with garlic powder, salt, and pepper. Coat with flour. Dip in beaten eggs and coat with bread crumbs. Melt ½ stick of butter in heavy skillet over medium heat. When bubbly, pan-broil fillets until golden brown. Remove to platter. Melt remaining butter, and pour over fillets. Arrange 3 or 4 slices of lemon on each fillet, and garnish with chopped egg and parsley. Serves 2.

The Columbia Restaurant Spanish Cookbook

Key Lime Grouper

This recipe won its author a ribbon at a Key lime cooking contest during the Indian Key Festival. It works with all firm, white fish.

Grouper fillets, cut into
   serving-size pieces
1 egg, beaten
Italian bread crumbs
1 key lime, sliced

1 stick butter, divided
½ pound chopped spinach
¼ pound chopped mushrooms
½ cup grated Parmesan cheese

Dip fish in beaten egg, then coat with bread crumbs. While coating sits, sauté lime in ½ stick butter in frying pan. When lime is cooked, remove it, then add fish, and heat on medium high. Turn fish when browned on first side. Add rest of butter; cover fillets with chopped spinach, chopped mushrooms, and cheese. Cover pan tightly, then turn heat to low, and let cook for 8–10 minutes, depending on thickness. Carefully remove fish from pan; stir drippings, and pour sparingly over each portion.

Historic Spanish Point: Cooking Then and Now

Grilled Swordfish Steaks in Packets, à la Grecque

This could be called a Florida Greek barbecue. Each packet contains one serving of wonderfully seasoned fish, crispy onions, and red bell peppers, and some great juices that you'll want to soak up with crusty bread or pour over hot buttered rice. Any firm fish can be used—try shark, tuna, redfish, ling, pompano, mullet . . . you name it. Serve the steaks in their packets so that the aroma can be savored as the foil is opened.

1 (8-ounce) swordfish steak
Salt and ground black pepper
Paprika
Fresh oregano leaves, or
  crumbled dried oregano

Thin slices of onion
Thin slices of red bell pepper
1 teaspoon lemon juice
2 tablespoons olive oil or melted
  butter

Place steak on a square of buttered or oiled aluminum foil and season with salt and pepper and a liberal sprinkling of paprika. Add oregano and top with onion and red bell pepper slices. Sprinkle with lemon juice and olive oil.

Fold over corners of foil securely to make packet. Grill about 12 inches above hot coals for about 20 minutes (cooking time will vary with type and thickness of fish). Serves 1.

Gulf Coast Cooking

Mahi Mahi with Spicy Mango Cilantro Sauce

½ cup chopped, dried mango
2 fresh serrano chiles, seeded
  and chopped
5 cloves garlic, chopped
½ white onion, chopped
¾ cup dry white wine
¼ cup orange juice

1 cup chopped fresh cilantro
8 (¾-inch-thick) mahi mahi fillets
Salt and pepper to taste
1 tablespoon olive oil
½ cup skim milk
2 tablespoons chopped macadamia
  nuts

Combine mango, chiles, garlic, onion, wine, and orange juice in a medium saucepan. Bring to a boil over medium heat. Cook 5 minutes. Reduce heat, and simmer until ingredients are tender and liquid is reduced by about half. Add cilantro. Purée mixture in a blender. Set aside.

Season fillets with salt and pepper. In a large skillet, heat oil. Add fillets, and cook 2 minutes on each side or until lightly browned. Turn off heat and cover. Add milk to sauce and purée again. Reduce sauce. Place fillets on a serving platter. Pour sauce over top, and sprinkle with nuts. Yields 8 servings.

Treasures of the Tropics

The mullet, a bottom-dwelling fish that inhabits local bayous, is celebrated in Florida. Each April at Perdido Beach, people gather on either side of the Florida-Alabama line to throw fish in the annual Mullet Toss. Donations are taken to benefit local charities. Niceville is home to the famous Boggy Bayou Mullet Festival celebrated in October.

Beer-Battered Mullet

1½ cups flour, divided
½ cup yellow cornmeal
12 ounces premium beer, such as
   Michelob or Old Milwaukee
1 tablespoon salt

1 tablespoon paprika
2 pounds fresh mullet fillets, skin
   on
Peanut oil for frying
Malt vinegar (optional)

In a bowl, mix ½ cup flour and yellow cornmeal. In second bowl, add 1 cup flour, beer, salt, and paprika. Blend well and let sit at room temperature for one hour.

Make sure mullet is dry. First dip fillet into dry mixture, then into batter. Shake off excess and fry in hot peanut oil in small batches until golden brown. Serve with malt vinegar, if desired. Serves 6.

The Mostly Mullet Cookbook

Foiled Mullet

4 (4-ounce) mullet fillets
1½ cups sliced fresh
   mushrooms
½ cup chopped onion
1 tablespoon olive oil

1 cup chopped tomatoes
2 tablespoons dry white wine
½ teaspoon dried, crushed
   thyme
⅛ teaspoon black pepper

For best results, skin fillets. In a large skillet, sauté mushrooms and onion in oil. Add all ingredients except fish. Cut a piece of foil twice the length of a baking pan. Place in pan and spray with a cooking oil spray. Arrange fish in a single layer on foil, and top with vegetable mixture. Bring foil up over fish, closing all edges. Bake at 350° for 10–15 minutes or until fish flakes readily when forked. Serve to 4 hungry people.

The Mostly Mullet Cookbook

Broiled Mackerel, Red and Hot

This fish can be as hot-tasting as you like. For a real taste-tingler, just add more horseradish.

2 pounds mackerel fillets
1 teaspoon salt
Dash freshly ground black
  pepper
1 cup grated sharp cheese
3 tablespoons chili sauce

1 tablespoon prepared Dijon
  mustard
2 teaspoons horseradish (or more
  to taste)
1/4 cup butter or margarine,
  melted

Thaw fish (if frozen). Wipe with a damp cloth and cut into serving portions. Sprinkle both sides with salt and pepper. Combine cheese, chili sauce, mustard, and horseradish. Brush fish with butter, then place on greased broiler pan about 2 inches below heating unit. Broil 5–8 minutes or until lightly browned. Turn carefully and brush other side with butter; broil 5–8 minutes longer, or until fish flakes easily with a fork. Spread cheese mixture on top of fish. Slide under broiler just long enough for cheese to melt and brown lightly, 1–2 minutes. Serves 4–6.

Florida Seafood Cookery

Potato Crusted Snapper

1/2 cup low-fat buttermilk
1/4 teaspoon salt
1/4 teaspoon black pepper
2 garlic cloves, minced
3/4 cup instant potato flakes
  (not granules)

4 (6-ounce) red snapper or mahi
  mahi fillets
1 tablespoon butter or margarine
4 lemon wedges

Combine first 4 ingredients in a shallow dish. Place potato flakes in another shallow dish. Dip fillets in buttermilk mixture, then dredge in potato flakes. Melt butter in a large nonstick skillet on medium-high heat. Add fish; cook 3 minutes on each side or until golden and fish flakes easily when tested with a fork. Serve with lemon wedges.

Good Cooking

Baked Snapper Fillets

2 large onions, finely chopped
¼ cup olive oil
2 garlic cloves, sliced
1 cup chopped celery
1 cup chopped carrots
½ cup chopped parsley

1 (28-ounce) can tomatoes
½ teaspoon salt
½ teaspoon pepper
6 snapper fillets
Juice of 1 lemon

Sauté onions in hot olive oil in a skillet. Add garlic, celery, carrots, and parsley, and mix well. Add tomatoes. Bring to a simmer. Simmer for 5 minutes. Season with salt and pepper. Arrange snapper in baking dish. Spoon sauce over snapper. Drizzle lemon juice evenly over top. Bake at 350° for 10 minutes per inch of thickness of snapper or until fish flakes easily. Yields 6 servings.

Entirely Entertaining in the Bonnet House Style

Baked Snapper with Bread Stuffing

BREAD STUFFING:
¼ cup chopped celery
¼ cup chopped onion
¼ cup butter or margarine,
  melted
1 quart dry bread cubes

1 egg, beaten
½ teaspoon salt
½ teaspoon thyme (optional)
½ teaspoon parsley
Pepper to taste

Sauté celery and onion in butter until tender. Combine with other ingredients. Makes 3 cups stuffing. Shrimp and crabmeat may be added to this stuffing to make it extra special, but it's good without.

FISH:
1 (3- to 4-pound) dressed snapper
  or other dressed fish (flounder
  is good)

Salt and pepper to taste
Bread Stuffing
2 tablespoons melted fat or oil

Clean, wash, and dry fish. Sprinkle inside with salt and pepper. Place fish on a well-greased bake-and-serve platter or aluminum foil. Stuff loosely with Bread Stuffing. Brush with oil. Bake at 350° for 45–60 minutes or until fish flakes easily when tested with a fork.

Crab Island Cookbook

Pompano Baked in Sour Cream Sauce

This recipe is of Russian origin. Pompano, red snapper and yellowtail are often caught in Florida waters and are perfect for this dish.

SOUR CREAM SAUCE:

½ stick butter

2 tablespoons flour

1 cup meat or vegetable stock, warmed

1 cup sour cream

Salt to taste

In a medium saucepan, melt butter, then add flour and blend until smooth. Gradually add warmed stock, stirring to blend, then add sour cream and blend thoroughly. Add salt as desired and simmer gently for 5–10 minutes.

2 pounds pompano fillets, boned and skinned

2 tablespoons flour

½ stick butter, divided

2 hard-boiled eggs, peeled and sliced

1 cup sliced mushrooms

1½ pounds potatoes, peeled and sliced

Salt and pepper to taste

Sour Cream Sauce

½ cup grated Cheddar cheese

Preheat oven to 350°. Cut fish fillets into 4 portions and roll in flour. In a large skillet, melt ¼ stick butter and sauté fillets for 3–4 minutes on both sides. Place fillets in a buttered baking dish and layer egg slices on top. In same large skillet, saute mushrooms for 4–5 minutes. Spoon mushrooms on top of eggs. In same skillet, melt remaining butter; add potatoes and cook until tender. Arrange potatoes around fish, eggs, and mushrooms. Sprinkle with salt and pepper. Pour Sour Cream Sauce over casserole, then sprinkle top with Cheddar cheese. Bake for 20–25 minutes.

Florida Cook Book

Pompano Papillot

1 onion, finely chopped
¼ pound butter
1 cup flour
2 cups boiled milk
2 eggs
Dash nutmeg
Dash Tabasco sauce

2 tablespoons Sauterne
½ pound shrimp, peeled,
  deveined, and chopped
½ pound crawfish or lobster
  meat, chopped
2 large or 4 small pompano
  steaks

Sauté onion in melted butter in large skillet for 5 minutes. Slowly add flour to form a roux. Let it cook dry, slowly. Add boiled milk and stir over medium heat to make thick cream sauce. Beat eggs with nutmeg, Tabasco sauce, and Sauterne; fold into cream sauce. Add shrimp and crawfish or lobster.

On buttered parchment paper or aluminum foil (large enough to make a bag enclosing fish), spread ⅓ sauce and top with a slice of skinned pompano steak. Spread another ⅓ sauce, then another slice of pompano. Spread remaining sauce over top. Close paper or foil over top; seal by folding edges together. Brush melted butter over paper and bake 20 minutes at 400°. This dish may also be made with snapper or grouper. Serves 2.

The Columbia Restaurant Spanish Cookbook

Lemon Marinated Orange Roughy

3 tablespoons lemon juice
1 clove garlic, crushed
1 tablespoon brown sugar
1 tablespoon oil

1 teaspoon finely chopped
  gingerroot
¼ teaspoon salt
1 pound orange roughy fillets

Combine all ingredients, except orange roughy, for marinade; mix thoroughly. Pour over fillets and marinate in refrigerator for 1 hour, turning once. Broil 4–5 inches from heat for 3–4 minutes on each side, basting frequently with marinade.

Crab Island Cookbook

Sesame-Crusted Yellowfin Tuna

4 (9-ounce) tuna steaks
1 cup sesame seeds, divided
¼ pound butter, whipped
2 tablespoons soy sauce
2 teaspoons sesame oil

1 teaspoon fresh chopped ginger
½ teaspoon minced fresh garlic
1 tablespoon wasabi
¼ cup thinly sliced chives
Lemon slices

Coat tuna steaks with ½ cup sesame seeds, and sear on both sides in hot oil until seeds are golden.

For sauce, toast remaining ½ cup sesame seeds. Mix butter with soy sauce, ginger, garlic and wasabi. Add toasted sesame seeds and heat until pourable. Slice steaks on diagonal; arrange on plates and drizzle wasabi sauce over. Garnish with chives and lemon slices, and serve with slaw. Serves 4.

Recipe from Ocean Grill, Vero Beach
Intracoastal Waterway Restaurant Guide & Recipe Book

Grilled Tuna with Tomato Basil Vinaigrette

6 (8-ounce) tuna steaks
¼ cup virgin olive oil
¼ cup dry white wine

1 tablespoon minced garlic
Salt and freshly ground pepper to taste

Arrange steaks in a single layer in a nonreactive dish. Whisk olive oil, white wine, garlic, salt and pepper in a bowl. Pour over steaks, turning to coat. Marinate, covered, at room temperature for 1 hour or up to 6 hours in refrigerator. Drain, reserving marinade. Bring reserved marinade to a boil in a saucepan. Boil for 2 minutes.

Grill steaks over hot coals for 5–7 minutes or until steaks flake easily, basting occasionally with cooked, reserved marinade. Drizzle with Tomato Basil Vinaigrette. Serves 6.

TOMATO BASIL VINAIGRETTE:

½ cup virgin or light olive oil
4 medium tomatoes, peeled, seeded, chopped
¼ cup finely chopped red onion
¼ cup drained finely chopped sun-dried tomatoes

¼ cup minced fresh basil
¼ cup drained small capers
1 teaspoon minced garlic
½ teaspoon salt
½ teaspoon freshly ground pepper

Combine olive oil, tomatoes, onion, basil, sun-dried tomatoes, capers, garlic, salt and pepper in a bowl, and mix gently.

Note: The vinaigrette may be prepared a day in advance and stored, covered, in the refrigerator, adding the basil and salt just before serving.

Made in the Shade

Fish Tacos

1 (12-ounce) bottle beer
1 cup salad oil
2–3 jalapeños, chopped
½ tablespoon finely ground
  black pepper

3 cloves garlic, minced
2 tablespoons soy sauce
1 teaspoon ground cumin
2–3 tuna steaks, ¾–1 inch thick
Flour tortillas

Mix all ingredients, except tuna steaks and tortillas, for marinade. Marinate tuna at least 12 hours or up to 3 days in refrigerator. Grill fish 10–12 minutes. Break into chunks. Wrap in warm flour tortillas.

TOPPINGS:

Sautéed onions
Cilantro
Salsa

Guacamole
Sour cream
Shredded cheese

Top taco with sautéed onions, cilantro sprigs, salsa, guacamole, sour cream, shredded cheese.

Country Club Cooks

Baked Salmon with Honey-Mustard Crunch Coating

4 salmon fillets
Salt and pepper to taste
4 tablespoons Dijon mustard
4 tablespoons butter, melted
3 tablespoons honey
⅓ cup soft bread crumbs

⅓ cup finely chopped pecans
2 tablespoons chopped fresh
  parsley
Lemon slices and parsley sprigs for
  garnish

Sprinkle salmon with salt and pepper. Place fillets, skin-side-down, in a lightly greased 9x13x2-inch baking dish. Combine mustard, butter, and honey, and spread over fillets. Combine bread crumbs, pecans, and chopped parsley; spoon mixture evenly over fillets. Bake at 450° for 10 minutes or until fish flakes easily when tested with fork. Garnish with lemon slices and fresh parsley sprigs.

Tastes from Paradise: A Garden of Eating

Stuffed Farm-Raised Catfish Almondine

8 small, pan-dressed, farm-raised catfish
½ cup white wine
1 tablespoon chopped onion
½ teaspoon salt
¼ teaspoon pepper
10 medium shrimp, cooked, chopped
1 (6-ounce) can crabmeat, well drained
¾ cup butter or margarine
1 (4-ounce) package sliced almonds
1 tablespoon lemon or lime juice
Cherry tomatoes
Parsley and lemon wedges

If frozen, thaw catfish in refrigerator. Clean thoroughly and dry with paper towels. Combine wine, onion, salt, pepper, shrimp, and crabmeat; marinate for 30 minutes. Drain and save liquid. If cavity of fish is small, enlarge it by cutting a small pocket along backbone. Stuff each fish with shrimp and crabmeat mixture. Sprinkle fish with salt. Fry in margarine until browned on each side and fish is done; it should flake easily when tested with a fork.

Remove fish from pan to a warm platter. Add almonds, lemon juice, and reserved marinade to frying pan; cook until almonds are lightly browned. Spread sauce over catfish and garnish with tomatoes, parsley, and lemon wedges. Serves 4.

Florida Seafood Cookery

Blackened Catfish

1 tablespoon paprika	1 teaspoon dried thyme
2 teaspoons dried basil	1/2 teaspoon salt
1 1/2 teaspoons garlic powder	4 catfish fillets, 4–6 ounces each
1 1/2 teaspoons black pepper	2 tablespoons butter or margarine
1 1/2 teaspoons sugar	Lemon wedges
1 1/2 teaspoons cayenne pepper, or to taste	

Combine all dry ingredients and spread evenly over a piece of waxed paper. Rinse catfish under cool, running water and pat dry with paper towels. Liberally coat both sides of catfish fillets with spice mixture.

Melt butter or margarine in an iron skillet over moderately high heat. Add fillets to hot skillet and cook 2–4 minutes on each side, turning once, until fish is no longer translucent at thickest part and flakes easily when tested with a fork. Cooking time will vary depending upon thickness of fish.

The Essential Catfish Cookbook

Editor's Extra: Good to have vent turned on, as this can be a little smoky.

Baked Catfish

1/4 cup yellow cornmeal	1/8 teaspoon ground red pepper
1/4 cup all-purpose flour	1 egg white
1/4 cup grated Parmesan cheese	2 tablespoons skim milk
1 teaspoon paprika	4 (4-ounce) catfish fillets
1/2 teaspoon salt	1/2 teaspoon sesame seeds
1/2 teaspoon black pepper	(optional)

Combine first 7 ingredients; set aside. Whisk together egg white and milk. Dip fillets in milk mixture, then dredge in cornmeal mixture. Place on a foil-lined baking sheet, coated with butter-flavored cooking spray. Sprinkle fillets with sesame seeds, if desired, and coat each fillet with cooking spray. Bake at 350° for 30 minutes or until fish flakes easily when tested with a fork. Serve with lemon wedges. Yields 4 servings.

Marion Dragoons Chapter 2311 Cookbook

Tequila-Lime Catfish

This very easy, inventive recipe conjures up visions of Mexico, sunshine, and salt air.

**4 catfish fillets, 4–6 ounces
  each
½ cup bread crumbs**

**Salt and pepper to taste
2 tablespoons vegetable oil or
  margarine**

Rinse catfish under cool, running water and pat dry with paper towels. Dredge fish in bread crumbs seasoned with salt and pepper. Heat oil or melt margarine in a heavy skillet over medium heat. Add catfish and sauté for 2–4 minutes on each side, turning once. The fish is done when it is no longer translucent at the thickest part and flakes easily when tested with a fork. Cooking time will vary depending upon thickness of fish. Remove catfish to a warm serving platter.

SAUCE:

**3 tablespoons tequila
Juice of 1 lime**

**Lime slices (optional)
Parsley (optional)**

Add tequila and lime juice to skillet, and cook an additional minute. Pour mixture over fish before serving. May be garnished with lime slices and chopped parsley, if desired. Serves 4.

The Essential Catfish Cookbook

Covering 730 square miles with an average depth of only ten feet, Lake Okeechobee is Florida's largest lake.

Traditional Southern-Fried Catfish

This catfish is served at fish fries and fish camps all over the South. Very easy.

Yellow or white cornmeal
Salt and pepper to taste
Catfish fillets or whole catfish,
  dressed

Vegetable oil or shortening
Lemon wedges or tartar sauce
  (optional)

Combine dry ingredients in a shallow bowl or pie pan. Rinse catfish under cool, running water and pat dry with paper towels. For whole fish, cut 3 slits in each side before cooking. Dredge catfish in dry ingredients. Shake off excess.

Fill a heavy skillet half full of vegetable oil or shortening. When using a Dutch oven, add oil to a depth of at least 1½ inches. Heat oil to 375° medium-high heat. Fry catfish in a single layer 2–4 minutes on each side, turning once, until fish is golden brown and flakes easily when tested with a fork. Cooking time will vary depending upon thickness of fish.

Drain fish on paper towels placed over a layer of newspaper or a brown paper bag. Serve with lemon wedges or tartar sauce, if desired.

The Essential Catfish Cookbook

Jamaican Grilled Fish

3–4 pounds fillets of snapper or
other fish
1 teaspoon plus 1 tablespoon
olive oil
3 large green peppers, chopped
or in slices
4 medium-size onions, sliced
3 medium-size carrots, cut in
lengthwise pieces about
2 inches long
2 bay leaves
1½ cups vinegar
2 teaspoons salt
½ teaspoon pepper

Brush fillets with 1 teaspoon oil and broil, turning as soon as brown on one side, and then browning the other. Depending on thickness of fillets, this will require 8–10 minutes for first side, and 5–8 minutes for remaining side. Put peppers, onions, carrots, bay leaves, vinegar, 1 tablespoon olive oil, salt and pepper in saucepan. Mix well and then bring to a boil. Allow to simmer for 20–30 minutes. Pour heated, blended sauce over the broiled fillets. Serves 4–6.

The Sunshine State Cookbook

Florida Fish

2 sea trout or grouper fillets
1 teaspoon mayonnaise
1 tablespoon fresh lemon juice
Salt and pepper to taste
1 onion, sliced thin
1 tomato, sliced thin
6 medium fresh mushrooms, sliced

Cut a piece of foil large enough to enclose fillets. Spray foil with nonstick cooking spray. Place fillets on foil. Coat fillets with mayonnaise. Add lemon juice, salt and pepper. Layer onion, tomato, and mushroom slices on fish, and bring corners of foil together to make a packet. Place on cookie sheet. Bake 20 minutes at 400°. Open packet and place under broiler until slightly browned. Fish is done when you can flake it with a fork.

Let's ACT Up in the Kitchen

Campfire Fish

This is my version of an old recipe for cooking fish over an open fire. The original recipe came from an old fishing camp on the lower Florida Keys.

¼ cup margarine, melted
  (½ stick)
⅓ cup firmly packed light
  brown sugar
⅓ cup fresh lime juice

3 tablespoons soy sauce
Dash liquid smoke
2–3 pounds fresh fish fillets
  (snapper, grouper, or dolphin)

Combine first 5 ingredients in a small bowl; stir until sugar is dissolved. This yields about 1 cup. Place fish in a plastic bag, pour marinade over, squeeze out excess air, and seal. Marinate 1–2 hours, turning once or twice during process to redistribute liquid. Place bag in a bowl as a precaution against leaks. Refrigerate.

Fashion a shallow pan out of heavy-duty aluminum foil, large enough to hold fish in a single layer. A grill basket can also be used.

On an outdoor grill, lay fish in foil pan; pour marinade over, then cook over a low fire, turning fish once during process. Baste frequently with marinade. Cooks in about 20 minutes. Serve at once. Serves 4–6.

Tropical Tastes and Tantalizing Tales

Broiled Fish Steaks Oriental

2 pounds fish steaks
¼ cup orange juice
¼ cup soy sauce
2 tablespoons ketchup
2 tablespoons oil

1 tablespoon lemon juice
½ teaspoon oregano
½ teaspoon pepper
1 clove garlic, finely chopped

Place fish in foil-lined baking dish. Combine remaining ingredients and pour over fish; let stand for 30 minutes, turning once. Remove and reserve sauce for basting. Place fish under broiler and broil about 4–5 minutes on each side, basting liberally with sauce at least twice on each side. Serves 3–4.

From Hook to Table

Sautéed Fish with Vegetables

2 pounds fish fillets
Seasoned salt
½ stick butter or margarine
1 medium onion, sliced
1 stalk celery, chopped
1 small yellow squash, sliced

1 small zucchini, sliced
1 red or green pepper, sliced
1 ripe but firm tomato cut in small
   wedges
¼ cup white wine

Sprinkle fillets with seasoned salt. Melt butter or margarine in a large sauté pan at medium heat, and continue heating until butter covers bottom of pan and turns dark brown. Add fish fillets. Turn after about 30 seconds and brown other side for another half-minute. Remove fillets to a nearby platter. Fish need not be done at this point, only browned on both sides.

Add onion and at least three of the remaining vegetables and cook, stirring frequently, until onion is opaque and other vegetables thoroughly heated. Do not overcook. Sprinkle vegetables lightly with seasoned salt (or salt and black pepper). Add wine. Place fish fillets atop vegetables; cover, then reduce heat and simmer for about 5 minutes. Check fish for doneness. All but the thickest fillets should be cooked; if not, simmer a few minutes more. Serves 4 or 5.

From Hook to Table

Mouth-Watering Fish

¼ cup diced onion
¼ cup diced celery
¼ cup diced green pepper
¼ cup diced red pepper
2 cloves garlic, crushed

2 orange roughy, grouper, or
  snapper fillets
Low-salt V-8 juice
White rice, uncooked
Black pepper to taste

Spray large frying pan with nonstick cooking spray; sweat veggies (keep crunchy), then add garlic. Place fish on top of veggies. Add enough V-8 juice to cover fish halfway. Cover pan and steam approximately 10 minutes. Serve over steamed white rice. Pepper to taste. Serves 2.

Cooking with 257

Fish Seminole

4 fish fillets
¼ cup seasoned flour
2 eggs, beaten
Oil for sautéing
½ pound scallops
½ pound fresh mushrooms,
  sliced

¼ cup diced shallot
½ teaspoon salt
1 teaspoon chopped garlic
¼ teaspoon white pepper
Butter for sautéing
½ pound cooked crabmeat

Dredge fish in flour and dip in egg. Sauté in a skillet in a small amount of oil until browned on both sides. Transfer to an oven and bake at 450° until fish flakes easily with a fork, about 7–10 minutes.

To make topping, sauté scallops and next 5 ingredients together in a small amount of butter. Add crabmeat and cook until hot. Spoon topping over cooked fish. Yields 4 servings.

Calypso Café

In 1947, Florida State College for Women began admitting male students, and was renamed Florida State University.

Sandy's Seafood Surprise

8 or 10 small fish fillets
(crappie or other pan fish)
Olive oil
1 pound bay scallops
Seasoned salt
1 medium onion, chopped
1 large tomato, ripe but firm,
chopped

¼ cup chopped celery
1 bell pepper, chopped
½ pound fresh mushrooms,
sliced
½ pound grated Swiss cheese
½ pound grated American
cheese

Rub fillets with olive oil. Spread fillets, intermingled with scallops, to cover bottom of a nonstick shallow baking pan. Deep-sea scallops may be substituted for bay scallops, but should be quartered or cut to approximate thickness of fish. Sprinkle fish and scallops very lightly with seasoned salt. Lightly toss together all chopped vegetables and distribute evenly over seafood. Mix grated cheeses together, and sprinkle over all. Bake at 450° for 10 minutes. Serves 6.

Note: This recipe is easily "customized" to your taste. For instance, you can use all fish or all scallops, or add other seafood of similar thickness. The mix of vegetables can be varied—sliced or chopped carrots, cauliflower, broccoli, etc. Use your favorites, or what you have on hand.

From Hook to Table

Seafood Crêpes Mornay

8 ounces small shrimp, peeled and deveined	1 cup whipping cream
1 tablespoon butter	1 cup half-and-half
1 tablespoon olive oil	⅓ cup shredded Gruyère cheese
Salt and pepper to taste	¼ cup dry white wine
Herbes de Provence to taste	½ teaspoon Worcestershire sauce
8 ounces lump crabmeat, shells and cartilage removed	Nutmeg to taste
	1 teaspoon tomato paste
¼ cup Madeira	12 crêpes
5 tablespoons butter	1 bunch fresh asparagus spears, blanched and drained
5 tablespoons flour	½ cup slivered almonds, toasted

Reserve a few shrimp for garnish. Heat butter and olive oil in a medium sauté pan over medium-high heat. Add remaining shrimp, salt, pepper, and herbes de Provence and mix well. Stir in crabmeat. Cook for 4 minutes or until the shrimp turn pink, stirring frequently. Stir in madeira. Let stand until cool.

Heat 5 tablespoons butter in 2½-quart saucepan over medium heat. Whisk in flour until blended. Cook until a soft paste forms, whisking constantly. Add whipping cream and half-and-half gradually, whisking constantly until smooth. Cook until slightly thickened, stirring frequently. Stir in cheese. Add white wine and mix well. Cook until thickened, stirring frequently. Season with salt, pepper, Worcestershire sauce, and generously with nutmeg. Combine ⅓ cup of sauce with tomato paste in a bowl and mix well. Keep both sauces warm.

To serve, layer each crêpe with 2 asparagus spears, some shrimp mixture and some mornay sauce and roll to enclose filling. Arrange crêpes in baking dish and warm to serving temperature in a 350° oven. Remove to serving platter and drizzle with tomato paste sauce. Sprinkle with almonds and reserved shrimp. Serves 6.

Bay Fêtes

Baked Seafood Au Gratin

1 onion, chopped	½ pound flounder fillets
1 green pepper, chopped	3 cups milk
1 cup butter or margarine, divided	1 cup shredded sharp Cheddar cheese
1 cup all-purpose flour, divided	1 tablespoon white vinegar
1 pound fresh crabmeat	1 teaspoon Worcestershire sauce
4 cups water	½ teaspoon salt
1 pound medium shrimp, peeled and deveined	1 pinch black pepper
	Dash hot pepper sauce
½ pound scallops	½ cup grated Parmesan cheese

Lightly grease a 9x13-inch baking dish. In a heavy skillet, sauté onion and green pepper in ½ cup butter or margarine. Cook until tender. Stir in ½ cup flour and cook over medium heat for 10 minutes, stirring frequently. Add crabmeat and stir well. Press this mixture into bottom of greased baking dish and set aside.

In a large saucepan, bring water to a boil. Add shrimp, scallops, and flounder. Simmer for 3 minutes. Drain and reserve one cup cooking liquid; set seafood aside.

Preheat oven to 350°. In a heavy saucepan, melt remaining ½ cup butter over low heat. Stir in remaining ½ cup flour. Cook and stir constantly for one minute. Gradually add milk plus one cup reserved cooking liquid. Raise heat to medium and cook, stirring constantly, until mixture is thickened and bubbly. Stir in Cheddar cheese, vinegar, Worcestershire sauce, salt, pepper, and hot sauce. Add cooked seafood and stir gently. Spoon seafood mixture over crabmeat crust and sprinkle with Parmesan cheese. Bake in preheated oven for 30 minutes or until lightly browned. Serve immediately. Makes 8 servings.

Feeding the Flock

South Florida Seafood Pasta

Enjoy this Florida combination of two of the most popular trends in today's cooking: seafood and pasta. You can vary the seafood, using the freshest available in your market.

1 pound uncooked linguine
2 tablespoons butter or
 margarine
Salt to taste
4 ounces fresh mussel meat
6 ounces fresh clams, chopped,
 cooked, drained

10 ounces fresh scallops
12 ounces fresh shrimp, peeled
¼ cup olive oil
¼ cup dry white wine
2 cups heavy cream
8 cloves garlic, finely chopped
Pepper to taste

Cook pasta al dente with butter in salted water in a saucepan. Drain and set aside. Combine mussel meat, clams, scallops, and shrimp in a bowl, and drain well. Bring olive oil, wine, cream, garlic, salt, and pepper to a boil in a large saucepan. Add seafood and pasta and mix well. Cook over medium heat for 10 minutes, or until seafood is cooked through and sauce is creamy. Serve immediately. Serves 6.

Tropical Settings

Pasta with Crab in White Sauce
(Pasta con Jaiba en Salsa Blanca)

1 onion, finely chopped	½ cup clam broth
2 shallots, finely chopped	½ cup white wine
1 teaspoon chopped garlic	Salt to taste
1 stick butter	½ teaspoon white pepper
½ cup extra virgin olive oil	¼ cup chopped parsley
2 pounds lump crabmeat, picked over to remove foreign particles	1 pound linguine, uncooked
	Grated Parmesan cheese to taste

Sauté onion, shallots, and garlic in butter and olive oil until limp. Add crabmeat; toss lightly. Add, in order, clam broth, wine, salt, pepper, and parsley. Boil linguine al dente, then drain. Ladle sauce over linguine. Sprinkle with Parmesan cheese. Serves 4.

The Columbia Restaurant Spanish Cookbook

Imperial Crab Casserole

1 pound backfin crabmeat	2 tablespoons mayonnaise
1 tablespoon chopped pimento	1 tablespoon prepared mustard
1 tablespoon chopped green pepper	1 egg, beaten
6 saltine crackers, crushed	Old Bay Seasoning

Grease 9x13-inch casserole. Mix together all ingredients, except Old Bay Seasoning. Pile ingredients loosely in casserole. Sprinkle seasoning on top.

TOPPING:

2 egg yolks	Paprika
2 cups mayonnaise	

Beat egg yolks with mayonnaise. Spread mixture over crabmeat mixture. Sprinkle paprika on top. Bake at 425° for 20–25 minutes.

Sing for Your Supper

Lobster Lisa with a Sherry-and-Brandy Mornay Sauce

A classic dish that uses the flavors of sherry, brandy, and Parmesan cheese to enhance the flavor of lobster.

PHYLLO BLOSSOMS:

½ sheet phyllo dough   Melted butter

Cut phyllo sheet in half, then cut each half into 6 equal squares. Brush melted butter onto each phyllo square. Repeat until you have 2 stacks. Grease 2 (2½-inch) muffin cup pans. Gently fit each stack into prepared muffin cups. Push down middle of blossom with the end of a cook's spoon. Bake 10–15 minutes at 350° or until lightly browned. Remove from muffin cups and place on wire rack to cool.

MORNAY SAUCE:

1 tablespoon butter   1 cup milk or cream
2 tablespoons flour   ¼ cup grated Parmesan cheese

Melt butter in saute pan and add flour to make a thick paste. Cook for 4 minutes over low heat. Let cool for a few minutes. Gradually add milk or cream to pan, stirring constantly. Add Parmesan cheese. Cook and stir for a few minutes. May add more milk or cream to thin it.

LOBSTER LISA:

1 tablespoon olive oil   ¼ cup brandy
½ ounce lobster meat, cut in   Small pinch of white pepper
   medium-size pieces   1 tablespoon chopped chives
¼ cup sweet sherry

In large saute pan over moderate heat, combine olive oil and lobster meat. Sauté 1–2 minutes. Remove saute pan 2 feet from stove to add sherry and brandy; using a long-handled match, ignite liquor (be careful of intensity of flame). Place back on stove. Next add white pepper, Mornay Sauce, and chives; cook until lobster meat is done.

Place Phyllo Blossoms in center of plates with equal amounts of lobster sauce on each plate. Pour excess sauce on each plate and blossom shell. Garnish with lemon crowns and parsley sprigs. Yields 2 servings.

Mastering the Art of Florida Seafood

Lobster Tails Grilled in Foil

6 spiny lobster tails, fresh or frozen	2 tablespoons lemon or lime juice
¼ cup butter or margarine, melted	½ teaspoon salt
	Pepper, freshly ground
	Melted butter for dipping

Thaw lobster tails in refrigerator (if frozen). Start fire in grill 30 minutes before cooking time. If lobster is fresh, remove swimmerettes and sharp edges. Cut 6 (12-inch) squares of heavy-duty aluminum foil. Place each lobster tail on half of each square of foil. Combine ¼ cup butter, lemon or lime juice, salt and pepper. Baste lobster meat with sauce. Fold other half of foil over lobster tail; seal edges by making double folds in foil.

Place packages of lobster tails on barbecue grill, shell-side-down, 5 inches above hot coals. Cook 20 minutes. Remove lobster tails from foil. On well-greased grill, place lobster tails, meaty-side-down, for 2–3 minutes, or until nicely browned. Serve at once with melted butter. Serves 6.

Note: This is equally good with 2 or 3 pounds fresh shrimp substituted for the lobster. For easy removal, place shelled shrimp on skewers before wrapping in foil and browning over the coals. You may also eliminate lemon butter, and instead combine white wine, soy sauce, and ground ginger with the black pepper for the marinade, for oriental-style shrimp.

Florida Seafood Cookery

The Dames Point Bridge on the St. Johns River is the longest concrete cablestayed bridge in the United States at 1,300 feet. (On a cablestayed bridge, the roadway hangs from cables connected directly to towers.) It was the second cablestayed bridge to be built in Florida. Tampa Bay's Sunshine Skyway was the largest, spanning 1,200 feet. Forty-three bridges traverse the 125 miles of islands in the Florida Keys.

Scallops in a Shell

This is a very easy dish to make, and cooking it in real scallop shells makes a very impressive dinner party presentation.

½ cup butter
2 pounds scallops, shrimp, or
  lobster, drained
1 green onion, finely chopped
1 cup heavy whipping cream
2 tablespoons all-purpose flour
3 tablespoons shredded Cheddar
  cheese

2 tablespoons pale dry sherry
Salt and pepper to taste
½ cup cheese croutons, finely
  crushed
Dried parsley flakes

Melt butter in a saucepan over medium heat; add scallops and sauté 3–4 minutes. Add green onion and sauté until tender. Combine cream and flour in a jar; cover tightly and shake vigorously. Pour cream mixture into scallop mixture and cook, stirring constantly, until thickened. Add cheese and sherry, stirring until smooth and creamy. Simmer 10 minutes. Season with salt and pepper to taste.

Spoon scallop mixture into small scallop shells or individual baking dishes coated with vegetable cooking spray. Top with crushed croutons and parsley flakes. Bake on a baking sheet at 325° for 15–20 minutes. Yields 6–8 servings.

Lighthouse Secrets

Suess Landing™, a theme park bringing the whimsical books of Dr. Seuss to life at Universal Orlando®, is called the "Land of No Right Angles." Every line you see, from the street lamps to the rail bars in queue lines, is curved. Universal even flew in trees bent from 1992's Hurricane Andrew to add detail.

Cakes

Dr. Seuss' whimsical children's tales come to life before your eyes at Seuss Landing™ at Universal Orlando®.

Easy Summer Cake

½ cup (1 stick) butter, softened
1 cup sugar
2 eggs
1 cup flour
1 teaspoon baking powder

Thin slices of fresh fruit such as
  apples, peaches or apricots
1 teaspoon lemon juice
1 teaspoon sugar
½ teaspoon cinnamon

Beat butter, sugar, and eggs in a mixing bowl until light and fluffy. Mix flour and baking powder in a bowl. Beat into the butter mixture until well mixed. Pour into a greased 9x9-inch baking pan. Arrange sliced fruit on top. Sprinkle with lemon juice, sugar, and cinnamon. Bake at 350° for one hour or until a wooden pick inserted in center comes out clean. Yields 4–6 servings.

An American Celebration

Paradise Cake

3 cups all-purpose flour
2 cups sugar
1 teaspoon baking soda
1 teaspoon salt
1 teaspoon ground cloves
3 eggs, beaten
1¼ cups vegetable oil

1 teaspoon almond extract
1 (8-ounce) can crushed pineapple,
  undrained
1 cup chopped toasted almonds
2 cups mashed bananas
1 (16-ounce) container cream
  cheese frosting

Combine flour, sugar, soda, salt, and cloves in a large mixing bowl; add eggs and oil, stirring until dry ingredients are moistened. Do not beat. Stir in almond extract, pineapple, almonds, and bananas. Spoon batter into a greased and floured 10-inch tube pan. Bake at 300° for 1 hour and 15 minutes. Cool in pan 10 minutes; remove cake from pan and cool completely before frosting.

Great Recipes from Near and Afar

Banana Cake

2 cups sugar
2 sticks butter, softened
2 eggs
½ cup milk

1½ teaspoons baking soda
2 cups flour
2 small bananas, mashed
1 teaspoon lemon juice

Cream together sugar, butter, and eggs. Add milk and soda, alternating with flour. Last, add bananas that have had lemon juice added to them. Bake in 2 large cake pans, greased and lined with wax paper rounds which you have cut to fit, at 350° for about 30 minutes. Cool.

FROSTING:

1 (8-ounce) package cream
  cheese, softened
1 (1-pound) box powdered sugar

1 teaspoon vanilla
Chopped nuts

Combine cream cheese, powdered sugar and vanilla. Spread on cooled cake layers, and sprinkle top layer with chopped nuts.

Village Royale: Our Favorite Recipes

Lemonade Cake

CAKE:

1 (3-ounce) package lemon
  gelatin
¾ cup boiling water
4 eggs

¾ cup cooking oil
1 (18¼-ounce) package yellow
  cake mix

Dissolve lemon gelatin in boiling water. Let cool. In a large mixing bowl, beat eggs thoroughly. Add cooking oil. Alternately add cake mix and dissolved lemon gelatin mixture. Pour into a greased tube pan. Bake in a 350° oven for 1 hour.

GLAZE:

1 (6-ounce) can lemonade
  concentrate

½ cup sugar

Dissolve sugar in heated lemon concentrate. Remove cake from oven, and leave in tube pan; drizzle with Glaze. Leave in pan 1 hour before removing.

Under the Canopy

Pineapple-Orange Sunshine Cake

1 (18¼-ounce) box yellow
  cake mix
¼ cup applesauce

4 eggs
1 (11-ounce) can mandarin
  oranges, in light syrup

Preheat oven to 350°. In a large bowl, stir together all ingredients until moist. Beat by hand for 2 minutes. Coat a 9x13-inch pan with nonstick spray. Pour batter into pan. Bake 30–40 minutes or until a toothpick inserted in center comes out clean. Cool completely.

FROSTING:

1 (8-ounce) container light
  whipped topping, thawed
1 (3-ounce) package instant
  vanilla pudding mix

1 (15½-ounce) can crushed
  pineapple, in juice

In a large bowl, mix together all Frosting ingredients until well blended. Spread over cake. Store in refrigerator.

Trinity Treats

Blueberry Cake

Serve this beautiful dessert with the whipped cream as suggested here, or omit the whipped cream for a delicious breakfast or brunch treat.

½ cup butter or margarine,
  softened
1 cup sugar, divided
1 egg
1½ cups flour
1½ teaspoons baking powder
2 teaspoons vanilla extract,
  divided

3½ cups fresh blueberries
16 ounces sour cream
2 egg yolks
1½ cups whipping cream
¾ cup sifted confectioners' sugar
Blueberries for garnish

Cream butter in a mixer bowl until light. Add ½ cup sugar gradually, beating at medium speed until fluffy. Beat in egg. Combine flour and baking powder. Add to creamed mixture, and mix just until moistened. Stir in 1 teaspoon vanilla. Spoon into a greased, 9-inch springform pan. Sprinkle with blueberries.

Combine sour cream, egg yolks, remaining ½ cup sugar, and remaining 1 teaspoon vanilla in a bowl, and mix well. Spoon over batter in pan. Bake at 350° for 1 hour or until edges are light brown. Cool in pan on wire rack. Chill, covered, in refrigerator. Place on a serving plate and remove side of pan.

Beat whipping cream in a mixer bowl until soft peaks begin to form. Add confectioners' sugar gradually, beating constantly. Spoon half the whipped cream over cake. Pipe remaining whipped cream around edge. Garnish with additional blueberries. Serves 8.

Tropical Settings

Esther Williams' 1953 movie *Easy to Love* featured Cypress Gardens' pool shaped like the state of Florida. Other movies filmed at central Florida's Cypress Gardens include *Moon Over Miami* and *Cinerama*.

Cranberry Applesauce Cake

½ cup Crisco, softened
1 cup white sugar
2 eggs
1 cup sweetened canned
  applesauce
1½ cup sifted flour
¾ teaspoon baking soda

½ teaspoon salt
½ teaspoon cinnamon
½ teaspoon cloves
¼ teaspoon nutmeg
1 cup uncooked oats
1 (16-ounce) can cranberry sauce
1½ cups chopped pecans

Beat Crisco until creamy; add sugar and eggs; mix well. Add apple-sauce (batter will look curdled). Blend well. Sift together flour, soda, salt, cinnamon, cloves, and nutmeg. Add to creamed mixture; blend well. Stir in oats and cranberry sauce; add pecans. Pour into lightly greased and floured Bundt pan, or 2 round glass cake pans. Bake in preheated oven at 325° for 60–65 minutes, watching carefully the last 10 minutes. Watch for cake to separate away from side of pan. Cool completely, about an hour, before trying to invert.

GLAZE:
1½ cups sifted powdered sugar   ¼ teaspoon salt
½ cup maple syrup

Mix ingredients well. Drizzle Glaze over cake, or leave off Glaze and sprinkle powdered sugar through doily placed on top of cake, then remove doily carefully.

Variation: Serve orange marmalade as a side dish and let each person use as they wish.

FCCD Cookbook

Orange Rum Cream Cake

1¾ cups sifted cake flour	1 cup sugar
1 tablespoon baking powder	8 egg yolks, beaten
¼ teaspoon salt	1 teaspoon grated orange rind
½ cup shortening	½ cup milk

Have all ingredients at room temperature. Sift together twice flour, baking powder, and salt. Cream shortening till fluffy; gradually add sugar. Blend till mixture is creamy. Stir in egg yolks and orange rind until well mixed. Alternately add dry ingredients and milk, beating after each addition. Turn into 2 greased 8-inch cake pans, and bake in 350° oven for 30 minutes. Cool 10 minutes; turn onto cake rack. Fill with Orange Rum Filling and frost with whipped cream.

ORANGE RUM FILLING:

3 tablespoons butter, softened	Dash salt
¾ teaspoon grated orange rind	2 tablespoons orange juice
1½ cups sifted confectioners' sugar, divided	1 teaspoon rum
	Whipped cream

Cream butter with grated orange rind. Gradually add ½ cup sifted confectioners' sugar, blending well. Add dash of salt; mix well. Add remaining 1 cup confectioners' sugar alternately with 2 tablespoons orange juice, beating till smooth after each addition. Blend in rum. Spread on cake layer. Frost with whipped cream.

Famous Florida Recipes

Florida Key Lime Pudding Cake

¾ cup sugar
¼ cup all-purpose flour
Dash salt
3 tablespoons butter or
    margarine, melted

¼ teaspoon grated Key lime peel
¼ cup Key lime juice
3 egg yolks
1½ cups milk
3 egg whites

In medium bowl, combine sugar, flour, and salt. Add melted butter, lime peel, and lime juice. Stir until blended. Set aside. Separate eggs into 2 bowls, being careful not to get any yolk in the whites. Beat egg yolks, then add the milk, stirring with a wooden or plastic spoon; stir into lime mixture.

In glass or china bowl (not plastic), beat egg whites until stiff. Fold gently into lime mixture. Pour batter into greased 8x8x2-inch baking pan. Pour hot water into a large, shallow baking pan to 1-inch depth. Set pan of pudding batter into the hot water. Bake in 350° oven 40 minutes or until lightly browned. Serve warm or chilled, topping with whipped cream or softened vanilla ice cream. Serves 6.

Florida Seafood Cookery

Key Lime Cake

1 (18¼-ounce) package
  Duncan Hines Lemon Supreme
  Cake Mix
½ cup water

½ cup Key lime juice
1 (3-ounce) package lime gelatin
½ cup vegetable oil
4 eggs

With electric mixer, blend all ingredients together on medium speed for about 2 minutes. Pour into a greased tube pan or 9x13-inch baking pan, and bake at 325° for 45 minutes. After removing from oven, use an ice pick and prick through cake, top to bottom, many times.

ICING:

2 cups powdered sugar   ¼ cup Key lime juice

Mix powdered sugar and lime juice. Drizzle cake with icing while cake is still warm.

Country Club Cooks

Editor's Extra: This can also be baked in a tube or Bundt pan for 7–10 minutes longer.

Hot Milk Cake

1 cup milk
2 tablespoons butter or
  margarine
4 eggs

2 cups sugar
2 teaspoons vanilla
2 cups flour
2 teaspoons baking powder

Grease and flour a Bundt pan. Heat milk and butter until hot stage—just hot enough to melt the butter. Beat eggs until creamy. Add sugar and beat again. Add vanilla and blend. Slowly add flour and baking powder. Mixture will be very thick. Slowly add hot milk mixture. Batter will then be thin. Pour into prepared pan. Bake at 350° for about 1 hour or until top springs back. No icing is needed. Can be lightly sprinkled with powdered sugar.

Centennial Cookbook

Nanny's Strawberry Cake

1 large box creamy white
frosting mix, or 2 small,
divided
2½ pints whipping cream

1 (18¼-ounce) box yellow
cake mix
1 quart fresh Florida strawberries,
divided

Set aside ½ cup creamy white frosting mix. Stir whipping cream into remaining frosting, mix; do not whip. Place in refrigerator to chill, preferably overnight. (If you want to make it in one day, you can put it in the freezer.)

Bake cake as directed on box. Use 2 (8- or 9-inch) cake pans. Cool. Slice crosswise, making 4 layers. Remove frosting mix from refrigerator and whip until very thick (like butter). Put a layer of cake, then a layer of frosting mix, then a thin layer of sliced strawberries (save about 7); continue until you have used all 4 layers. Use plenty of frosting on each layer.

For top layer, crush a few sweetened strawberries and use juice to mix with ½ cup frosting mix. Spread over top layer and let drizzle down sides of cake. Garnish with 4 strawberries in center of cake.

Simply Florida...Strawberries

Fat Man's Misery

CAKE:

4 eggs, lightly beaten
2 cups granulated sugar
½ pound butter, softened
1½ cups self-rising flour

2 cups chopped pecans
1 teaspoon vanilla
2 tablespoons cocoa

Preheat oven to 325°. Mix together eggs, sugar, butter, flour, pecans, vanilla, and cocoa. Pour into ungreased 9x13-inch baking pan and bake 45 minutes.

ICING:

1 (1-pound) bag miniature
  marshmallows
4 teaspoons cocoa

½ pound butter, melted
1 (1-pound) box powdered sugar
8 teaspoons whipping cream

Place marshmallows on top of cake layer as soon as it comes out of the oven. Place back into oven until marshmallows are melted. Mix cocoa, butter, powdered sugar, and whipping cream together; blend until of spreading consistency. Pour this mixture evenly over marshmallows. Let set at least 2 hours before cutting into squares. Makes 24 bars.

The Best of Sophie Kay Cookbook

Plant City, the Winter Strawberry Capital of the World, holds the Guinness record for the world's largest strawberry shortcake. The 827-square-foot cake weighed over 6,000 pounds. It took 300 sheet cakes, 7,800 pints of strawberries, 450 pounds of sugar, and 600 pounds of whipped cream. More than 300 volunteers worked on this project.

Darn Good Chocolate Cake

1 (18¼-ounce) package devil's
  food chocolate cake mix
1 (3½-ounce) package
  chocolate instant pudding
1¾ cups sour cream

¾ cup vegetable oil
½ cup warm water
4 eggs
1½ cups milk chocolate chips

Mix together the cake mix and pudding mix. Add sour cream, vegetable oil, water, and eggs; mix well. Stir in chocolate chips. Spray Bundt pan with cooking spray; pour in batter and bake at 350° for 50–60 minutes, or until firm to touch, or when toothpick comes out clean.

Heaven in a Pot

Cinnamon Chocolate Cake

1½ sticks margarine
1 cup water
¼ cup cocoa
2 cups flour
2 cups sugar

1 teaspoon baking powder
1 teaspoon cinnamon
½ cup buttermilk
2 eggs

Boil margarine, water, and cocoa. Mix in flour, sugar, baking powder, and cinnamon. Add buttermilk and eggs. Pour into a greased 9x13-inch pan. Bake at 400° for 25 minutes.

FROSTING:
1 stick butter
1 (1-pound) box powdered sugar

¼ cup cocoa

Melt butter. Add powdered sugar and cocoa. Beat well, and pour over hot cake. Serves 12–16.

Village Royale: Our Favorite Recipes

Oatmeal Cake
with Broiled Coconut Topping

1½ cups boiling water
1 cup quick-cooking rolled oats
1½ cups sifted all-purpose
  flour
1 teaspoon baking soda
1 teaspoon salt
1 teaspoon ground cinnamon
½ teaspoon baking powder

½ cup butter or margarine,
  softened
1 cup granulated sugar
1 cup firmly packed light brown
  sugar
2 large eggs
Coconut Topping

Preheat oven to 350°. Combine 1½ cups boiling water and oats; set aside. Sift together flour and next 4 ingredients. Beat butter and sugars at medium speed with an electric mixer until mealy; add eggs, one at a time, beating until light and fluffy. Stir in oats; add flour mixture, beating well. Pour batter into a greased and floured 9-inch-square pan.

Bake at 350° for 40 minutes. Let cool in pan 10 minutes. Transfer cake to a baking sheet, and cool completely. Spread Coconut Topping over cake. Broil 2–3 minutes or until topping is lightly browned. Yields 8 servings.

COCONUT TOPPING:

1⅓ cups flaked coconut
¼ cup butter or margarine,
  melted

½ cup firmly packed brown sugar
¼ cup heavy cream or milk
1 teaspoon vanilla

Combine all ingredients in a bowl.

Lighthouse Secrets

Sawgrass, endless stretches of which fill the Florida Everglades, is not a grass at all, but a member of the sedge family.

Kahlúa Cake

CAKE:

1 (18¼-ounce) box chocolate
  fudge cake mix without pudding
1 (3-ounce) box instant vanilla
  pudding
1 pint sour cream

4 eggs
⅓ cup Kahlúa
1 (6-ounce) package chocolate
  chips
¾ cup oil

Stir all ingredients for Cake together; do not beat. Bake in a 350° oven for 45–50 minutes.

FROSTING:

1 cup sifted powdered sugar
½ tablespoon cocoa

¼ cup Kahlúa
1 teaspoon milk

Mix all ingredients together. Cool cake 10–15 minutes before frosting.

GARNISH:

Mint leaves
Fresh strawberries

Mini chocolate chips

Garnish with mint leaves, fresh strawberries, and/or mini chocolate chips.

Hints: To thicken Frosting, add powdered sugar; to thin, add milk; to make more chocolate-y, add cocoa; to spice up, add more Kahlúa; for almond flavor, add amaretto. Any other liqueur may be substituted for the coffee liqueur.

Under the Canopy

While searching for the legendary Fountain of Youth, Hernando de Soto discovered the historic Espiritu Santo Springs or "Springs of the Holy Spirit" in 1539 in Safety Harbor. The springs are thought to have curative powers.

Delmonico Nut Cake

1 stick butter, softened
½ cup vegetable shortening
2 cups sugar
5 eggs, separated
1 teaspoon vanilla
2 cups cake flour

1 teaspoon baking soda
1 cup buttermilk
1 (7-ounce) can shredded coconut
1 cup chopped nuts (½ pecans
   and ½ walnuts)

In large bowl of electric mixer, cream butter and shortening thoroughly. Gradually add sugar, and beat until light and fluffy. Add egg yolks and vanilla. Sift flour with soda, then add to batter alternately with buttermilk, beginning and ending with dry ingredients. By hand, stir in coconut and nuts.

Beat egg whites until stiff but not dry. Stir a heaping tablespoon into batter, and beat by hand vigorously until blended. Then carefully fold in remaining egg whites. Turn into greased 9x13x2-inch baking pan. Bake at 325° (350° if metal) for 1 hour or until cake tests done. Or bake in 3 greased (nonstick vegetable spray) 8-inch layer pans at 350° for 25 minutes or until cake tests done. Frost with Delmonico Cake Icing.

DELMONICO CAKE ICING:
1 (8-ounce) package cream
   cheese, softened
½ stick butter, softened
¾ (16-ounce) box confectioners'
   sugar

1 teaspoon vanilla
½ cup finely chopped pecans
   and walnuts

In a small bowl, beat cream cheese and butter until smooth. Gradually add sugar and beat well again. Blend in vanilla. Spread on top and sides of 9x13-inch cake or between layers and on top and sides of layer cake. Sprinkle nuts on top.

Sand in My Shoes

Italian Cream Cake

1 teaspoon baking soda	5 eggs
1 cup buttermilk	1 teaspoon vanilla
½ cup butter, softened	1 (3-ounce) can coconut
2 cups sugar	1 teaspoon baking powder
½ cup shortening	2 cups all-purpose flour

Preheat oven to 350°. Grease 3 (9-inch) round cake pans. Dissolve baking soda in buttermilk. Cream butter, sugar, and shortening together until light and fluffy. Mix in eggs, buttermilk, vanilla, coconut, baking powder, and flour. Stir until just combined. Pour batter into prepared pans. Bake at 350° for 30 minutes. Let cakes cool before frosting and assembling.

FROSTING:

1 (8-ounce) package cream cheese, softened	4 cups confectioners' sugar
½ cup butter, softened	Cream
1 teaspoon vanilla	Chopped nuts
	Flaked coconut

Cream together the cream cheese, butter, vanilla, and confectioners' sugar until light and fluffy. Mix in a small amount of cream to attain the desired consistency. Stir in chopped nuts and flaked coconut to taste. Spread between layers and on top and side of cooled cake.

A Taste of Heaven

Created in 1925, Coral Gables was one of the first fully planned communities in the United States. There you will find the Florida Museum of Hispanic and Latin American Art, the first and only museum in the United States dedicated to the preservation, diffusion, and promotion of Hispanic and Latin American Art.

Molly's Pumpkin Pie Cake

CRUST:

1 box yellow cake mix (reserve
  1 cup for topping)

1 stick butter, melted
1 large egg, unbeaten

Mix ingredients with a fork and press into a 9x13x2-inch pan.

FILLING:

1 (15-ounce) can pumpkin
½ cup brown sugar
⅔ cup milk

2 teaspoons cinnamon
3 eggs

Mix well and spread over cake mixture.

TOPPING:

Reserved 1 cup cake mix
1½ cups chopped nuts
  (pecans or walnuts)

¼ cup butter
½ cup sugar

Mix reserved cake mix and remaining ingredients with a pastry blender. Spread evenly over Filling. Bake at 375° for 40 minutes.

The Woman's Exchange Classic Recipes

Pumpkin Sheet Cake

1 (16-ounce) can pumpkin
2 cups sugar
1 cup vegetable oil
4 eggs, lightly beaten

2 cups all-purpose flour
2 teaspoons baking soda
1 teaspoon ground cinnamon
½ teaspoon salt

In a mixing bowl, beat pumpkin, sugar, and oil; add eggs. Mix well. Combine dry ingredients; add to pumpkin mixture, and beat until well blended. Pour into a greased 10x15x1-inch sheet cake pan. Bake at 350° for 25–30 minutes or until cake tests done. Cool.

FROSTING:

1 (3-ounce) package cream
  cheese, softened
5 tablespoons butter, softened
1 teaspoon vanilla extract

1¾ cups confectioners' sugar
3–4 teaspoons milk
Chopped nuts

Beat cream cheese, butter, and vanilla until smooth. Gradually add sugar; mix well. Add milk till Frosting reaches desired consistency. Frost cake; sprinkle with nuts. Yields 20–24 servings.

Treasured Recipes from Near and Far

Brown Sugar Pound Cake

1 cup butter, softened	3 cups flour
½ cup shortening	½ teaspoon baking powder
1 cup white sugar	1 cup milk
1 pound light brown sugar	1 teaspoon vanilla
5 large eggs	1 cup chopped nuts

Cream butter and shortening; add sugars and cream again. Add eggs. Sift dry ingredients. Add alternately with milk. Add vanilla and nuts. Bake in greased and floured Bundt pan for 1 hour and 30 minutes at 325°.

A Collection of Favorite Recipes

Eggnog Pound Cake

2 sticks butter, softened	1 teaspoon almond extract
½ cup shortening	1 teaspoon butternut extract
3 cups sugar	1 teaspoon lemon extract
5 large eggs	1 teaspoon rum extract
1 teaspoon vanilla extract	3 cups cake flour
1 teaspoon coconut extract	1 cup evaporated milk

Cream butter, shortening, and sugar. Add eggs, one at a time, beating well after each. Add extracts, one at a time, mixing thoroughly after each addition. Alternately add flour and milk, beginning and ending with flour. Pour into a greased and floured 10-inch tube pan. Bake at 300° for 1 hour and 45 minutes.

Sand in My Shoes

Florida is home to the largest population (about 3,000) of West Indian manatees. The manatee, which can live up to 60 years, is classified as an endangered species.

Florida Orange Fruit Cake

¾ cup butter or margarine,
  softened
1½ cups white sugar
3 whole eggs
1 tablespoon orange juice
Grated rind of 1 orange

3 cups flour
1½ teaspoons baking soda
1 cup buttermilk
1½ cups chopped dates
1 cup chopped pecans

Cream butter and sugar; add eggs and mix until fluffy. Add orange juice and rind. Sift flour and soda; add to mixture, alternately with buttermilk. Flour dates and nuts and fold into cake mixture. Pour into a greased and floured 10x14-inch pan, or divide and pour into 2 small greased and floured bread pans. Bake in 350° oven for one hour.

ORANGE SYRUP:

1 cup sugar   1½ cups orange juice

While cake is baking, stir 1 cup sugar into 1½ cups orange juice; mix thoroughly. Turn cake out of pan, bottom-side-up, and gradually sprinkle with Orange Syrup until mixture is used.

Marion Dragoons Chapter 2311 Cookbook

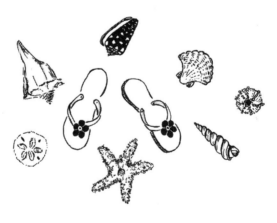

Blueberry Cheesecake

1 (8-ounce) package cream cheese, softened	1 (8-ounce) tub Cool Whip
1 cup powdered sugar	1 (21-ounce) can blueberry pie filling

Mix cream cheese, sugar, and Cool Whip and pour in a glass dish. Top with pie filling. Refrigerate. May also be placed in crumb crust for pie.

4-U: 400 Recipes of 4 Ingredients

Black Forest Cheesecake

CRUST:

1½ cups chocolate cookie crumbs	¼ cup butter, melted

Combine crumbs and butter; blend well. Press into bottom and 1 inch up sides of a 9-inch springform pan.

FILLING:

3 (8-ounce) packages cream cheese, softened	4 eggs
1½ cups sugar	⅓ cup cherry-flavored liqueur

Beat cream cheese with mixer until fluffy; add sugar gradually, blending well. Add eggs, one at a time, mixing well. Add liqueur, continuing to beat until mixed. Spread into prepared Crust, and bake at 350° for 55–60 minutes or until set. Cool completely.

TOPPING:

4 (1-ounce) squares semisweet chocolate	12 maraschino cherries with stems
½ cup sour cream	

In the top of a double boiler, melt chocolate; allow to cool, then stir in sour cream. Spoon over top of cheesecake, and chill thoroughly before serving. Slice and garnish each slice with a cherry.

Christmas Memories

Chocolate Cheesecake

CRUST:

1 (8½-ounce) package chocolate
  wafers, finely crushed
⅓ cup butter, melted

¼ cup sugar
¼ teaspoon nutmeg

Combine ingredients for Crust and mix well. Press mixture evenly over bottom and sides of 9-inch springform pan. Refrigerate Crust while preparing Filling.

FILLING:

3 eggs
1 cup sugar
3 (8-ounce) packages cream
  cheese, softened
1 teaspoon vanilla

12 ounces semisweet chocolate
  chips, melted
⅛ teaspoon salt
1 cup dairy sour cream

Combine eggs and sugar in a large bowl or food processor. When eggs and sugar are light and foamy, beat in cream cheese until smooth. Add vanilla, melted chocolate, salt, and sour cream, and beat until smooth. Pour into Crust. Bake in preheated 350° oven for 1 hour.

After removing cheesecake from oven, allow it to cool in the pan on a wire rack. Cover and refrigerate cheesecake overnight. Cake may be decorated with a combination of 1 cup heavy cream, whipped, and 2 tablespoons confectioners' sugar, or may be served without topping. Serves 16.

Let's Talk Food from A to Z

With more than 43 million visitors annually, Orlando attracts more visitors than any other amusement park destination in the United States. People from all over the world plan repeated vacations here. Major parks include Disney World's Magic Kingdom®, Epcot®, MGM Studios®, Animal Kingdom®, Blizzard Beach® and Typhoon Lagoon®; Universal Orlando's® Universal Studios Florida® and Universal's Islands of Adventure®; and SeaWorld Orlando®.

Irish Cream Cheesecake

CRUMB CRUST:

½ pound cookies (vanilla wafers, coconut cookies, ginger snaps, or any other cookies of choice)

¼ pound butter (1 stick)

Crush cookies to crumbs with a rolling pin, food processor, or blender. Melt butter; add crumbs and mix well. Press mixture onto base and sides of an 8-inch springform cake pan. Chill while preparing the Filling.

FILLING:

½ pound cottage cheese
½ pound cream cheese, softened
2 tablespoons cold water
1 teaspoon plain gelatin
Juice and rind of 2 lemons

6 tablespoons Irish cream liqueur
1 cup heavy whipping cream
2 egg whites
½ cup castor sugar* (or regular sugar)
2 ounces melted chocolate

Push cottage cheese through sieve, then combine in mixing bowl with cream cheese. Beat together well. Put cold water into a cup and sprinkle gelatin on top. Leave about 5 minutes to soak, then put the cup over or in a small amount of hot water until gelatin has dissolved completely. Blend into creamed mixture with lemon juice and rind. Continue beating until mixture is very smooth. Beat in liqueur. Whip cream until thick, and fold into creamed mixture. Whisk egg whites until stiff, then gradually whisk in sugar. Fold them carefully into cake batter. Pour into prepared Crumb Crust. Refrigerate 6 hours or overnight.

Just before serving, drizzle melted chocolate over surface of cheesecake. Serves 8.

Note: *Castor sugar is very fine sugar often used in baking. If not available, place sugar in a blender or food processor and work for about a minute or two. You may also use regular sugar, if preferred.

Let's Talk Food from A to Z

White Chocolate Raspberry Cheesecake

CRUST:

1 cup vanilla wafer crumbs
½ cup ground almonds
2 tablespoons sugar

⅛ teaspoon almond extract
3 tablespoons butter or margarine,
   melted

Preheat oven to 350°. Combine all ingredients in a small bowl or food processor until mixture resembles coarse crumbs. Press into bottom of an 8- or 9-inch springform pan. Bake for 10 minutes; cool completely. Reduce oven temperature to 325°.

FILLING:

4 ounces white chocolate,
   chopped
16 ounces cream cheese,
   softened

3 large eggs
¾ cup sugar
2 teaspoons flour
1 teaspoon vanilla

Melt white chocolate in double boiler. Cool to lukewarm. In a medium bowl, beat cream cheese with electric mixer until smooth. Add eggs, one at a time, mixing well after each addition. Mix in sugar, flour, and vanilla. Gently but thoroughly blend in melted white chocolate. Pour filling over Crust. Bake until cheesecake hardens around edges, but still moves slightly in center when gently shaken (approximately 40 minutes); cool completely. Cover and refrigerate 8 hours or overnight.

GLAZE:

¼ cup heavy cream

½ cup chopped white chocolate

In small saucepan, bring cream to simmer over low heat. Add white chocolate and stir until smooth. Spread Glaze evenly over top of cooled cheesecake. Refrigerate until set. Cake may be made ahead to this point, up to 2 days in advance.

SAUCE:

12 ounces frozen raspberries
½ cup white wine
⅓ cup sugar

Fresh raspberries for garnish
   (optional)

(continued)

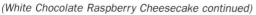

(White Chocolate Raspberry Cheesecake continued)

Thaw raspberries in a sieve placed over a bowl, reserving juice. In a small saucepan, boil wine and sugar until reduced to $\frac{1}{4}$ cup (approximately 10 minutes). Purée through a sieve to remove seeds. Sweeten purée with 2 tablespoons each wine syrup and reserved raspberry juice, adding more to taste.

To serve, spoon a pool of raspberry Sauce onto individual plates. Slice cheesecake and place on top of Sauce. Drizzle more Sauce over top, if desired. Garnish plates with fresh berries. Yields 12–16 slices.

A Slice of Paradise

White Chocolate Key Lime Cheesecake

CRUST:

2 tablespoons butter, melted
2 tablespoons sugar
1½ cups graham cracker
  crumbs

Mix ingredients and pat into bottom of 10-inch springform pan.

FILLING:

2 pounds cream cheese, softened
½ pint heavy cream
1 cup sour cream
4 eggs, beaten
2 cups sugar
1 tablespoon butter, melted
4 tablespoons flour
1 tablespoon cornstarch
9 ounces white chocolate, melted
Juice from 4 Key limes
2 tablespoons vanilla

Beat cream cheese until smooth and add remaining ingredients. Pour into crumb-lined springform pan. Bake at 350° for 1 hour; turn oven off and leave for ½ hour. Chill for 12 hours.

Roberts Ranch Museum Cookbook

Toffee Cheesecake Temptations

Creamy and rich bite-size cheesecakes. Ideal to serve on a buffet.

⅔ cup butter or margarine,
  softened
¾ cup packed brown sugar
2 cups flour
½ cup chopped pecans
16 ounces cream cheese,
  softened

¾ cup sugar
2 large eggs
1 tablespoon lemon juice
2 teaspoons vanilla extract
1 (7-ounce) Heath Bar, crushed

Beat butter at medium speed in mixing bowl until light. Add brown sugar gradually, beating until fluffy. Add flour and mix well. Stir in pecans. Set aside 1 cup mixture. Press remaining mixture over bottom of a greased 9x13-inch baking pan. Bake at 350° for 14–15 minutes or until light brown.

Beat cream cheese at medium speed in mixing bowl until smooth. Add sugar gradually, beating until light and fluffy. Beat in eggs one at a time. Stir in lemon juice and vanilla. Pour over hot crust. Sprinkle reserved crumb mixture evenly over batter. Bake at 350° for 25 minutes or until nearly set; cheesecake will firm when chilled. Sprinkle candy over hot cheesecake. Cool on a wire rack. Chill, covered, for 8 hours. Cut into bars to serve. Makes 3 dozen.

Savor the Moment

Cookies and Candies

Founded in 1565, picturesque St. Augustine is the oldest continuously occupied settlement of European origin in the United States.

Wongalara Lemon Fingers

This is a perfect choice for a hot day, as it requires no baking whatsoever. Serve these lemon fingers with a cool glass of lemonade!

8 ounces vanilla wafer cookies
2⅔ cups flaked coconut
⅔ cup butter, melted
½ cup plus 2 tablespoons
  sweetened condensed milk

Juice of 1 lemon
1½ cups confectioners' sugar

Crush vanilla wafers with a rolling pin in a sealable plastic bag. Remove to a bowl. Add coconut and melted butter and stir to mix. Add sweetened condensed milk and mix thoroughly. Press into bottom of a 9x9-inch baking pan. Combine lemon juice and confectioners' sugar in a bowl; mix until smooth. Pour over crumb mixture. Chill for one hour. Cut into squares. Yields 2–3 dozen bars.

An American Celebration

Lemon-Cream Cheese Cookies

1 cup butter, softened
1 (3-ounce) package cream
  cheese, softened
1 cup sugar
1 egg, beaten

1 tablespoon lemon juice
1 teaspoon grated lemon rind
2½ cups flour
1 teaspoon baking powder
Food coloring (optional)

Blend butter and cream cheese. Add sugar; cream thoroughly. Add egg, lemon juice, and rind; blend well. Mix flour and baking powder. Add to cream cheese mixture, along with food coloring, if desired, and mix until well blended. Chill dough at least 30 minutes.

Preheat oven to 375°. Force dough through cookie press onto ungreased baking sheet. Bake 8–10 minutes, or until slightly browned. These freeze well. Yields 5 dozen (2-inch) cookies.

Some Like it South!

Crunchy Key Lime Cookies

Mouth-watering cookies with a tropical flair, made with the juice and rind of the Key lime—a small yellow lime native to Florida.

½ cup (1 stick) butter or margarine, softened	2 teaspoons grated Key lime zest
1½ cups confectioners' sugar	1 cup flour
1 egg	1 teaspoon baking powder
1 tablespoon Key lime juice	¼ teaspoon salt
	2 cups cornflakes, crushed

Cream butter and confectioners' sugar in a mixing bowl until light and fluffy. Stir in egg, Key lime juice, and zest (mixture may appear curdled). Add flour, baking powder, and salt, and mix well.

Drop dough by teaspoonfuls into cornflakes, and turn to coat. Place on ungreased cookie sheets. Bake at 350° for 16 minutes. Remove to a wire rack to cool. Makes 2 dozen.

Savor the Moment

Peanut Butter Cookies

1 (14-ounce) can sweetened condensed milk	2 cups biscuit mix
¾ cup peanut butter, smooth or crunchy	1 teaspoon vanilla
	¼ cup sugar

Preheat oven to 375°. In a large mixing bowl, beat condensed milk and peanut butter until smooth. Add biscuit mix and vanilla and mix well. Put a large teaspoonful of the cookie dough in your hand and roll it around until it is fairly smooth (no big lumps). Put the ¼ cup sugar in a little dish and roll the ball of cookie dough until it is covered with sugar. Place cookies about 2 inches apart on a cookie sheet and press down lightly, just a little, with a fork.

Place cookie sheet in oven on top shelf and bake for 6–8 minutes or until lightly browned; do not overbake. Take from cookie sheet and place on cooling rack. Cool, then store in ziploc bags.

Kids at Work

Hamantashen

Cookies for Purim Jewish holiday.

2 cups flour	¼ cup shortening
½ cup sugar	1 egg
2 tablespoons baking powder	1 tablespoon vanilla

Combine flour, sugar and baking powder. Cut in shortening; add egg and vanilla. Divide into 4 parts. Put on wax paper. Refrigerate 3 or 4 hours or overnight.

   Roll out. Cut in circles (use shot glass).

FILLING:

Pecans	Jam
Raisins	

Chop pecans and raisins and add jam; mix well. Put teaspoonful of mixture on each dough circle. Bring dough together to form a triangle; pinch at top. Bake at 400° on greased cookie sheet for 10–12 minutes.

Tastes from Paradise: A Garden of Eating

Butter Cookies

2 (3-ounce) boxes (any flavor) instant pudding	2½–2¾ cups flour
	3 sticks margarine, softened

Mix all ingredients and roll into walnut-size balls. Place on ungreased cookie sheet. Flatten with fork or bottom of glass dipped in flour. Bake at 350° for 10–15 minutes.

Variation: Add chopped nuts with chocolate pudding. Cut up cherries with pistachio pudding. Add red cherries in green cookies for Christmas.

4-U: 400 Recipes of 4 Ingredients

Star Speck Cookies

2 cups all-purpose flour
2 tablespoons sugar (optional)
½ teaspoon salt
¾ cup (1½ sticks) unsalted
   butter, chilled and chopped

6–8 tablespoons ice water
1 (12-ounce) jar raspberry
   preserves

Mix flour, sugar, and salt in a food processor. Add butter and pulse until mixture resembles cornmeal. Add water gradually, mixing just until mixture is moist enough to be pressed together; do not mix until it forms a ball. Press mixture together on a lightly floured surface. Set aside ¼ of the dough. Roll the large portion into a ¼-inch-thick rectangle, and place on a cookie sheet. Freeze for 30 minutes.

Prick pastry all over with a fork. Bake at 400° for 10 minutes. Cool on a wire rack. Spread with preserves.

Roll the smaller dough portion less than ¼ inch thick on a lightly floured surface. Cut into star shapes with a cookie cutter. Place close together over the preserves so that each cookie square will have a star.

Bake at 350° for 15–20 minutes or until light brown. Cool on a wire rack and cut into squares. Makes 4 dozen.

By Invitation Only

Coconut Macaroons

3 egg whites
1 cup sugar
3 cups shredded coconut

2 tablespoons cornstarch
1 tablespoon vanilla

Beat egg whites until stiff, but not dry. Gradually beat sugar into egg whites. Fold in shredded coconut mixed with cornstarch. Cook in double boiler over hot water, stirring often, for 15 minutes. Add vanilla to mixture. Drop by teaspoonfuls onto greased cookie sheet, 1 inch apart. Bake at 300° for 20–25 minutes or until delicately browned. Yields 2½ dozen.

Historic Spanish Point: Cooking Then and Now

Coconut Dreams

1 cup (2 sticks) butter, softened
½ cup sugar

2 cups flour
1 (4-ounce) can flaked coconut

Cream butter and sugar in a mixing bowl until light and fluffy. Beat in flour and coconut. Shape into 2 logs, 1½-inches in diameter. Chill, covered, until firm. Cut the logs into ¼-inch-thick slices. Place slices on nonstick cookie sheet. Bake at 300° for 25 minutes or until coconut is browned. Cool on wire rack. Store in an airtight container. Yields 5 dozen.

Entirely Entertaining in the Bonnet House Style

There is no state income tax in Florida. The corporate income tax rate is 5.5 percent, one of the lowest in the country.

Kahlúa Nut Bars

½ cup (1 stick) butter, softened
2 eggs
2½ cups packed light brown
  sugar
¼ cup Kahlúa
1 teaspoon vanilla extract

1½ cups flour
2 tablespoons baking powder
1 teaspoon salt
1 cup chopped nuts
1 (4-ounce) can flaked coconut

Combine butter, eggs, and brown sugar in a bowl and mix well. Add Kahlúa, vanilla, flour, baking powder, and salt, and mix well. Stir in nuts and coconut. Spoon into a greased 9x13-inch baking pan. Bake at 350° for 25 minutes. Cool in the pan. Cut into squares. Yields 2 dozen.

Entirely Entertaining in the Bonnet House Style

Lemon Crumb Squares

1 (15-ounce) can sweetened
  condensed milk
1 teaspoon grated lemon rind
½ cup lemon juice
1½ cups flour

½ teaspoon salt
1 teaspoon baking powder
1 cup uncooked oatmeal
⅔ cup butter, softened
1 cup dark brown sugar

Blend milk, lemon rind, and juice for filling. Set aside. Sift flour, salt, and baking powder. Add oatmeal to flour mixture. Cream butter and sugar. Mix with flour mixture until crumbly. Spread half the mixture in buttered pan and pat down. Spread condensed milk mixture over it. Cover with remaining crumbly mixture. Bake at 350° for about 25 minutes. Cool in pan for 15 minutes. Cut into squares. Chill in pan until firm.

Recipes for Lori's Lighthouse

Brownie Lady Heavenly Brownies

BROWNIES:

2 cups all-purpose flour, sifted
½ cup baking cocoa, sifted
¼ teaspoon salt
2 cups (4 sticks) butter, chopped
4 ounces semisweet chocolate
  chunks

4 ounces unsweetened chocolate
  chunks
3 cups sugar
2 teaspoons vanilla extract
8 eggs

Line miniature muffin cups with gold foil liners. Sift flour, baking cocoa, and salt together. Melt butter and chocolates in a double boiler, stirring frequently until smooth; remove from heat. Whisk in sugar and vanilla. Whisk in eggs 1 at a time. Add dry ingredients and whisk until smooth. Spoon batter into prepared muffin cups, filling cups to the rim. Bake at 350° on lower oven rack for 25–30 minutes or until a wooden pick inserted in center comes out clean. Cool in pan on a wire rack.

PEPPERMINT FROSTING:

1 cup heavy cream
2 tablespoons light corn syrup
1 pound white chocolate,
  chopped

8 ounces peppermint candies,
  broken

Bring cream and corn syrup to a simmer over low heat in a saucepan; remove from heat. Add chocolate, and stir until melted and smooth. Spread on Brownies, and immediately sprinkle with peppermint candies. Remove from muffin cups. Makes 4 dozen.

By Invitation Only

With easy access, shallow waters, and a variety of marine biology, the Benwood Shipwreck on French Reef in the Florida Keys is considered the most popular dive site in the Florida Keys.

Zucchini Brownies

2 cups grated zucchini	1/2 teaspoon salt
1/2 cup oil	1/2 cup cocoa
1 1/2 cups sugar	1/2 cup chocolate chips
1 egg	1/2 cup chopped nuts (optional)
2 cups flour	1/2 teaspoon baking soda
1 teaspoon vanilla	

Mix all ingredients together. Pour into a greased 9x13-inch baking pan. Bake at 350° until done, about 25–30 minutes. Cut into squares.

A Taste of Heaven

Chocolate Toffee Bars

1 3/4 cups crushed chocolate graham teddy bear cookies	1 (6-ounce) package white chocolate chips
1/2 cup butter or margarine, melted	1 cup chopped walnuts
1 (6-ounce) package milk chocolate chips	1 cup chopped pecans
1 (6-ounce) package almond brickle chips	1 (14-ounce) can sweetened condensed milk

Line a 9x13-inch pan with heavy-duty aluminum foil. Spread crushed cookies in pan, and pour melted butter over. Bake at 325° for 5 minutes. Remove from oven. Layer all chips and nuts over cookie layer, pressing into bottom layer. Pour sweetened condensed milk over all. Bake at 325° for 30 minutes. Cool completely. Cut into squares, removing foil.

Recipes for Lori's Lighthouse

Butter Pecan Turtle Cookies

CRUST:

2 cups flour
1 cup packed brown sugar

½ cup sweet butter, softened
1 cup pecan halves

Preheat oven to 350°. Combine flour, brown sugar, and butter, and mix at medium speed for 2–3 minutes. Pat into 9x13-inch ungreased pan. Sprinkle pecans over Crust.

CARAMEL LAYER:

⅔ cup sweet butter (not
  margarine)

½ cup packed brown sugar
1 cup milk chocolate chips

Combine butter and brown sugar in saucepan. Cook over medium heat, stirring constantly until mixture boils. Boil 1½ minutes, stirring. Pour over Crust. Bake at 350° for 18–22 minutes. Remove from oven. Immediately sprinkle with chips. Swirl slightly. Do not spread. Cool, then cut into bars.

Tastes from Paradise: A Garden of Eating

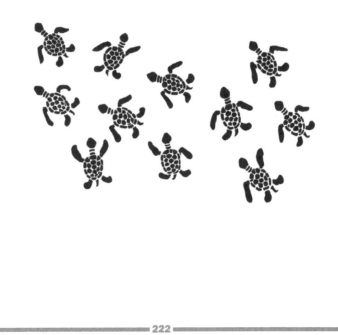

Eggnog Holiday Fudge

1 cup eggnog
2 cups sugar
2 tablespoons white corn syrup
1/4 teaspoon salt

2 tablespoons butter
1/2 cup chopped walnuts
1/2 cup sliced candied red cherries

Combine first 4 ingredients in large saucepan. Cook over medium to high heat, stirring constantly until it reaches a soft-ball stage (235° on candy thermometer). Cool to lukewarm. Add butter; beat until no longer glossy (starts to thicken). Stir in nuts and cherries. Pour quickly into greased 8x8x2-inch pan. Cut into one-inch squares.

Garden of Eatin'

Key Lime Fudge

3 cups (18 ounces) white chocolate chips
1 (14-ounce) can sweetened condensed milk
2 tablespoons Key lime juice or lime juice

2 teaspoons finely grated lime zest
1 cup chopped macadamia nuts, toasted
Coarsely chopped macadamia nuts to taste

Line an 8x8-inch or 9x9-inch dish with foil, allowing a 4- to 5-inch overhang. Coat foil with butter. Combine white chocolate chips and condensed milk in heavy saucepan. Cook over low heat just until chocolate melts and mixture is smooth, stirring frequently. Remove from heat. Stir in lime juice and lime zest. Add 1 cup macadamia nuts and mix well. Spread chocolate mixture in prepared dish and sprinkle with coarsely chopped macadamia nuts. Chill, covered, for 2 hours or until firm. Lift fudge out of dish using edges of foil. Cut the fudge into squares and store in an airtight container at room temperature for 1 week or freeze for up to 2 months. Makes 64 squares.

Bay Fêtes

Premium Bonbons

1 cup peanut butter chips	½ teaspoon vanilla extract
1 cup semisweet chocolate chips	1½ cups crushed saltine
1 tablespoon butter	crackers (about 36)
1 ounce unsweetened chocolate,	½ cup pecan meal or very fine
chopped	pecans

Place peanut butter chips, chocolate chips, butter, and chocolate in a medium pan and cook over very low heat until melted. Stir frequently. Remove from heat; add vanilla. Stir in cracker crumbs gradually to make a stiff dough. Roll into large marble-size balls. Spread pecan meal on wax paper; roll each bonbon in meal to coat. Let stand on wax paper 30 minutes to set. Store in airtight container at room temperature or in freezer. Makes about 50.

Strictly Scratch

Triple Chocolate Peanut Clusters

Simple, but elegant!

1 (12-ounce) package semisweet	2 pounds white chocolate
chocolate chips	1 (24-ounce) jar unsalted dry
1 (12-ounce) package milk	roasted peanuts
chocolate chips	

Melt all chocolate in an electric skillet on lowest setting, or in double boiler, stirring until melted. Cool for 5 minutes and stir in peanuts. Drop onto wax paper by tablespoons. Let cool completely. Wrap and keep in refrigerator until ready to serve. Makes 3 pounds.

Thymes Remembered

Wonderful Chocolate Truffles

4 (1-ounce) squares unsweetened
  chocolate
4 (1-ounce) squares semisweet
  chocolate
¾ cup butter or margarine,
  room temperature

2 cups confectioners' sugar
Yolk of a large egg
2 tablespoons rum or coffee

Melt both chocolates together. Cool to room temperature. In medium bowl, beat butter, sugar, egg yolk, and rum with electric mixer until pale and fluffy. Mix in melted chocolate.

To make rosettes, line a baking sheet with waxed paper or small fluted candy cups. Spoon chocolate mixture into a 6-inch pastry bag, fitted with a large star or rosette tip. Pipe large rosettes onto paper or into cups. Refrigerate or freeze until firm.

To make balls, shape truffle mixture into a 10½x15½-inch foil-lined jellyroll pan and spread to ⅓–½ inch thick. Place in freezer at least 45 minutes, or until firm enough to shape. With hands, roll rounded teaspoons into 1-inch balls. Roll in cocoa or sprinkles; place on wax paper-lined baking sheet and refrigerate or freeze until firm. Transfer to tightly covered container to store in refrigerator or freezer. Serve chilled. Makes 50. If refrigerated, will keep up to 3 weeks.

A Taste of Heaven

Peanut Butter Balls

1 pound butter, softened
2 pounds peanut butter
3 pounds confectioners' sugar

4 (12-ounce) packages chocolate
   chips
⅔ bar paraffin wax

Mix first 3 ingredients together. Roll into 1- or 2-inch balls. Melt chocolate and paraffin wax in a double boiler. Using a toothpick, dip balls in chocolate and place on wax paper. Refrigerate to cool. Makes approximately 180 balls.

Under the Canopy

Praline Crunch

1 stick margarine
1 cup firmly packed brown sugar

½ cup chopped pecans
2½ cups cornflakes

Melt margarine and brown sugar in pan. Bring to a boil and immediately remove from heat. Add pecans and cornflakes and toss together with fork to coat mixture. Spread on waxed paper and let cool. Store in airtight container. Serve over ice cream.

Cooking with People to People

Chow Mein Candies

1 (6-ounce) package butterscotch
   chips
1 (6-ounce) package chocolate
   chips

1 (5-ounce) can chow mein
   noodles
½ pound cashews, broken

Melt chips together. Pour over combined noodles and nuts. Drop from teaspoon onto cookie sheet or wax paper. Cool until hardened. Yields 36 pieces.

4-U: 400 Recipes of 4 Ingredients

Pies and Other Desserts

PHOTO © ANDY NEWMAN / FLORIDA KEYS TDC

Spanning from Key Vaca to Sunshine Key, the Seven Mile Bridge is one of the longest segmental bridges in the world. The Old Seven-Mile Bridge, running parallel to the modern span, is also known as the world's longest fishing pier.

Margaritaville Key Lime Pie

This tropical dessert recipe comes from singer Jimmy Buffett's Margaritaville Café.

CRUST AND FILLING:

1 (9-inch) graham cracker pie crust
2 egg yolks
1 (14-ounce) can sweetened condensed milk
1 egg white
½ cup Key lime juice

Bake pie crust at 350° for 5 minutes. Beat egg yolks with an electric mixer 2 minutes. Blend yolks into milk. In separate bowl, beat egg white with electric mixer until fluffy. Gently fold white into mixture. Fold in lime juice. Pour filling into pie crust. Refrigerate 2–3 hours before adding Topping.

TOPPING:

5 egg whites
2 teaspoons cream of tartar
½ cup sugar

Whip egg whites and cream of tartar with electric mixer until foamy. Continue to whip while slowly adding sugar. Beat until peaks form. Score filling with a fork. Spread Topping over Filling. Bake at 425° for 5 minutes or until topping starts to brown. Yields 8 servings.

Calypso Café

Key limes, abundant in the Florida Keys, are much smaller and rounder than regular limes, ranging in size from a ping-pong ball to a golf ball. The peel is thin, smooth and greenish-yellow when ripe. The flesh is yellow and quite juicy with a higher acidity than regular limes. That is why a true Key Lime Pie is yellow—not green.

No-Bake Key Lime Pie

1 (8-ounce) package cream
  cheese, softened
1 (14-ounce) can sweetened
  condensed milk
3 ounces Key lime juice

1 graham cracker pie shell, baked
Sliced strawberries, kiwi fruit,
  or other fresh fruit, or fruit pie
  filling
Whipped cream

Blend cream cheese and condensed milk (it will have some tiny lumps of cheese). Add one ounce of lime juice at a time, blend well each time. Pour into pie shell; chill.

At serving time, top with one or more of the fruit slices or pie filling. Then top with whipped cream.

The Cruising K.I.S.S. Cookbook II

Lemon Luscious Pie

1 cup sugar
4 tablespoons cornstarch or
  Clear Jel
1 tablespoon or less grated
  lemon rind
¼ cup lemon juice

3 egg yolks, unbeaten
¼ cup butter or margarine
1 cup milk
1 cup sour cream
Whipped cream
2 tablespoons chopped walnuts

Combine sugar, cornstarch or Clear Jel, rind, juice, egg yolks, and butter; stir in milk. Cook over medium heat, stirring until thick (can be done in microwave). Cool; fold in sour cream. Place in pastry shell. Chill at least 2 hours. Serve with whipped cream and chopped walnuts.

Treasured Recipes from Near and Far

Strawberry Drizzle Pie

1 (8-ounce) package light cream
  cheese, softened
⅓ cup sugar
¼ teaspoon almond extract
1 cup whipping cream

1 pie shell, baked and cooled
4 cups fresh Florida strawberries
½ cup semisweet chocolate chips
1 tablespoon shortening

Beat cream cheese until fluffy. Gradually add sugar and extract. Blend well. Whip whipping cream stiff, then add to first mixture. Place mixture in pie shell, then starting at outer edge, arrange strawberries pointing up on top of mixture. Melt chocolate and shortening together. Stir constantly until smooth. Pour chocolate mixture into a zip lock bag. Squeeze chocolate out of cut corner of bag to drizzle chocolate onto strawberries. Refrigerate. Serves 6–8.

Simply Florida...Strawberries

Orange Pecan Pie

1 fresh medium-size orange
1½ cups brown sugar
1 cup light corn syrup
3 tablespoons butter

3 eggs, well beaten
1½ cups broken pecans
1 (9-inch) pie shell, unbaked

Cut orange into quarters and remove any seeds. Put orange quarters, peel, and pulp through a food chopper. Combine ground orange with sugar and corn syrup in saucepan. Bring to a full hard boil. Remove from heat. Cool slightly, stirring occasionally.

    Add butter and cool a little more, still stirring, about 5 minutes. Blend in eggs and pecans, mixing thoroughly. Pour into unbaked pie shell, and bake in 350° oven approximately 40–45 minutes, or until set.

Citrus Lovers Cook Book

Florida Orange Pie

FILLING:

2 cups orange juice
1 cup sugar
2 tablespoons cornstarch
¼ cup water
½ teaspoon salt

1 tablespoon butter or margarine
3 egg yolks
3 tablespoons grated orange rind
1 cup orange sections
1 (9-inch) pie shell, baked

Combine orange juice and sugar, and boil until sugar dissolves. Mix cornstarch and water; add to orange juice mixture. Add salt and butter. Beat egg yolks and add a little of hot mixture and stir together, then combine and stir until thickened. Add grated orange rind and sections just before removing from heat. Pour into pie shell and let cool.

TOPPING:

3 egg whites
3 tablespoons ice water

Pinch of salt
6 tablespoons sugar

Beat egg whites until frothy; add ice water, then salt. Add sugar slowly while beating eggs until stiff, but not dry. Mound lightly on filled pie shell and spread to edge of crust. Bake at 300° for 15–20 minutes or until brown. Yields 8 servings.

Historic Spanish Point: Cooking Then and Now

Grapefruit Pie

1 (3-ounce) package strawberry
  Jell-O
3 tablespoons cornstarch
1 cup sugar

1½ cups water
2 ruby red grapefruits, sectioned
1 pie crust, baked
Cool Whip

Cook Jell-O, cornstarch, sugar, and water until thickened. Place pieces of grapefruit on bottom of pie crust. Pour prepared mixture over grapefruit; cool. Add Cool Whip just before serving.

Garden of Eatin'

Crumb-Top Apple Pie

FILLING:
⅔ cup sugar
½ teaspoon cinnamon
¼ teaspoon nutmeg
8 large tart apples, peeled, cored,
  and thinly sliced (12 cups;
  about 4 pounds)

2 tablespoons water
2 tablespoons lemon juice
2 tablespoons butter

Preheat oven to 350°. In large bowl, combine sugar, cinnamon, and nutmeg. Add apples; sprinkle on water and lemon juice. Toss until evenly coated. Spoon into a 10-inch deep-dish pie pan, without pastry. Dot with butter.

CRUMP TOPPING:
½ cup firmly packed brown
  sugar

½ cup butter, softened
1 cup all-purpose flour

Cream sugar and butter until light and fluffy. Add flour and stir until smooth. Dab on apples. Bake 50–60 minutes. Serve warm, plain, or with ice cream.

Trinity Treats

Celebration of Liberty Chocolate Pie

Everyone raves about the rich flavor of this chocolate pie, and to serve it with coffee is divine!

1½ cups (3 sticks) unsalted butter

6 cups (36 ounces) semisweet chocolate chips

8 eggs

1 (9-inch) chocolate crumb pie shell

Chocolate Glaze

Fresh raspberries, strawberries or blueberries for garnish

Melt butter in a saucepan. Melt chocolate chips slowly in another saucepan. Add melted butter to melted chocolate, and stir to blend. Beat eggs vigorously in a bowl for 5 minutes. Add chocolate mixture to eggs in 3 additions, stirring well after each addition. Pour into chocolate crumb shell. Bake at 350° for 15–20 minutes. The filling will look soft. Remove to a wire rack to cool. Chill for 8 hours. Spread Chocolate Glaze over chilled pie. Garnish with raspberries, strawberries or blueberries.

CHOCOLATE GLAZE:

3 tablespoons unsalted butter

1½ tablespoons dark rum

1 tablespoon plus 1 teaspoon light corn syrup

Pinch of salt

½ cup (3 ounces) white chocolate chips

Combine butter, rum, corn syrup, and salt in a small heavy saucepan. Cook over low heat, stirring constantly, until butter melts. Increase heat to medium and bring to a boil, stirring constantly. Remove from heat and add white chocolate chips. Stir until melted. Cool at room temperature for 5 minutes or until mixture coats a spoon and does not drip off edge. Yields 16–18 servings.

Note: The pie can be made ahead and frozen before glazing. Thaw before topping with Chocolate Glaze.

An American Celebration

Located 15 miles east of Lake City on the southern perimeter of Osceola National Forest, Olustee Battlefield Historic State Park is Florida's first state park and the site of the largest battle fought in Florida during the Civil War.

Green Coconut Pie

Large green coconuts picked from the tree yield a softer meat, producing a smooth-textured pie. You'll know if you have the magic coconut when you pry the meat from the shell. The skin will be a pale tan instead of brown. But any coconut can be used. This pie is magnificent.

1 Memorable Pie Crust
  (see opposite page)
Meat from 1 coconut, or 2 cups
  commerically prepared, flaked
  coconut
1 cup sugar
$\frac{1}{2}$ cup cornstarch

$\frac{1}{4}$ teaspoon salt
3 cups skim or whole milk
3 large egg yolks, beaten
$\frac{1}{2}$ teaspoon almond extract
1 teaspoon vanilla extract
2 cups heavy whipping cream

Prepare and bake Memorable Pie Crust according to instructions on opposite page.

In a food processor or blender, grind up fresh coconut as finely as possible. (I do not pare off the brown skin on the outside of the nut, but you may if you wish.)

In a 2-quart saucepan, combine sugar, cornstarch, and salt. Stir until well blended. Add milk slowly, stirring until smooth. Cook over medium heat, stirring constantly until mixture boils and begins to thicken. Remove from heat. Remove about 1 cup of mixture from pan, and slowly stir into egg yolks. When well blended, pour into saucepan, return to heat, and continue cooking until custard is thick enough to mound on the spoon.

Remove from heat; stir in extracts and coconut, reserving a handful for top of pie. Pour into a bowl, and cover with wax paper laid directly on custard. Refrigerate to completely chill, about 3 hours.

Three hours later, chill bowl and beaters for 15 minutes in freezer. Whip heavy cream in chilled bowl with electric mixer until stiff. Fold $\frac{3}{4}$ whipped cream into custard. Pour into baked pie shell. Spread remaining whipped cream on top. Sprinkle reserved coconut on top. Refrigerate 3 hours before serving. Store leftovers in refrigerator. Serves 8–10.

Tropical Tastes and Tantalizing Tales

Memorable Pie Crust

A few words about pie crust . . . I started using margarine in my crust to avoid the annoyance of measuring shortening. Once I tasted crust made with margarine, well that was a memorable experience. If you think margarine won't make a difference, try shortening on your toast in the morning.

ONE CRUST:

6⅓ tablespoons margarine
1 cup sifted all-purpose flour

½ teaspoon salt
2½ tablespoons cold water

TWO CRUST:

¾ cup margarine
2–2½ cups sifted all-purpose
   flour

1 teaspoon salt
5 tablespoons cold water

Preheat oven to 450°. Cut margarine into flour and salt with pastry cutter until crumbly. Mix in 2 tablespoons water. Work in with your hands. If it is too dry, add enough water to give dough a nice pliable consistency.

Roll out between 2 pieces of well-floured wax paper. Turn into plate. If you are baking an empty shell, prick bottom liberally with a fork. Bake for 10–15 minutes or until golden, unless your recipe calls for an unbaked shell.

Tropical Tastes and Tantalizing Tales

Sweet Potato Pie

3 large sweet potatoes
1½ sticks margarine
1½ cups sugar
½ cup evaporated milk
4 eggs, beaten

1 tablespoon vanilla
1 tablespoon lemon extract
2 tablespoons cinnamon
2 tablespoons nutmeg
2 (9-inch) unbaked pie shells

Boil potatoes until done. Drain, and use beater to mash potatoes. Add margarine, sugar, and milk. Add eggs and extracts. Last add cinnamon and nutmeg. Pour into pie shells and bake 45 minutes at 325°.

Tip: To prevent crust from becoming soggy with any creme pies, sprinkle crust with powdered sugar.

FCCD Cookbook

Ricotta Pie with Chocolate Marbled Filling

CRUST:

3 cups flour
1 cup confectioners' sugar
½ teaspoon baking powder
½ cup shortening
½ teaspoon vanilla
2 egg yolks
¼ cup water

Mix flour, sugar, and baking powder. Cut shortening into flour mixture. Add vanilla to egg yolks, and blend in water. Add egg mixture to flour and mix well by hand. Roll out dough, and line bottom of a 3-quart oblong baking dish. Save some dough for lattice strips.

FILLING:

8 egg whites
3 pounds ricotta
1½ teaspoons lemon extract
1 tablespoon vanilla
1 tablespoon diced citron
 (optional)
1 cup sugar
⅛ teaspoon salt

Beat egg whites until fluffy; blend in all other ingredients. Set to one side.

CHOCOLATE MIXTURE:

4 (1-ounce) squares chocolate
2 tablespoons sugar
1 egg yolk (reserve white)

Melt chocolate. Blend in sugar and egg yolk. Set aside. Pour half of the Filling over Crust. Drop Chocolate Mixture with a teaspoon (randomly) over Filling. Pour remaining Filling over top. Swirl with a spoon to give a marbled effect.

Roll and cut remaining dough in strips, and form a lattice top. Brush with egg white. Bake in preheated oven 350° for 1 hour.

Preserving Our Italian Heritage

Triple Layer Mud Pie

2 squares semisweet baking
  chocolate, melted
¼ cup sweetened condensed
  milk
1 ready-made chocolate pie crust
¾ cup pecans, toasted

2 (4-ounce) packages
  chocolate-flavored instant
  pudding and pie filling
2 cups cold milk
1 (8-ounce) carton Cool Whip,
  thawed

Pour chocolate and condensed milk into bowl; stir until smooth. Pour into crust. Press nuts in chocolate. Refrigerate 10 minutes.

Add pudding mix into milk then beat until smooth. Spread 1½ cups pudding over chocolate in crust. Stir ½ of whipped topping into remaining pudding. Spread over pudding in crust. Top with remaining whipped topping.

Good Cooking

Eggnog Pie

1 (9-inch) pie shell, baked
1 envelope unflavored gelatin
3 tablespoons cold water
2 cups eggnog
1 cup heavy cream

¼ cup sugar
¼ teaspoon salt
2 tablespoons vanilla extract
½ teaspoon almond extract
Ground nutmeg

Prepare and cool pie shell. Soften gelatin in cold water. Heat eggnog in a saucepan over moderately low heat for 1–2 minutes. Stir in softened gelatin, and continue heating until gelatin is completely dissolved, about 1–2 minutes. Chill until the consistency of unbeaten egg whites.

Combine heavy cream, sugar, and salt in a chilled bowl. Whip until cream holds its shape. Stir in vanilla and almond extracts. Fold the whipped cream mixture into the gelatin and eggnog mixture. Pour mixture into baked pie shell. Chill 2–4 hours until set. Serve with nutmeg sprinkled on top.

Heaven in a Pot

Walnut Pie

Give this pie a try. You will love it.

3 egg whites
1 cup plus 2 tablespoons sugar, divided
½ teaspoon baking powder
18 saltines, crumbled

1 cup chopped walnuts
1 teaspoon vanilla
½ pint whipping cream
Cherries for garnish

Beat egg whites until stiff, then add 1 cup sugar and baking powder. Fold in saltines, walnuts, and vanilla. Pour into well-buttered 9-inch pie plate and bake at 325° for 25 minutes. Cool. Beat whipping cream, gradually adding 2 tablespoons sugar, then pour over pie. Spread whipping cream to edges of pie pan. Whipping cream must be added at least 4–5 hours before serving. Refrigerate. Garnish with cherries before serving.

Florida Fixin's

Lost Creek Sawdust Pie

1½ cups flaked coconut
1½ cups graham cracker crumbs
1½ cups chopped pecans or walnuts

1½ cups sugar
1 cup egg whites (unbeaten)
1 unbaked pie shell

Combine coconut, graham cracker crumbs, nuts, and sugar. Mix with egg whites. Pour mixture into pie shell. Bake at 350° for 30–35 minutes. Serve warm with ice cream.

Let's ACT Up in the Kitchen

Peanut Butter Pie

1 cup powdered sugar	2 cups milk, scalded
1/2 cup peanut butter	2 tablespoons butter
3 egg yolks	1 teaspoon vanilla
2/3 cup sugar	Whipped cream
1/8 teaspoon salt	1 (9-inch) pie shell, baked and
1/4 cup cornstarch	cooled

Blend powdered sugar and peanut butter. Mixture will be crumbly. Set aside. Beat egg yolks in top of double boiler until fluffy. Combine sugar, salt, and cornstarch; beat into egg yolks. Add milk gradually. Cook in double boiler until smooth and thick, stirring constantly. Remove from heat; add butter and vanilla. Cover the bottom of pie shell with 2/3 of the peanut butter mixture. Pour hot custard over this, then cool. Top with whipped cream, and sprinkle remaining peanut butter mixture on top.

Heaven in a Pot

Kool-Aid Pie

1 (6-ounce) package pre-	1 (8-ounce) container Cool Whip,
sweetened Kool Aid (any flavor)	divided
3 tablespoons water	1 (9-inch) graham cracker pie shell
1 (14-ounce) can condensed milk	

Empty package of Kool Aid into a large bowl. Heat water in microwave for one minute; add to Kool Aid. Add condensed milk and blend well. Add half of Cool Whip to mixture and mix well. Pour mixture into graham cracker pie crust. Take remainder of Cool Whip and spread over top of pie. Chill for at least 2 hours. It will set better if prepared the day before you plan to serve it.

Feeding the Flock

Mango Cobbler

Anyone who has lived in the southern part of the United States knows fruit cobblers, the most popular ones being blackberry, dewberry, or peach. A warm cobbler served with cold heavy cream is summer's most delectable dessert. Along most of the Gulf Coast, mangoes are plentiful in the markets during the season, so for a change, try making the following cobbler from this delicious fruit.

**6 cups sliced ripe mangoes
 (about 5, depending on size)
½ cup sugar
½ teaspoon cardamom seeds,
 crushed**

**2 tablespoons flour
4 tablespoons lime juice
Basic pastry dough**

In a deep pie dish or other 2-quart baking dish, toss together mangoes, sugar, cardamom seeds, flour, and lime juice.

Roll out pastry dough to cover top of baking dish, crimping edges to seal. Cut slits for steam to escape. Preheat oven to 425° and bake for 45–50 minutes, or until crust is brown and crisp. If necessary, cover edges of crust with strips of foil to prevent burning. Serves 6–8.

Gulf Coast Cooking

Cherry Cobbler

This is a delicious dessert, and so very easy to make.

**1 (21-ounce) can cherry pie
 filling
1 cup chopped or broken pecans
½ (18¼-ounce) package
 yellow cake mix**

**1 stick margarine, melted
Vanilla ice cream**

Pour pie filling into an 8x8x2-inch baking dish, then sprinkle pecans over cherries. Cover with dry cake mix (that's right, just open up the package and pour ½ of it over the cherries), and pour melted margarine over top. Bake at 350° for 25–30 minutes. Serve while hot with a scoop of vanilla ice cream on top.

Kids at Work

Editor's Extra: A Jiffy cake mix works fine.

Guava Cobbler

1 stick butter
¾ cup sugar
¾ cup flour
2 teaspoons baking powder

½ teaspoon salt
¾ cup milk
2½ cups chopped guavas

Melt butter in 9-inch square pan. Mix together the sugar, flour, baking powder, salt, and milk. Pour batter over melted margarine. Add guavas. Do not stir. Bake 45 minutes at 325°.

SAUCE:

⅔ cup chopped guavas
2 tablespoons sugar

¼ cup water
2 teaspoons cornstarch

Heat all ingredients in saucepan. Pour hot Sauce over warm cake.

Note: Fresh peaches mixed with a little sugar can be substituted for guavas.

Marion Dragoons Chapter 2311 Cookbook

Peach Crisp

4 cups peaches, peeled and
   sliced
1 cup all-purpose flour
1 cup sugar or honey
1 teaspoon baking powder

1 teaspoon allspice
1 large egg
⅓ cup butter or margarine, melted
½ cup chopped walnuts

Line a greased 8x8x2-inch baking dish with peach slices. Sift dry ingredients together and work in egg with pastry blender until mixture is like cornmeal. Sprinkle over peach slices. Drizzle butter and nuts on top. Bake at 350° for 45 minutes or until brown.

Exotic Foods: A Kitchen & Garden Guide

Mango Tarts

4 ripe mangoes	1 teaspoon cinnamon
1 teaspoon cornstarch	1 cup sugar
2 egg yolks, beaten	2 tablespoons butter
½ cup water	6 tart shells, previously cooked

Slice mangoes thinly. Heat in saucepan with water and sugar and cook at a moderate heat for 15 minutes. Mix cornstarch and egg yolks with small amount of water and add to the mango sauce. Continue to cook for several minutes, stirring constantly. Add cinnamon and butter while stirring. Fill previously cooked tart shells. Serve while still warm.

The Sunshine State Cookbook

Easy Oreo Peanut Butter Squares

1 (1-pound) package Oreo cookies	1 (3½-ounce) box vanilla instant pudding
1 cup margarine, melted	
1 (16-ounce) carton Cool Whip	1 (16-ounce) package semisweet chocolate chips
2 cups creamy peanut butter	

Grease a 9x13-inch pan with margarine. Grind Oreo cookies in a blender until gravel-like in texture. Add melted margarine; blend some more. Pat cookie mixture lightly in greased pan. Bake for 10–15 minutes at 350°. Let cool. With a mixer, blend Cool Whip, peanut butter, dry vanilla pudding, and chocolate chips until a brownish color. Spread carefully over cookie crust. Refrigerate. Cut into squares. Delicious.

A Collection of Favorite Recipes

Snow Peak Lemon Squares

2½ cups graham cracker
  crumbs
1 stick butter or margarine,
  softened
1¼ cups sugar, divided
1 (3-ounce) package lemon Jell-O
1 cup boiling water

1 (8-ounce) package cream
  cheese, softened
1 (12-ounce) can evaporated milk,
  chilled overnight
2 tablespoons lemon juice
½ pint whipping cream,
  whipped

Mix cracker crumbs, butter, and ½ cup sugar (reserve ¾ cup for topping) and press into a 9x13-inch dish. Dissolve Jell-O in boiling water and mix with cream cheese. Whip chilled evaporated milk, and add to remaining ¾ cup sugar and lemon juice. Fold into Jell-O mixture. Pour into crust and chill until set. Top with remaining crumbs and whipped cream. Garnish with a twist of lemon.

The Woman's Exchange Classic Recipes

Apricot Noodle Dessert

2 eggs, beaten
¼ cup sugar
1 pound broad egg noodles,
  cooked and drained
1 (12-ounce) jar apricot
  preserves

1 cup sour cream
½ cup creamed cottage cheese
½ cup seedless raisins
1 teaspoon vanilla
¼ cup butter, melted
¼ teaspoon cinnamon

Preheat oven to 375°. In a large bowl, combine eggs and sugar. Add noodles, preserves, sour cream, cottage cheese, raisins, vanilla, and butter; blend well. Turn into buttered 2-quart baking dish and sprinkle with cinnamon. Bake 1 hour.

Recipes of Spruce Creek

Timmy's Firework Trifle

1 (4-ounce) package vanilla
pudding mix (not instant)
3 cups skim milk
2 pints blueberries, divided
1/3 cup plus 3 tablespoons
sugar, divided
1/4 cup plus 2 tablespoons
orange juice, divided

1 pint strawberries, divided
1 (18 1/4-ounce) package Pillsbury
Moist Supreme White Cake Mix
1 1/4 cups water
1/4 cup oil
3 egg whites
1 cup whipping cream
2 tablespoons powdered sugar

In medium saucepan, combine pudding mix and milk. Prepare as directed on package. Cover; refrigerate until cool. Meanwhile, reserve 1/2 cup blueberries, 1/3 cup sugar, and 1/4 orange juice; stir to mix, crushing berries slightly. Set aside. Reserve 1/2 cup strawberries for garnish. In another non-metal bowl, combine remaining 1 1/2 cups strawberries, 3 tablespoons sugar, and 2 tablespoons orange juice; stir to mix, crushing berries slightly. Set aside.

Heat oven to 350°. Spray 2 (8- or 9-inch) round cake pans with nonstick cooking spray. Prepare cake mix as directed on package using water, oil, and egg whites. Pour batter evenly into sprayed pans. Bake at 350° for 30–40 minutes or until toothpick inserted in center comes out clean. Cool in pans on wire racks for 15 minutes. Remove cake from pans; cool 30 minutes or until completely cooled. Cut cakes in half horizontally to make 4 layers.

Place 1 layer in bottom of clear 2 1/2-quart soufflé dish or glass trifle bowl, trimming sides of cake to fit, if necessary. Spread with half of crushed blueberry mixture; top with 1/3 of pudding. Top with second cake layer, trimmed if necessary, all the crushed strawberry mixture, and 1/3 pudding. Top with third cake layer, trimmed if necessary, remaining crushed blueberry mixture, and remaining pudding. Top with fourth cake layer. Cover; refrigerate at least 1 hour before serving. In medium bowl, whip cream until soft peaks form. Gradually add powdered sugar, beating until stiff peaks form. Top trifle with whipped cream. Sprinkle with reserved blueberries and strawberries. Store in refrigerator. Makes 12 servings.

Simply Florida...Strawberries

Praline Banana Pudding

PECAN PRALINES:

1½ cups sugar
½ teaspoon baking soda
1 stick butter

½ cup buttermilk
1 cup whole pecans
1 teaspoon vanilla

In large saucepan, combine sugar, baking soda, butter, and buttermilk. Heat on medium-high heat, stirring constantly. When mixture begins to spread when dropped into cold water, add pecans, then vanilla. Using a candy thermometer, cook until mixture reaches 235°. Remove from heat and continue to stir until mixture starts to cool. Spoon by tablespoon onto greased cookie sheet. When cool, crush.

2 large packages French vanilla
instant pudding, prepared
according to directions,
minus ½ cup milk
2 (8-ounce) containers Cool
Whip, divided

1 (16-ounce) box vanilla wafers
6 bananas, sliced
1 cup crushed Pecan Pralines
Chopped pecans for garnish

Combine prepared pudding and 1 container Cool Whip. Layer wafers, sliced bananas, pudding mixture, and crushed Pecan Pralines twice. Top with remaining Cool Whip and pecans.

Steinhatchee Village Seafood and Etc!

Quick Chocolate Mousse

10 ounces whipping cream
5 ounces semisweet Couverture or
  good-quality dark chocolate,
  broken into pieces

Heat whipping cream in a saucepan; do not boil. Add chocolate. Cook until blended, stirring frequently; do not boil. Let stand until cool. Chill, covered, for 24 hours.

   Beat chocolate mixture in a mixer bowl until firm. Dip a spoon in hot water and scoop the chocolate mousse into individual dessert bowls. Serves 4.

Note: May add one teaspoon Kahlúa or Grand Marnier to chocolate mixture before cooling.

Made in the Shade

Low-Fat Raspberry Cheesecake Parfaits

¼ cup light ricotta cheese
¼ cup nonfat cream cheese,
  softened
2 tablespoons sugar
1 cup fresh raspberries

2 tablespoons all-fruit raspberry
  spread
8–10 vanilla wafers, crushed
¼ cup reduced-calorie whipped
  topping

Combine ricotta cheese, cream cheese, and sugar in a blender or food processor, and process until smooth. Reserve 8 raspberries for topping. Combine remaining raspberries and raspberry spread in a bowl and mix gently. Layer raspberry mixture, cheese mixture, and cookie crumbs in 4 parfait glasses. Top with reserved raspberries and whipped topping. Chill for 2 hours. Serves 4.

Tropical Settings

Banana Split Cake

This no-cook dessert is even better if prepared a day ahead. The tart pineapple keeps the bananas "happy."

2 cups graham cracker crumbs
1 stick butter or margarine, softened
1 (1-pound) box confectioners' sugar
1 (8-ounce) package cream cheese, softened
1 egg (or egg substitute)

4–6 bananas
1 (20-ounce) can crushed pineapple, drained
1 (16-ounce) carton Cool Whip, room temperature
Few chopped nuts, pecans, or walnuts
Cherries for decoration

Mix graham cracker crumbs with margarine and press into 8x11-inch glass dish. Combine confectioners' sugar, cream cheese, and egg. Beat together until smooth. Pour over graham cracker crumbs. Slice bananas over mixture. Pour crushed pineapple over bananas. Spread Cool Whip over pineapple. Sprinkle nuts over top. Add cherries now, or just before serving. Place in refrigerator until ready to cut and serve. Serves 12–16.

Christmas Memories

Citrus Sundae

2 cups orange sections or tangerine sections, drained
¼ cup orange-flavored liqueur

1 pint vanilla ice cream
1 pint orange sherbet

In a shallow leakproof covered container, marinate orange or tangerine sections in liqueur for a day. Turn container upside-down once during the period.

At serving time, scoop a ball of ice cream and one of sherbet into each individual serving dish. Top with oranges and marinade. Serves 6.

Citrus Lovers Cook Book

Vanilla Ice Cream Crêpes with Strawberry Sauce

Crêpes are tissue-thin pancakes that can be used to make any number of delicious desserts. In this recipe, you will fill crêpes with ice cream and smother with Strawberry Sauce and whipped cream.

CRÊPE SHELLS:

¼ cup all-purpose flour
7 tablespoons milk
1 large egg

½ tablespoon vegetable oil
1 pinch salt
Vegetable spray or oil

Combine flour, milk, egg, oil, and salt in a blender or food processor. Blend into a smooth batter, stopping motor a few times to scrape down the sides of the bowl. Cover and refrigerate batter for 1 hour. Blend batter well before making crêpes.

Over moderate heat, lightly oil a preheated, 6-inch, nonstick sauté pan. Add enough batter to make a thin coat, tilt pan so batter forms a thin, even covering over bottom of saute pan. Cook each crêpe until it sets, about 45 seconds, flip over and cook other side for 30 seconds.

Place cooked crêpe on wax paper or clean, dry surface. Do not stack crêpes while hot. Cooled crêpes may be stacked, wrapped in aluminum foil, and refrigerated for a few days or frozen for a few months. If frozen, thaw in refrigerator for 6 hours before use.

STRAWBERRY SAUCE:

1 pint strawberries, washed
2 tablespoons granulated sugar
6 tablespoons water

3 cups vanilla ice cream
4 cups whipped cream

Pick stems off strawberries and slice; place in mixing bowl with sugar and water. Lay crêpes out flat and place a scoop of ice cream in middle. Roll up crêpes and place on plates. Smother with strawberries and sauce. Garnish with whipped cream, and serve immediately. Yields 4 servings.

Mastering the Art of Florida Seafood

Mango or Peach Frost

Deceptively simple, this recipe is an all-time favorite. 'Specially good after a heavy meal, it has marvelous tropical flavor and a texture like soft sherbet.

1 heaping cup sliced mangoes or
  peaches
2 tablespoons powdered milk
Juice of 1 lime

1 tablespoon sugar
1 tablespoon light rum
Crushed ice
Mint sprigs for garnish

Combine first 5 ingredients in blender. Add crushed ice to fill container. Blend at high speed until mixture thickens to the consistency of soft sherbet. Serve immediately topped with a sprig of mint, with a spoon or straw, depending on thickness.

Famous Florida Recipes

Mocha Almond Fudge Girdlebuster

1¼ cups graham cracker
  crumbs
3 tablespoons sugar
⅓–½ cup butter, softened
1 gallon vanilla ice cream,
  softened, divided

8 Skor candy bars, broken,
  divided
1½ cups flaked coconut, divided
½ gallon mocha almond fudge
  ice cream, softened
Chocolate sauce

Mix graham cracker crumbs, sugar, and butter in a bowl. Press crumb mixture over bottom of a springform pan.

Layer ½ vanilla ice cream, 3 broken candy bars, ½ cup coconut, mocha almond fudge ice cream, 3 broken candy bars, ½ cup remaining coconut, remaining vanilla ice cream, remaining broken candy bars, and remaining coconut in prepared pan.

Freeze, covered with plastic wrap, for 24 hours or longer. Top with chocolate sauce just before serving.

Made in the Shade

Fresh Mango Sorbet

2 large ripe mangoes, pitted and chopped
1 cup canned mango nectar
½ cup fresh lime juice
¾ cup sugar
Zest of one small lime

In a food processor, combine all ingredients and purée. Transfer mixture to a medium-size bowl; cover with plastic wrap and refrigerate until very cold.

Place mixture in an ice cream machine, and freeze according to manufacturer's directions. Makes 6 servings.

Gracious Gator Cooks

Tiramisu Ice Cream

4 cups milk
1 vanilla bean, split lengthwise into halves
6 egg yolks
1¼ cups sugar
2 cups mascarpone cheese
1 tablespoon instant espresso granules or instant coffee granules
¼ cup coffee liqueur
½ cup shaved bittersweet chocolate

Combine milk and vanilla bean in a heavy saucepan. Bring just to boiling point over medium heat. Whisk egg yolks and sugar in a bowl until blended. Add hot milk mixture to egg yolk mixture gradually, whisking constantly. Return egg yolk mixture to saucepan.

Cook over medium-low heat for 7 minutes or until mixture just barely coats the back of a spoon, stirring constantly; do not boil. Remove from heat. Scrape seeds from vanilla bean into egg yolk mixture, discarding bean. Add cheese gradually and mix well. Chill, covered, for 2 hours or until completely cooled. Stir in espresso granules. Pour cooled custard into an ice cream freezer. Freeze using manufacturer's directions, stirring in liqueur and chocolate after 20 minutes. Spoon ice cream into a freezer container and freeze until firm. Serves 6–8.

Bay Fêtes

Tobacco Road's Carambola Ice Cream

3–4 ripe carambola (star fruit)
2½ cups milk, divided
2 cups heavy cream
1½ cups sugar
3 egg yolks
4 teaspoons vanilla

Cut fruit into slices. Purée carambola in a food processor with half of the milk. In a mixing bowl, combine all ingredients and mix with a whisk until sugar dissolves. Pour mixture into an ice cream machine and let it run until mixture is smooth, creamy, and thick, without a granular texture. Take ice cream out of machine, and let it harden in freezer, or eat as is. Yields ½ gallon.

Florida's Historic Restaurants and Their Recipes

Mock Ice Cream

1 (8-ounce) package cream
  cheese, softened
1 (10-ounce) tub Cool Whip
1 (10-ounce) package frozen
  strawberries
½ cup sugar
1 (8-ounce) can crushed pineapple,
  drained

Blend cream cheese, Cool Whip, strawberries, sugar, and pineapple. Freeze. Serve as ice cream or serve chilled as mousse.

Country Club Cooks

In 1889, thousands of prospectors poured into central Florida, hoping to reap fortunes by mining phosphate. Not only did the miners benefit from selling phosphate for use in fertilizer, they also made a fortune selling land. Prices went from $1.25 to $5.00 an acre to as high as $300 an acre. The Phosphate Boom lasted until 1896.

Key Lime Ice Cream

2 cups sugar
¼ cup fresh Key lime juice
1 tablespoon Key lime zest

5 cups heavy cream
¼ teaspoon green food coloring

Combine sugar, juice, and zest in a large bowl. In separate bowl, lightly whip the cream to the point where it begins to thicken (just beyond the frothy stage, but before it begins to whip). Gently stir cream mixture into sugar mixture until the granules of sugar break down. Add food coloring and chill in refrigerator for at least 4 hours. Churn in an ice cream maker according to manufacturer's directions.

Note: May substitute fresh lemons and yellow food coloring.

Cookin' on Island Time

Praline Crème Brûlée

2 cups heavy cream
3 large egg yolks
¼ cup granulated sugar
1 teaspoon vanilla

¼ cup firmly packed light brown
  sugar
¼ cup finely chopped pecans

Preheat oven to 300°. Scald cream. Beat egg yolks with granulated sugar and vanilla until sugar has dissolved. Stir in hot cream. Strain into 6 ramekins or other individual serving dishes. Place ramekins in a roasting pan and pour hot water halfway up sides of ramekins. Bake in water bath for 20–25 minutes or until just set. Remove from water bath and cool.

Heat broiler. Mix together brown sugar and pecans, and sprinkle in an even layer over top of custards. Place under broiler about 5–6 inches from the source of heat, and cook gently until topping has melted and caramelized. If sugar begins to burn, move ramekins further away from heat. The caramelizing will take 4–5 minutes. Cool and chill before serving.

Recipes and Remembrances

Frozen Key Lime Pie

½ cup lime juice
1 cup sweetened condensed milk
1 cup chopped pecans
1 (20-ounce) can crushed
 pineapple, drained

1 (16-ounce) carton Cool Whip
4–6 drops green food coloring
2 (8-inch) prepared graham
 cracker crusts

Mix together all ingredients, except crusts. Divide mixture evenly between pie shells. Place in freezer to set. Keep frozen until ready to serve.

Let's ACT Up in the Kitchen

Strawberries Rebecca

2 quarts fresh strawberries,
 washed and stemmed
2 cups sour cream
1 cup light brown sugar

1 tablespoon vanilla
1 tablespoon cinnamon
Fresh mint for garnish

Place berries in large bowl or small dessert dishes. Combine sour cream, light brown sugar, vanilla, and cinnamon. Spoon over berries; garnish with mint. Sauce can be made ahead and refrigerated. Serves 8.

Simply Florida...Strawberries

Blueberry Delight

1 (15¼-ounce) can crushed
   pineapple with juice
3 cups fresh blueberries
¾ cup sugar

1 (18¼-ounce) box Duncan
   Hines Golden Butter Cake Mix
1½ sticks margarine

In a 9x13-inch baking pan, combine pineapple with juice, blueberries, and sugar. Sprinkle cake mix over this mixture. Melt margarine, and pour over cake mix. Bake at 350° for 45–50 minutes or until golden brown.

Treasures

Pineapple Delight

1 (20-ounce) can crushed
   pineapple
1 (18¼-ounce) butter pecan
   cake mix

1 stick butter

Spread crushed pineapple, including juice, into a 9x13-inch baking dish. Sprinkle cake mix, dry, over pineapple. Cut butter into thin slices and lay over cake mix. Bake at 350° for 30–35 minutes.

Garden of Eatin'

Catalog of Contributing Cookbooks

Set aside in 1968, Biscayne National Park is the largest marine park in the National Park System, with 95% of its 173,000 acres covered by water.

PHOTO COURTESY OF NATIONAL PARK SERVICE

Catalog of Contributing Cookbooks

All recipes in this book have been selected from the cookbooks shown on the following pages. Individuals who wish to obtain a copy of any particular book may do so by sending a check or money order to the address listed by each cookbook. Please note the postage and handling charges that are required. State residents add tax only when requested. Prices and addresses are subject to change, and the books may sell out and become unavailable. Retailers are invited to call or write to same address for discount information.

AN AMERICAN CELEBRATION

Celebration Women's Club   866-899-2665
P. O. Box 470471   Fax 407-566-2455
Celebration, FL 34747   www.anamericancelebration.com

This cookbook is a legacy to the beautiful town of Celebration. The 208 pages provide 319 recipes that reflect the diversity of the community. Every chapter opener describes a tradition of Celebration. Original watercolor artwork by Lynn Sands and Kathleen McNally. Proceeds directly benefit charitable organizations of the club.

$29.95 Retail price   Visa/MC accepted
  $2.10 Tax for FL residents   ISBN 0-972-0812-0-8
  $5.00 Postage and handling

Make check payable to Celebration Women's Club

BAY FÊTES

Junior Service League of Panama City
P. O. Box 404   850-785-7870
Panama City, FL 32402   www.bayfetes.com

Bay Fêtes is an entertainment cookbook. It features 288 pages of vivid color pictures and recipes highlighting the flavors and history of the Gulf Coast. There are seven sections with 22 different themed entertainment menus. *Bay Fêtes* takes its readers on a multifaceted tour through different parts of Bay County.

$34.95 Retail price   Visa/MC accepted
  $2.62 Tax for FL residents   ISBN 0-9615014-2-1
  $3.50 Postage and handling

Make check payable to Bay Publications

THE BEST OF SOPHIE KAY COOKBOOK

by Sophie Kay
2904 River Point Drive   386-756-3783 or 386-212-9491
Daytona Beach, FL 32118   cooksmart1@aol.com

An outstanding collection of over 200 exciting and delicious recipes from appetizers to desserts that Sophie Kay, nationally known food authority, has created for her cookbooks, over 3,500 television cooking shows, and fine dining restaurants throughout her forty years of experience in the food world.

$19.95 Retail price   ISBN 0-9667263-0-8
  $1.30 Tax for FL residents

Postage and handling included in the price

Make check payable to Sophie Kay Petros

BY INVITATION ONLY

Junior League of Pensacola   850-433-4353
3298 Summit Boulevard, Suite 44   Fax 850-438-9738
Pensacola, FL 32503   www.juniorleagueofpensacola.org

Artful entertaining, southern style • More than 275 mouth-watering recipes • Eight themed sections • Twenty-four creative, hand-painted invitation ideas for innovative parties with accompanying menus and recipes • Featuring nine beautiful renderings of local landmarks by renowned watercolorist Paul Jackson

$29.95 Retail price   Visa/MC accepted
  $2.25 Tax for FL residents   ISBN 0-9613622-9-4
  $4.50 Postage and handling (UPS)

Make check payable to Junior League of Pensacola

CALYPSO CAFÉ

by Bob Epstein
Wimmer Companies   800-727-1034
4650 Shelby Air Drive   Fax 800-794-9806
Memphis, TN 38118   www.wimmerco.com

Soak up the island spirit; mix up a pitcher of Jimmy Buffett's famous margaritas and learn to create fantastic feasts. With a variety of recipes from the Caribbean, including conch, fish, and shellfish sections, and a variety of mixed drinks, you'll be taken to the islands—right in your own backyard.

$19.95 Retail price   Visa/MC/Amex accepted
  $6.00 Postage and handling   ISBN 1-879958-29-5

Make check payable to Wimmer Cookbooks

CENTENNIAL COOKBOOK

Spring Glen United Methodist Church
Barbara Crosby   904-725-2391
1412 Glendale Road West
Jacksonville, FL 32216

The cookbook was created to celebrate the centennial of Spring Glen Methodist Church. The recipes were submitted by members, former members, and pastors. It consists of 120 pages and 356 recipes. These recipes are a mixture of southern favorites and family traditions.

$12.00 Retail price
  $3.00 Postage and handling

Make check payable to Spring Glen United Methodist Church

CHILIMANIA!

by Herb and Chris Geltner
Geltner Books   321-453-8315
915 Koloa Drive   Fax 321-453-1516
Merritt Island, FL 32953

Chilimania! A collection of chili recipes from Floridians as well others from across the country—over 955 unique recipes with "chili." If you're into exploring the world of chili, this book's for you. Happy chili!

$14.95 Retail price   ISBN 0-9631162-0-7
  $.90 Tax for FL residents
  $3.25 Postage and handling

Make check payable to Geltner Books

CHRISTMAS MEMORIES

by Jeannine Browning
8552 Sylvan Drive
Melbourne, FL 32904-2426

321-723-5111
Fax 321-725-3354

If you are looking for wonderful and delicious recipes for the holiday season, or a special gift for someone you love, then *Christmas Memories* is the perfect cookbook for you. You will enjoy having this cookbook in your collection.

$22.95 Retail price
$1.38 Tax for FL residents
$2.50 Postage and handling

Visa/MC accepted
ISBN 0-9710006-0-3

Make check payable to Cookbooks by Jeannine

CITRUS LOVERS COOK BOOK

by Al and Mildred Fischer
Golden West Publishers
4113 N. Longview
Phoenix, AZ 85014

800-658-5830
Fax 602-279-6901
www.goldenwestpublishers.com

More than 280 mouth-watering recipes for drinks, salads, breads, meats, seafood, pies, cakes, desserts, sauces, preserves, marinades, and salad dressings! Sample Grapefruit Chiffon Pie, Sunny Morning Bread, Orange Fried Chicken...and many more. Oranges, tangerines, grapefruits, lemons, limes—oh my! Citrus has never tasted so good. 128 pages.

$6.95 Retail price
$4.00 Postage and handling

ISBN 0-914846-90-6

Make check payable to Golden West Publishers

A COLLECTION OF FAVORITE RECIPES

Deercreek Home and Garden Club
7816 McLaurin Road North
Jacksonville, FL 32256

904-363-2360

Deercreek Country Club is a very ethnically varied community and our 483-recipe cookbook reflects this diversity. The easel makes the three-ring-binder-style book "user friendly" as do the extra subcategories. Whether you need a simple recipe or one more exotic, you'll find what you need in our cookbook.

$15.00 Retail price
$5.00 Postage and handling

Make check payable to Deercreek Home and Garden Club

THE COLUMBIA RESTAURANT SPANISH COOKBOOK

by Ferdie Pacheco and Adela Gonzmart
University Press of Florida
15 NW 15th Street
Gainesville, FL 32611-2079

352-392-1351 or 800-226-3822
Fax 352-392-7302
www.upf.com

A cookbook of recipes used in the 100-year history of the famous Spanish restaurant. This compilation was started by Pijuan, chef for the king of Spain, and it is a combination of Spanish and Cuban cuisine. It includes recipes by the owner, Adela Gonzmart.

$24.95 Retail price
$5.00 Postage and handling

Visa, MC, Amex accepted
ISBN 0-8130-1403-4

Make check payable to University Press of Florida

COOKIN' IN THE KEYS

by William Flagg
Palm Island Press   305-294-7834
411 Truman Avenue   Fax 305-296-3102
Key West, FL 33040   www.junekeith.com

This cookbook covers the various local cuisines of the Florida Keys, including seafood, Cuban conch, and island originals. Try such dishes as Black Beans and Rice, Key Lime Pie, Honey Baked Bananas, and Conch Fritters. Simple instructions on food preparation are provided, along with information on buying and storing island ingredients.

$9.95   Retail price   Visa/MC accepted
 $.75   Tax for FL residents   ISBN 0-9643434-60
$2.00   Postage and handling

Make check payable to Palm Island Press

COOKIN' ON ISLAND TIME

Palm Island Estates Association, Inc.
P. O. Box 5244
Grove City, FL 34224   www.piecesofpie.org

A fun cookbook containing almost 500 recipes! A delightful blend of recipes which reflects the cultural diversity of the island residents themselves, as well as our "laid back" island lifestyle.

$12.50   Retail price
 $2.50   Postage and handling

Make check payable to Palm Island Estates (PIE)

COOKING FOR TWO, NO NONSENSE COOKBOOK

by James McNaughton
367 Ashton Court   850-875-3222
Quincy, FL 32352   www.jamesmcnaughton.net

A cookbook with 150 recipes that are designed to be low in fat, yet tasty. They are also made with gluten-free products. Over 30 entrées can be made in advance and frozen. Recipe portions are designed for two people, when practical.

$6.00   Retail price
$1.50   Postage and handling

Make check payable to James McNaughton

COOKING IN PARADISE

Key West Power Squadron   305-872-9244
612 Blackbeard Road
Summerland Key, FL 33042

Many recipes in this delightful cookbook are marked with an anchor identifying that recipe as one that can easily be taken along on a small boat with limited cold storage and cooking facilities. All of the recipes are guaranteed to please the palate. Illustrations by local Key West artists.

$9.95   Retail price
 $.75   Tax for Florida residents
$1.30   Postage and handling

Make check payable to KWPS

COOKING WITH CLASS

Park Maitland School
1450 S. Orlando Avenue   407-647-3038
Maitland, FL 32751   Fax 407-645-4755

Cooking with Class is a must-have for your cookbook collection. This array of family favorites is sure to tantalize even the most discriminating taste buds. "Restaurant Recipes" and "Through the eyes of a Child" sections complete the *Cooking with Class* package. Tasting is believing!

$15.00 Retail price
 $1.05 Tax for FL residents
 $2.25 Postage and handling

Make check payable to Park Maitland School

COOKING WITH PEOPLE TO PEOPLE

2002 Student Ambassadors
20 Cotton Creek Road
McDavid, FL 32568

This cookbook was compiled by student ambassadors from Pensacola, Florida, to Tallahassee, Florida. It includes over 200 recipes. These recipes are simple to prepare and delicious to eat.

$10.00 Retail price
 $.75 Tax for FL residents
 $2.50 Postage and handling

Make check payable to Susan Winters

COOKING WITH 257

Boy Scout Troop 257
2855 Alger Street   941-429-1558
North Port, FL 34286

Our book is a collection of family recipes, some 75 years old. Our book has 114 pages of 350 great recipes.

$10.00 Retail price
 $3.00 Postage and handling

Make check payable to Boy Scout Troop 257

COUNTRY CLUB COOKS

Spanish Lakes Country Club Homeowners Association
c/o J. Camino
35 Azul   727-460-8997
Ft. Pierce, FL 34951

An interesting collection of 350 recipes plus 24 pages of helpful information. The recipes range from those passed down for generations like "War Cake" to the new generation "White Chili." It spans the globe from Tex-Mex to Japanese and Italian dishes. Something for every cook—from beginner to gourmet.

$8.00 Retail price
 $.48 Tax for FL residents
 $2.00 Postage and handling

Make check payable to SLCCV HOA

CRAB ISLAND COOKBOOK

Collected, Sorted, and Edited by Chef Rebecca Watkins
c/o Thomas Hughes
284 Twin Lakes Lane   850-650-3673
Destin, FL 32541   Fax 850-650-4592

Succulent seafood recipes, appetizers, and spicy sauces, the *Crab Island Cookbook* contains delicious crab, shrimp, oysters, scallops, and fish recipes that can be found on the Gulf Coast. Includes 148 recipes, shopping list, and unique stand-up feature.

$14.95 Retail price   ISBN 0-9678051-0-4
 $1.50 Postage and handling

Make check payable to *Crab Island Cookbook*

THE CRUISING K.I.S.S. COOKBOOK II

by Corinne C. Kanter
SAILco Press, Inc.   Phone and Fax 305-743-0626
234 49th Streat, Ocean   Corinne@sailcopress.com
Marathon, FL 33050-2608   www.sailcopress.com

Includes 645 exciting recipes that are delicious, nutritious, economical and convenient; 480 pages; charts; illustrations; guides; using a pressure cooker; identifying uncommon and common vegetables; starting from scratch; making your own mixes; and a how-to section for cruisers, campers, and busy people on the go.

$24.95 Retail price   Visa/MC/Amex/Disc accepted
 $1.75 Tax for FL residents   ISBN 0-9618406-7-6
 $3.75 Postage and handling

Make check payable to SAILco Press

ENTIRELY ENTERTAINING IN THE BONNET HOUSE STYLE

Bonnett House Alliance   954-563-5393
Box 460117   Fax 954-561-4174
Ft. Lauderdale, FL 33346   www.bonnethouse.com

This charming cookbook contains 144 wonderful recipes compiled by Bonnet House Alliance members, plus interesting tidbits about the lifestyle of two artists, Frederic and Evelyn Bartlett who wintered in Florida. The home they built has been turned into a house museum, and this book raises funds to continue its upkeep.

$22.95 Retail price   ISBN 0-9624757-4-2
 $1.38 Tax for FL residents
 $4.00 Postage and handling

Make check payable to Bonnet House Cookbook

THE ESSENTIAL CATFISH COOKBOOK

by Shannon Harper and Janet Cope
Pineapple Press, Inc.   800-746-3275
P. O. Box 3889   Fax 941-351-9988
Sarasota, FL 34230   www.pineapplepress.com

Includes tasty sauces, soups, stews, side dishes, and sandwiches, as well as hints for healthy eating. Recipes are rated Very Easy, Easy, or Moderately Easy, and all have been kitchen-tested for convenience, accuracy, and taste. 83 recipes. Softcover, 6x9, 144 pages.

$8.95 Retail price   Visa/MC/Amex/Disc accepted
 $.58 Tax for FL residents   ISBN 1-56164-201-0
$3.00 Postage and handling for 1st book, $1.00 each additional

Make check payable to Pineapple Press

EXOTIC FOODS: A KITCHEN & GARDEN GUIDE

by Marian Van Alta
Pineapple Press, Inc.   800-746-3275
P. O. Box 3889   Fax 941-351-9988
Sarasota, FL 34230   www.pineapplepress.com

A wealth of sumptuous and nutritious recipes are sure to inspire you to serve your bounty. Whether you're a cook who likes to garden, a gardener who likes to cook, or simply someone who loves good food, this guide is guaranteed to have something for you. Over 150 recipes. 6x9, 224 pages.

$9.95 Retail price   Visa/MC/Amex/Disc accepted
$.65 Tax for FL residents   ISBN 1-56164-215-0
$3.00 Postage and handling for 1st book, $1.00 each additional

Make check payable to Pineapple Press

FAMOUS FLORIDA RECIPES

by Lewis Carlton
Great Outdoors Publishing Company
4747 28th Street N.
St. Petersburg, FL 33714

Florida cooks' treasured recipes—southern, Spanish, Jewish, Greek—using tropical fruits, vegetables, and seafood. Sample Orange Rum Cream Cake, Shrimp-Stuffed Avocados, and Florida Green Ice Cream. Thumbnail sketches of Florida's turbulent history. 80 pages, 166 tested recipes, softcover.

$4.95 Retail price   ISBN 0-8200-0804-4
$.30 Tax for FL residents
$1.50 Postage and handling

Make check payable to Great Outdoors Publishing Company

FAVORITE FLORIDA RECIPES

Florida Wildlife Hospital & Sanctuary, Inc.   321-254-8843
4560 North U.S. Highway 1   Fax 321-255-2213
Melbourne, FL 32935   www.floridawildlife.org

Tasty favorites and long-held secret family recipes from supporting members and friends of Florida Wildlife Hospital. Features 88 pages of delicious regional and traditional recipes, including a special Low-Calorie section. Adorned with original artwork and famous quotations highlighting the beauty of nature and wildlife.

$8.00 Retail price
$.48 Tax for FL residents
$3.52 Postage and handling

Make check payable to Florida Wildlife Hospital

FCCD COOKBOOK

Florida Council on Crime and Delinquency Chapter XVII
Luthers Publishing   386-423-1600
1009 North Dixie Freeway   Fax 386-423-1600
New Smyrna Beach, FL 32168-6221   www.lutherspublishing.com

Over 350 recipes are featured in this 160-page, 5½"x8½" paperback. Includes many old-time Florida favorites from original family recipes, plus helpful hints to ensure delicious success. With index.

$9.95 Retail price   ISBN 1-877633-04-6
$.65 Tax for FL residents
$3.00 Postage and handling

Make check payable to Luthers

FEEDING THE FLOCK

St. Joseph Catholic Church
140 W. Government Street   850-436-6461
Pensacola, FL 32501   Fax 850-436-6462

This culinary delight reflects a variety of historical recipes from our parishioners. The church is over 100 years old and the recipes have been passed down from generation to generation. Significant examples are Mississippi Mud, Creole Gumbo, Egg Nog, Shrimp and Mushroom Stuffed Potatoes, etc. All are tried-and-true favorites!

$10.00 Retail price
$2.00 Postage and handling

Make check payable to St. Joseph Booster

FLORIDA COOK BOOK

Golden West Publishers   800-658-5830
4113 N. Longview   Fax 602-279-6901
Phoenix, AZ 85014   www.goldenwestpublishers.com

Mention Florida and think citrus—oranges and grapefruits, as well as many more exotic types, such as mangos and kumquats—and seafood from two coasts, the Atlantic Ocean and the Gulf of Mexico, featuring delicacies like shrimp, crab, clams, sea bass and swordfish. This cookbook features Florida cuisine at its best! 96 pages.

$6.95 Retail price   ISBN 1-885590-55-5
$4.00 Postage and handling

Make check payable to Golden West Publishers

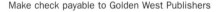

FLORIDA FIXIN'S

by Jeannine Browning
Melbourne, FL

A great cookbook with southern recipes! Contains easy-to-follow recipes with most ingredients already in the average kitchen. Many recipes have been in Jeannine's family for generations. A special gift for a teacher, sister or friend! Currently out of print.

FLORIDA SEAFOOD COOKERY

by Lowis Carlton
Great Outdoors Publishing Company
4747 28th Street North
St. Petersburg, FL 33714

An award-winning food editor presents tempting ways with Florida fish and seafood—such tropical delights as Coconut Fried Shrimp with Mango Sauce, Keys Conch Chowder, and Palm Beach Dolphin Soufflé. Softcover. 144 pages. Nutrition chart for lean or oily fish. 175 tested recipes.

$7.95 Retail price   ISBN 0-8200-0809-5
$.50 Tax for FL residents
$1.50 Postage and handling

Make check payable to Great Outdoors Publishing Company

FLORIDA'S HISTORIC RESTAURANTS AND THEIR RECIPES

by Dawn O'Brien and Becky Roper Matkov
John F. Blair, Publisher   800-222-9796
1406 Plaza Drive   Fax 336-768-9194
Winston-Salem, NC 27103

This cookbook celebrates fifty restaurants housed in buildings at least fifty years old. The cuisines include exquisite French fare, seafood favorites, Hispanic flavor, and southern comfort foods. Florida's historic restaurants mirror the wide range of tastes offered in the Sunshine State. From grandeur to down-home, this book has it all!

$14.95 Retail price   Visa/MC accepted
  $5.00 Postage and handling   ISBN 0-89587-120-3

Make check payable to John F. Blair

4-U: 400 RECIPES OF 4 INGREDIENTS

by Carmel M. Yacoboni
Mama Gallo
418 Holmes Avenue   863-465-2463
Lake Placid, FL 33852   www.mamagallocookbooks.com

A beautiful hardback book for cooks of all ages and with little time or storage space for many ingredients. A portion of the proceeds from the sale of this book have helped (and will continue to help) Headstart, Migrant Children, September 11 New York Firemen, and the local Jaycees.

  $8.00 Retail price
  $2.00 Postage and handling

Make check payable to Mama Gallo

FROM HOOK TO TABLE

by Vic Dunaway
Florida Sportsman/Primedia   772-219-7400
2700 S. Kanner Hwy   Fax 772-219-6900
Stuart, FL 34994   www.floridasportsman.com

Angler's guide to field care, cleaning and cooking of fish, with instructional chapters on various cooking procedures plus more than 100 recipes.

  $9.95 Retail price   ISBN 0-936240-15-6
   $.70 Tax for FL residents
  $3.00 Postage and handling

Make check payable to Florida Sportsman

THE GALLEY K.I.S.S. COOKBOOK

by Corinne C. Kanter
SAILco Press, Inc.
Marathon, FL   www.sailcopress.com

Contains 400 proven recipes, helpful hints, provisioning, galley gear. Recipes are based on a theme of delicious, nutritious, economical, and convenient. For busy people on the go, campers, boaters. The best selling nautical cookbook. Keep it simple system is the essence of simplicity. A companion to *The Cruising K.I.S.S. Cookbook II*. This cookbook is currently out of print.

GARDEN OF EATIN'

Book Review Club of Sorrento East
464 Leger Drive
Nokomis, FL 34275

Sorrento East Book Reviewers meet once monthly to report on and share books they read. An additional monthly eatin' meetin' for food and fellowship resulted in this cookbook. The 350 delicious recipes in the 132 pages were gleaned from the files of over 100 excellent cooks. Books are nonprofit.

$4.00 Retail price
$2.00 Postage and handling

Make check payable to Doris Dittmar

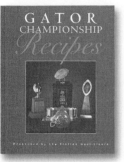

GATOR CHAMPIONSHIP RECIPES

Florida Goal-Liners
Sue Goodwin
P. O. Box 543   352-591-1476
McIntosh, FL 32664   Fax 352-591-0751

This hardcover book, depicting a day at a Gator football game, features 270 pages of delicious recipes submitted by University of Florida coaches, wives, former athletes, and members of Florida Goal-Liners, an all women's booster club for UF sports. Proceeds are to fund a UF scholarship.

$10.00 Retail price (Reduced from $19.96)   Visa/MC accepted
$.60 Tax for FL residents   ISBN 0-965934I-0-I
$3.00 Postage and handling

Make check payable to *Gator Championship Recipes*

GOOD COOKING

Grand Lagoon Yacht Club   850-492-0255
P. O. Box 34350   Fax 850-492-0255
Pensacola, FL 32507   www.glyc.addr.com

Over 150 pages of recipes and ideas. This book contains the favorite recipes from our members. There are recipes from appetizers to desserts. If you love seafood, included are many different ways to prepare it.

$9.95 Retail price
$.74 Tax for FL residents
$3.00 Postage and handling

Make check payable to GLYC

2000

GRACIOUS GATOR COOKS

Junior League of Gainesville   352-376-3805
P. O. Box 970   Fax 352-371-4994
Gainesville, FL 32602-0970   www.gainesvillejrleague.org

The essential cookbook for every cookbook for every Florida fan, *Gracious Gator Cooks* is a delectable compilation of sumptuous recipes for planning the perfect menu. There is also a delightful chapter of Children's Choices. Tidbits of information and photographs about our community are sprinkled throughout the book.

$19.95 Retail price   Visa/MC accepted
$1.40 Tax for FL residents   ISBN 0-9606616-3-8
$4.00 Postage and handling

Make check payable to Junior League of Gainesville

GREAT RECIPES FROM NEAR AND AFAR

Special Forces Association, Chapter 44
Navarre, FL

Great Recipes from Near and Afar is a book of favorite recipes compiled by members and wives of active and retired soldiers of the U.S. Army Special Forces. This book is currently out of print.

GULF COAST COOKING

by Virginia Elverson
Shearer Publishing   800-458-3808
406 Post Oak Road   Fax 830-997-9752
Fredericksburg, TX 78624   www.shearerpub.com

Gulf Coast Cooking gathers all the delicious bounty of the Gulf of Mexico into one coherent collection of 300 mouth-watering recipes. Author Virginia Elverson has skimmed the cream of her own recipe files and those of other cooking professionals from Tampa Bay to Tampico and all points between.

$34.95 Retail price   Visa/MC/Amex/Disc accepted
 $7.00 Postage and handling   ISBN 0-940672-56-1

Make check payable to Shearer Publishing

HEAVEN IN A POT

Wesley United Methodist Women
350 South Barfield Drive   941-394-3734
Marco Island, FL 34145   Fax 239-394-6092

The 140 pages of recipes are all favorites from the United Methodist Women of Marco Island, Florida. They include many of our "potluck" favorites, as well as a wonderful selection of salads and desserts.

$7.75 Retail price
 $.47 Tax for FL residents
$3.25 Postage and handling

Make check payable to Wesley United Methodist Church

HISTORIC SPANISH POINT: COOKING THEN AND NOW

Gulf Coast Heritage Association, Inc.   941-966-5214
P. O. Box 846   Fax 941-966-1355
Osprey, FL 34229-0846   www.historicspanishpoint.org

Historic Spanish Point: Cooking Then and Now was chosen the 1994 National Winner of the Tabasco Community Cookbook Award. A truly regional cookbook, recipes feature fish, fruits and vegetables and every sort of food native to the Gulf Coast of Florida.

$13.95 Retail price   Visa/MC/Disc accepted
 $.98 Tax for FL residents   ISBN 0-9660576-1-9
$4.00 Postage and handling

Make check payable to Gulf Coast Heritage Association, Inc.

HORSE TAILS: A COLLECTION OF OLD & NEW RECIPES

The Florida Thoroughbred Farm Managers, Inc. 352-401-3535
6998 NW Hwy. 27, Suite 106 B Fax 352-401-3533
Ocala, FL 34482 www.ftfarmmanagers.com

Over 250 recipes including favorite dishes of Florida's top thoroughbred owners, managers, and trainers. From Alligator Piquante to White Chocolate Créme Brûlée, this cookbook has it all, including some fabulous black-and-white horse photos. Net proceeds benefit our scholarship programs.

$15.00 Retail price Visa/MC/Amex accepted
$1.05 Tax for FL residents
$3.00 Postage and handling

Make check payable to Florida Thoroughbred Farm Managers, Inc.

INTRACOASTAL WATERWAY RESTAURANT GUIDE & RECIPE BOOK

by Charles and Susan Eanes 800-330-9542
Espichel Enterprises
P. O. Box 1017 Fax 727-734-8179
Dunedin, FL 34697 www.cruisingguides.com

This guide features 135 restaurants along the aquatic highway from Virginia to Key West. It is invaluable for those who love to cook, travel and enjoy unique and exceptional cuisines. Restaurants and recipes are profiled with color photographs. Coffee-table quality; 180 pages.

$14.95 Retail price Visa/MC/Amex/Disc accepted
$1.05 Tax for FL residents ISBN 1-890494-05-4
$4.00 Postage and handling

Make check payable to Cruising Guide Publications

KIDS AT WORK

by Jeannine Browning
8552 Sylvan Drive 321-723-5111
Melbourne, FL 32904-2426 Fax 321-725-3354

A cookbook for children of all ages! It is also a handy book for those who need to know more about cooking...at any age. A great gift for that special child in your life.

$12.95 Retail price Visa/MC accepted
$.78 Tax for FL residents ISBN 0-9627729-2-5
$2.50 Postage and handling

Make check payable to Cookbooks by Jeannine

LES SOUPS FANTASTIQUES

by Monique Fisher
Strawberry Press
3712 Woodmont Drive 941-377-9786
Sarasota, FL 34232 Fax 941-377-5328

Includes 101 easy one-pot soups. No heavy cream, butter, or flour in any of these delicious recipes. Most are healthy and low in fat, yet very tasty. Monique Fisher has perfected soup making to an art. Her flavor combinations are ingenious.

$12.00 Retail price ISBN 0-9640198-5-X
$.84 Tax for FL residents

Make check payable to Strawberry Press

LET'S ACT UP IN THE KITCHEN

Abuse Counseling and Treatment, Inc.   239-939-2553
P. O. Box 60401   Fax 239-939-4741
Fort Myers, FL 33906   www.actabuse.com

Let's Act Up in the Kitchen is a cookbook by Abuse Counseling and Treatment, Inc., a nonprofit agency serving victims of domestic violence and their children and survivors of sexual assault in Lee, Hendry, and Glades Counties. The cookbook has over 125 pages of recipes.

$15.00 Retail price   Visa/MC accepted
 $.90 Tax for FL residents
$2.00 Postage and handling

Make check payable to Abuse Counseling and Treatment, Inc.

LET'S TALK FOOD FROM A TO Z

by Doris Reynolds
P. O. Box 875   239-261-8054
Naples, FL 34106   Fax 239-261-7866

A collection of columns written by Doris Reynolds for the *Naples Daily News*. Columns included a request and the book is an outgrowth of answers to various questions, along with essays regarding food history and lore. There are 267 recipes in the 302 pages.

$14.95 Retail price   ISBN 0-9628173
 $.90 Tax for FL residents
$2.15 Postage and handling

Make check payable to D. Reynolds Enterprises Inc.

THE LIFE OF THE PARTY

Junior League of Tampa
87 Columbia Drive   813-254-1734 ext. 502
Tampa, FL 33606   www.jltampa.org

First in a series from THE JUNIOR LEAGUE OF TAMPA CULINARY COLLECTION, *The Life of the Party* embraces the attitude that less is more—less time spent in the kitchen and more time with your guests. You will find party menus, presentation ideas, entertaining tips and creative twists on classic recipes.

$17.95 Retail price   Visa/MC accepted
$1.26 Tax for FL residents   ISBN 0-9609556-3-1
$4.95 Postage and handling

Make check payable to Junior League of Tampa

LIGHTHOUSE SECRETS

Junior Service League of St. Augustine, Inc.
P. O. Box 374   904-824-3939
St. Augustine, FL 32085

With 256 pages and 250+ recipes, this beautiful cookbook is overflowing with regional tradition and history, as well as a variety of recipes that will make your mouth water. The recipe compilation of local favorites and specialties, combined with the delicious contributions of St. Augustine families, is a cookbook worthy of any collection.

$19.95 Retail price   Visa/MC accepted
$1.20 Tax for FL residents   ISBN 0-9670320-0-8
$3.50 Postage and handling

Make check payable to Junior Service League of St. Augustine, Inc.

MADE IN THE SHADE

Junior League of Ft. Lauderdale
704 Southeast First Street   954-462-1350
Ft. Lauderdale, FL 33301

Reflecting the lives of members who contributed to this book, Junior League of Ft. Lauderdale brings you *Made in the Shade*. Discover unique recipes from appetizers to desserts, with a tropical flair, and a creative kids play chapter, as well as a "Best of" *Sunny Side Up*, our original cookbook.

$22.95 Retail price   Visa/MC accepted
 $1.38 Tax for FL residents   ISBN 0-9604158
 $4.00 Postage and handling

Make check payable to Jr. League of Ft. Lauderdale

MARION DRAGOONS CHAPTER 2311 COOKBOOK

United Daughters of the Confederacy, Marion Dragoons Chapter #2311
Mrs. Paul A. Mott   352-753-7856
1227 La Paloma Place
Lady Lake, FL 32159-5758

A 445-page cookbook featuring mouth-watering recipes, many of which have been handed down through several generations. Plenty of quick and easy recipes to fit today's tastes and lifestyles are also included, making this book a must have.

$10.00 Retail price
 $2.00 Postage and handling

Make check payable to Marion Dragoons Chapter #2311

MASTERING THE ART OF FLORIDA SEAFOOD

by Lonnie Lynch
Pinepple Press, Inc.   800-746-3275
P. O. Box 3889   Fax 941-351-9988
Sarasota, FL 34230   www.pineapplepress.com

Includes tips on purchasing, preparing, and serving seafood. Handy information such as the nutritional value and the right tools and equipment to prepare seafood. Full of recipes (over 150) from appetizers to desserts that complement these tantalizing seafood dishes. 6x9, 144 pages, 50 illustrations.

$12.95 Retail price   Visa/MC/Amex/Disc accepted
  $.84 Tax for FL residents   ISBN 1-56164-176-6
 $3.00 Postage and handling for 1st book, $1.00 each additional

Make check payable to Pineapple Press, Inc.

THE MONGO MANGO COOKBOOK

by Cynthia Thuma
Pinepple Press, Inc.   800-746-3275
P. O. Box 3889   Fax 941-351-9988
Sarasota, FL 34230   www.pineapplepress.com

Discover mouth-watering recipes that feature mangoes in salads, meat and seafood dishes, desserts, drinks, and even salsas and chutneys. There is also a compendium of mango history, legend, literature, and lore, tracing the fruit's proliferation throughout the world's warm climates. 6x9, 160 pages, 53 recipes.

$12.95 Retail price   Visa/MC/Amex/Disc accepted
  $.85 Tax for FL residents   ISBN 1-56164-239-8
 $3.00 Postage and handling for 1st book, $1.00 each additional

Make check payable to Pineapple Press, Inc.

THE MOSTLY MULLET COOKBOOK

by George "Grif" Griffin
Pinepple Press, Inc.
P. O. Box 3889   800-746-3275
Sarasota, FL 34230   Fax 941-351-9988
                                        www.pineapplepress.com

Inventive mullet recipes plus mullet-friendly sides and sauces and other great southern seafood such as Wicked Wokked Scallops & Veggies, Ybor City Street Vendor's Crab Cakes, and Judy's Mullet Butler. Over 80 recipes. $5\frac{1}{2}$x$8\frac{1}{2}$, 112 pages, softcover.

$7.95   Retail price   Visa/MC/Amex/Disc accepted
 $.52   Tax for FL residents   ISBN 1-56164-147-2
$3.00   Postage and handling for 1st book, $1.00 each additional

Make check payable to Pineapple Press, Inc.

PRESERVING OUR ITALIAN HERITAGE

Sons of Italy Florida Foundation
87 Northeast 44 Street, Suite 5   877-435-6742 or 954-771-2445
Fort Lauderdale, FL 33334   Fax 954-771-2446
                                                   www.osiafl.org

More than just a cookbook, this spiral-bound, hard-cover collection of over 300 recipes in 222 pages preserves recipes from the hearts and minds of our forefathers, handed down for generations. Wonderful foods, nostalgic and heartwarming.

$14.95   Retail price   ISBN 0-9629303-0-X
 $3.00   Postage and handling

Make check payable to Sons of Italy Florida Foundation

RECIPES AND REMEMBRANCES

GFWC Santa Rosa Woman's Club
P. O. Box 423
Gulf Breeze, FL 32561

More than a cookbook, it features the history of Gulf Breeze and the Santa Rosa peninsula, section dividers with historic photographs and text, and 500 irresistible recipes reflecting the heritage of Florida's Gulf Coast and use of local seafood. A custom-color, loose-leaf design allows additional recipes to be added.

$19.95   Retail price

Make check payable to GFWC Santa Rosa Woman's Club

RECIPES FOR LORI'S LIGHTHOUSE

Lori's Lighthouse Youth Center   850-968-5472
Smyrna Baptist Church
1504 Templemore Drive
Cantonment, FL 32533

This cookbook is dedicated to the memory of Lori Weekley Dwelle. Recipes were collected from Lori's family and friends. The proceeds from sales go to the youth center, Lori's Lighthouse, at Smyrna Baptist Church.

$16.00   Retail price
 $3.50   Postage and handling

Make check payable to Lori's Lighthouse

RECIPES OF SPRUCE CREEK

Spruce Creek Garden Club
3177 Royal Birkdale Road
Daytona Beach, FL 32128   Fax 386-322-8762

Treasured recipes, cooking tips, and helpful hints (including napkin folding) sprinkled throughout the book make this a wonderful addition to a cookbook collection. Recipes range from appetizers and beverages to soups, salads, vegetables, main courses, breads, and desserts. Easily add your favorite recipes to the 8½"x5½" three-ring binder.

$15.00   Retail price

Make check payable to Spruce Creek Garden Club

ROBERTS RANCH MUSEUM COOKBOOK

Friends of the Collier County Museum
Collier County Museum   239-739-8393
3301 Tamiami Trail East   Fax 239-774-8580
Naples, FL 34112   www.colliermuseum.com

This book is dedicated to the pioneers and settlers of Southwest Florida who helped the area grow and prosper. From this group and other families settling in this area came good cooks who have shared their "treasured" recipes. Proceeds benefit the restoration of the Immokalee Pioneer Museum at Roberts Ranch.

$15.00   Retail price   Visa/MC accepted
   $.90   Tax for FL residents
$2.00   Postage and handling

Make check payable to Friends of the Collier County Museum

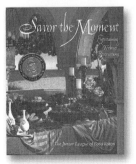

SAND IN MY SHOES

by Jeannine Browning
8552 Sylvan Drive   321-723-5111
Melbourne, FL 32904-2426   Fax 321-725-3354

Florida Cracker cooking from a fourth generation Florida Cracker. Wonderful recipes for everyone who enjoys baking, and those who want quick, delicious meals and raves from your family.

$14.95   Retail price   Visa/MC accepted
   $.90   Tax for FL residents   ISBN 0-9627729-0-9
$2.50   Postage and handling

Make check payable to Cookbooks by Jeannine

SAVOR THE MOMENT:
ENTERTAINING WITHOUT RESERVATIONS

Junior League of Boca Raton, Inc.   866-574-9229
P. O. Box 811676   Fax 561-241-6348
Boca Raton, FL 33481   www.jlbr.org

This James Beard Award-winning cookbook of Junior League of Boca Raton includes more than 300 recipes, creative entertaining ideas, and great cooking tips, and showcases 280 pages reflecting the beauty and elegant lifestyle for which Boca Raton is known. The *Savor the Moment* CD ROM is also available.

$28.95   Retail price   Visa/MC/Amex accepted
  $1.74   Tax for FL residents   ISBN 0-9670944-0-2
$6.50   Postage and handling

Make check payable to Junior League of Boca Raton, Inc.

SIMPLY FLORIDA...STRAWBERRIES

Florida Strawberry Grower's Association   813-752-6822
P. O. Drawer 2550   Fax 813-752-2167
Plant City, FL 33564   www.straw-berry.org

Over 267 strawberry recipes featuring drinks, salads, cookies, cakes, pies, short-cakes, breads and spreads. Includes unique recipes including strawberry dips, sauces and salsas, great ideas from strawberry growers/spouses on how to decorate with this diverse fruit, tips on growing your own strawberries, and great ideas for gifts and holiday parties.

$12.50 Retail price   Visa/MC accepted
  $3.00 Postage and handling   ISBN 0-9702239-0-0

Make check payable to FSGA

SING FOR YOUR SUPPER

Venetian Harmony Chorus
411 Blue Springs Ct.
Englewood, FL 34223   941-473-3937

Sing for Your Supper has 250 recipes in eight categories, with an alphabetical index of recipe titles by category. Also contains cooking tips, measurements, equivalency chart, calorie counter, and much more! Our award-winning Sweet Adelines cook as well as they sing!

$10.00 Retail price
  $1.00 Postage and handling

Make check payable to Venetian Harmony Chorus

A SLICE OF PARADISE

Junior League of the Palm Beaches, Inc.   561-689-7562
470 Columbia Drive, Bldg. F   Fax 561-640-3955
West Palm Beach, FL 33409   www.jlpb.org

A Slice of Paradise contains a collection of over 300 unique treasures from the Palm Beaches. Each recipe, painting and thought is a little piece of paradise which we, the Junior League of the Palm Beaches, would like to share with you.

$19.95 Retail price   Visa/MC accepted
  $1.20 Tax for FL residents   ISBN 0-9608090-1-5
  $3.50 Postage and handling

Make check payable to Junior League of the Palm Beaches

SOME LIKE IT SOUTH!

Junior League of Pensacola   850-433-4353
3298 Summit Boulevard, Suite 44   Fax 850-438-9738
Pensacola, FL 32503   www.juniorleagueofpensacola.org

Some Like It South! contains 366 pages of over 550 delectable recipes thoroughly tested by discriminating cooks. This attractive, hardcover edition is Smythe-sewn to lie flat. Here is a colorful and appealing entertainment book designed with ideas from some of the best cooks and hostesses on the Gulf Coast.

$16.95 Retail price   Visa/MC accepted
   $.72 Tax for FL residents   ISBN 0-9613622-0-0
  $3.00 Postage and handling

Make check payable to Junior League of Pensacola

Steinhatchee
Village Seafood
and Etc!

Steinhatchee

Special Recipe Collection by
Preceptor Theta Chi Sorority of
Beta Sigma Phi
of Steinhatchee, Florida

STEINHATCHEE VILLAGE SEAFOOD AND ETC!

Theta Chi Sorority of Beta Sigma Phi
Attn: Doris Bishop
P. O. Box 276   352-498-3489
Steinhatchee, FL 32359

Enjoy Steinhatchee Village seafood from our locals, mostly the catch of the Gulf. One hundred thirteen pages of delicious recipes, some floating around Steinhatchee for years and kept secret until now, are just waiting for you to try on your next seafood catch. Also includes bits of Steinhatchee history.

$8.00   Retail price
$3.00   Postage and handling

Make check payable to Theta Chi Sorority of Beta Sigma Phi

Strictly
Scratch

A Treasury of Timeless Recipes
by Dianne C. Mahlert

STRICTLY SCRATCH

by Dianne C. Mahlert
106 Hoffman Drive   850-386-2955
Tallahassee, FL 32312   www.cookingfromscratch.com

Strictly Scratch features 337 recipes, 78 original/prize winners, plus a collection of family treasures. Only basic ingredients are used so that all are timeless and can be adjusted to suit individual tastes or medical requirements. Easy enough for the novice, interesting enough for the accomplished cook.

$12.00   Retail price
$.90   Tax for FL residents

Make check payable to Dianne C. Mahlert

The
Sunshine
State
Cookbook
george s. fichter

THE SUNSHINE STATE COOKBOOK

by George S. Fichter   800-746-3275
Pinepple Press, Inc.
P. O. Box 3889   Fax 941-351-9988
Sarasota, FL 34230   www.pineapplepress.com

Part Deep South, part subtropical, part Latin, part everywhere that its immigrants have come from, Florida is unique in its variety. And Florida's kitchens reflect this delicious diversity. In this collection you will find easy-to-follow recipes that range from the comforting to the fantastical. Over 250 recipes, 6x9, 224 pages.

$9.95   Retail price   Visa/MC/Amex/Disc accepted
$.65   Tax for FL residents   ISBN 1-56164-214-2
$3.00   Postage and handling for 1st book, $1.00 each additional

Make check payable to Pineapple Press

A Taste of
Heaven

A TASTE OF HEAVEN

St. Francis of Assisi Church
834 South Orange Blossom Trail   407-886-4602
Apopka, FL 32703   Fax 407-886-9758

A collection of recipes by our many parishioners. Many of these delicious recipes have been handed down throughout the families. We hope you enjoy!

$10.00   Retail price
$2.00   Postage and handling

Make check payable to St. Francis of Assisi Church

TASTES FROM PARADISE

Naples Woman's Club
570 Park Street   239-262-6331
Naples, FL 34103   Fax 239-262-2302

This cookbook contains A-Z recipes from Ambrosia to Zucchini Dill Cream Sauce. A three-ring binder with easel and over 200 treasured recipes from the Naples Woman's Club, has the price to suit every pocket—$10.00. From Florida's famous Key Lime Pie to Five Fibre Casserole are the *Tastes from Paradise*.

$10.00 Retail price
 $3.00 Postage and handling

Make check payable to Naples Woman's Club

TASTES FROM PARADISE: A GARDEN OF EATING

Sisterhood, Jewish Congregation of Marco Island
901 Winterberry Drive   239-642-0800
Marco Island, FL 34145   Fax 239-642-1031

Tastes from Paradise: A Garden of Eating contains over 350 delicious recipes incorporating ethnic, holiday, and other delectable delights put together by the Sisterhood of Jewish Congregation of Marco Island. We are an integral part of the Congregation and help to further community relations on the Island and vicinity.

$12.50 Retail price
 $3.50 Postage and handling

Make check payable to JCMI Sisterhood

THYMES REMEMBERED

Junior League of Tallahassee   850-224-9161
P. O. Box 13428   Fax 850-224-9306
Tallahassee, FL 32317   jlt@jltallahassee.org

Thymes Remembered, our classic cookbook of 399 southern-born recipes, just got a new addition. "Finding Thyme," its CD-Rom companion, adds 90 new recipes plus all of the old. Plan, shop and create all from your IBM computer. Let us show you the way to find more "thyme" for food, family and friends.

$18.95 Retail price, cookbook only (ISBN 0-9620166-0-8)
$29.95 Retail price, CD-Rom/Cookbook Set (ISBN 0-9620166-1-6)
 $1.43 Tax for FL residents (cookbook only) $2.25 for the set
 $5.00 Postage and handling   Visa/MC accepted

Make check payable to Junior League of Tallahassee

TREASURED RECIPES FROM NEAR AND FAR

Bahia Vista Mennonite Church   941-377-4041
4041 Bahia Vista Street   Fax 941-378-9674
Sarasota, FL 34232   www.bahiavista.org

A collection of favorite recipes honoring 50 years of a Mennonite Church's life: worshipping and sharing meals and fellowship together. Attractively compiled with 265 pages of appetizers, beverages, breads, desserts, main dishes, salads, sandwiches, soups, and vegetables. Traditional recipes from Mennonite families passed on from generation to generation.

$10.00 Retail price
  $.70 Tax for FL residents
 $3.00 Postage and handling

Make check payable to Bahia Vista Mennonite Church

TREASURES

by Laura F. Wheeler
P. O. Box 729
Malone, FL 32445

Treasures is a collection of favorite and easy-to-prepare recipes from the kitchen of Laura F. Wheeler. It includes nine categories of 191 recipes collected from family, friends, and personal creations. From the simplest to the most elegant, the cookbook is filled with proven *Treasures*.

$10.00   Retail price
  $.75   Tax for FL residents
 $3.85   Postage and handling

Make check payable to Laura F. Wheeler

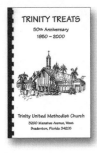

TREASURES OF THE TROPICS

Hibiscus Children's Center
P. O. Box 305   772-334-9311
Jensen Beach, FL 34958   Fax 772-334-1991
                                                  www.hibiscuschildren.org

Treasures of the Tropics features over 400 taste-tingling recipes for any occasion— from an elegant dinner party to a football tailgate picnic, an afternoon luncheon for thirty, or a quick evening meal for two.

$19.95   Retail price   ISBN 0-9704715-0-5
 $1.20   Tax for FL residents
 $4.00   Postage and handling

Make check payable to Hibiscus Children's Center

TRINITY TREATS

Trinity United Methodist Women
3603 16th Avenue W
Bradenton, FL 34205   941-746-2500

A collection of recipes from people who have come to the Sunshine State from all over the United States. 181 pages, 443 recipes.

$10.00   Retail price
 $2.50   Postage and handling

Make check payable to Trinity United Methodist Women

TROPICAL SETTINGS

Junior League of Ft. Myers
12995 S. Cleveland Ave., Suite 157   239-227-1197
Ft. Myers, FL 33907   Fax 239-277-1125
                                                       www.jlfm.org

A collection of more than 250 tested recipes and photos that reflect the flavor of Southwest Florida. Recipes include preparation and cooking times along with ideas and hints to make meals effortless. For the health conscious, nutritional profiles for each recipe is included in the back of the cookbook.

$19.95   Retail price   Visa/MC accepted
 $1.20   Tax for FL residents   ISBN 0-9613314-1-0
 $2.00   Postage and handling

Make check payable to Junior League of Ft. Myers

TROPICAL TASTES AND TANTALIZING TALES

by Carol Garvin   305-444-4717
1815 Tigertail   Fax 305-858-0702
Coconut Grove, FL 33133   www.carolgarvin.com

Written and illustrated by popular watercolorist Carol Garvin. Join her and wander these pages for exotic food, humor, tales of old Florida and perhaps even adventure. Guaranteed to entertain, softcover, 250 recipes, 160 illustrations, 196 pages. All books are signed and personalized upon request. Print recipient's name.

$16.95   Retail price   Visa/MC accepted
$1.10   Tax for FL residents   ISBN 0-9633461-1-3
$4.75   Postage and handling

Make check payable to Carol Garvin

UNDER THE CANOPY

GFWC–Tallahassee Junior Woman's Club
P. O. Box 944   850-847-5158
Tallahassee, FL 32302   www.tjwc.org

Broaden your knowledge of Florida history while cooking some favorite recipes of the residents around the historic Canopy Roads area. There's even a wild game section, including recipes for duck, venison, and quail. Benefits philanthropic projects by the GRWC Tallahassee Junior Woman's Club. 300 pages. 372 recipes.

$16.95   Retail price   ISBN 0-9644244-0-1
$1.28   Tax for FL residents
$3.00   Postage and handling

Make check payable to *Under the Canopy*

VILLAGE ROYALE: OUR FAVORITE RECIPES

by Nancy Carden
2141 NE 1st Ct. #104
Boynton Beach, FL 33435   561-737-1812

This 90-page book is full of delicious recipes I have collected over the past three years. Also included are some of the old Village Royale Cookbook recipes. Enjoy!

$5.00   Retail price
$1.50   Postage and handling

Make check payable to Nancy Carden

THE WOMAN'S EXCHANGE CLASSIC RECIPES

The Woman's Exchange of St. Augustine
143 St. George St.   904-829-5064
St. Augustine, FL 32084   Fax 904-829-6210

This third volume of *Classic Recipes* includes 361 recipes—members' own and those of the flavor of St. Augustine, founded in 1565. The Woman's Exchange of St. Augustine, founded in 1892 and a member of the National Federation of Woman's Exchanges, offers spring luncheons and catering in the historic Peña-Peck House.

$12.00   Retail price   Visa/MC/Amex/Disc accepted
$.72   Tax for FL residents
$3.50   Postage and handling

Make check payable to The Woman's Exchange of St. Augustine

Index

PHOTO © ANDY NEWMAN / FLORIDA KEYS TDC

Known as the "Sportfishing Capital of the World," Islamorada in the Florida Keys offers some of the most competitive and diverse fishing in the world.

Best of the Best State Cookbook Series

Best of the Best from
ALABAMA
288 pages, $16.95

Best of the Best from
ALASKA
288 pages, $16.95

Best of the Best from
ARIZONA
288 pages, $16.95

Best of the Best from
ARKANSAS
288 pages, $16.95

Best of the Best from
BIG SKY
Montana and Wyoming
288 pages, $16.95

Best of the Best from
CALIFORNIA
384 pages, $16.95

Best of the Best from
COLORADO
288 pages, $16.95

Best of the Best from
FLORIDA
288 pages, $16.95

Best of the Best from
GEORGIA
336 pages, $16.95

Best of the Best from the
GREAT PLAINS
North and South Dakota,
Nebraska, and Kansas
288 pages, $16.95

Best of the Best from
HAWAI'I
288 pages, $16.95

Best of the Best from
IDAHO
288 pages, $16.95

Best of the Best from
ILLINOIS
288 pages, $16.95

Best of the Best from
INDIANA
288 pages, $16.95

Best of the Best from
IOWA
288 pages, $16.95

Best of the Best from
KENTUCKY
288 pages, $16.95

Best of the Best from
LOUISIANA
288 pages, $16.95

Best of the Best from
LOUISIANA II
288 pages, $16.95

Best of the Best from
MICHIGAN
288 pages, $16.95

Best of the Best from the
MID-ATLANTIC
Maryland, Delaware, New
Jersey, and Washington, D.C.
288 pages, $16.95

Best of the Best from
MINNESOTA
288 pages, $16.95

Best of the Best from
MISSISSIPPI
288 pages, $16.95

Best of the Best from
MISSOURI
304 pages, $16.95

Best of the Best from
NEVADA
288 pages, $16.95

Best of the Best from
NEW ENGLAND
Rhode Island, Connecticut,
Massachusetts, Vermont,
New Hampshire, and Maine
368 pages, $16.95

Best of the Best from
NEW MEXICO
288 pages, $16.95

Best of the Best from
NEW YORK
288 pages, $16.95

Best of the Best from
NO. CAROLINA
288 pages, $16.95

Best of the Best from
OHIO
352 pages, $16.95

Best of the Best from
OKLAHOMA
288 pages, $16.95

Best of the Best from
OREGON
288 pages, $16.95

Best of the Best from
PENNSYLVANIA
320 pages, $16.95

Best of the Best from
SO. CAROLINA
288 pages, $16.95

Best of the Best from
TENNESSEE
288 pages, $16.95

Best of the Best from
TEXAS
352 pages, $16.95

Best of the Best from
TEXAS II
352 pages, $16.95

Best of the Best from
UTAH
288 pages, $16.95

Best of the Best from
VIRGINIA
320 pages, $16.95

Best of the Best from
WASHINGTON
288 pages, $16.95

Best of the Best from
WEST VIRGINIA
288 pages, $16.95

Best of the Best from
WISCONSIN
288 pages, $16.95

All cookbooks are 6x9 inches, ringbound, contain photographs, illustrations and index.

Special discount offers available! *(See previous page for details.)*

To order by credit card, call toll-free **1-800-343-1583** or visit our website at **www.quailridge.com.**
Use the form below to send check or money order.

Call 1-800-343-1583 or email <u>info@quailridge.com</u> *to request a free catalog of all of our publications.*

 **Order form**   Use this form for sending check or money order to:
QUAIL RIDGE PRESS • P. O. Box 123 • Brandon, MS 39043

❑ Check enclosed

Charge to: ❑ Visa ❑ MC ❑ AmEx ❑ Disc

Card # _____

Expiration Date _____

Signature _____

Name _____

Address _____

City/State/Zip _____

Phone # _____

Email Address _____

Qty.	Title of Book (State) or Set	Total

Subtotal _____

7% Tax for MS residents _____

Postage ($4.00 any number of books) **+   4.00**

Total _____